James Edwards

James Edwards

African American Hollywood Icon

PAMALA S. DEANE

McFarland & Company, Inc., Publishers
Jefferson, North Carolina, and London

I wish to acknowledge University Libraries at the University of Maryland, College Park. Without access to this facility with its splendid services and helpful staff, this book could not have been written.

All of the photographs were supplied by Photofest.

LIBRARY OF CONGRESS CATALOGUING-IN-PUBLICATION DATA

Deane, Pamala Suzette.
  James Edwards : African American Hollywood icon / Pamala S. Deane.
      p.   cm.
  Includes bibliographical references and index.

  ISBN 978-0-7864-4415-1
  softcover : 50# alkaline paper ∞

  1. Edwards, James, 1918 Mar. 6–1970. 2. African American actors — Biography. 3. Actors — United States — Biography.
  I. Title
  PN2287.E387D43   2010
  791.4302'8092 — dc22   2009039809
  [B]

British Library cataloguing data are available

©2010 Pamala S. Deane. All rights reserved

No part of this book may be reproduced or transmitted in any form or by any means, electronic or mechanical, including photocopying or recording, or by any information storage and retrieval system, without permission in writing from the publisher.

On the cover: James Edwards in *Home of the Brave*, 1949 (United Artists/Photofest)

Manufactured in the United States of America

McFarland & Company, Inc., Publishers
  Box 611, Jefferson, North Carolina 28640
      www.mcfarlandpub.com

To my favorite uncle, Walter Winfree,
who showed me golf

Table of Contents

Preface   1

1. Inner Rage   3
2. The Greatest Break of His Life   10
3. A *Brave* Picture   16
4. "Hollywood's Boldest Stroke for Democracy"   26
5. James Edwards Had Arrived   31
6. "Triple-Threat Edwards"   36
7. Soldier Stories   41
8. Reading, Writing, and Radio   52
9. "I Am Arrogant and Shall Remain So"   59
10. "Mad Behavior"   63
11. Scandalize My Name   68
12. "It Wasn't a Damn Bit Funny"   75
13. *The Joe Louis Story*   78
14. Some of His Best Work   83
15. Negro Products   92
16. "Hollywood: So What!"   101
17. A Khaki-Clad Stereotype?   112
18. Tarzan, Eartha Kitt, and the Strip Scene   128
19. "The Role Was a Cheat"   139
20. Black Cowboys on a *Mission*   145

21. Comeback in a Big Picture	151
22. The Black Revolution	163
23. Final Curtain	175
24. "James Edwards Was a Pioneer"	185
Appendix 1: Morse v. Morse	193
Appendix 2: Film, Television, and Radio Performances	195
Chapter Notes	203
Bibliography	217
Index	223

Preface

This book explores the career of James Edwards (1918–1970), an African American actor who achieved Hollywood stardom during the period after the Second World War.

In America, the war years saw the passage of significant civil rights legislation. Black citizens, many of whom had participated in the war against bigotry and totalitarianism, cast a hopeful eye towards the postwar period with its continued assault on discriminatory practices, Jim Crow, and racial prejudice. However, years after the war ended, Black citizens were still regarded with mistrust and suspicion; they were targets of racial profiling, police brutality, and lynching; and, struggled under a system of overt and covert discrimination in housing, education, government, industry, business, and professional sports. In the entertainment field, including film, radio, and the new medium of television, Black citizens were routinely depicted as caricatures that served to denigrate the race as a whole.

It is against this backdrop that James Edwards, a recently discharged Army veteran, and a regular guy from Indiana as he liked to call himself, took the bold step of taking on life as an actor. With a primary focus on his professional activities, this book examines some of the challenges, triumphs, successes, and disappointments of this versatile, complicated, and multi-faceted individual.

A quasi-chronological sequence of chapters, which include commentary on the historical and cultural backdrop, follow Edwards from his beginnings as a stage actor and his appearance in the hit play *Deep Are the Roots*. In 1949, Edwards achieved celebrity status via his role as an anguished soldier in the Stanley Kramer production *Home of the Brave*. Though he would never again be cast in another picture that would feature him as prominently and afford him as much positive notice, he nonetheless earned parts in perhaps two dozen more pictures, some completely forgettable and a scant few, for one reason or another, now considered film landmarks.

Edwards performed on radio, made spoken word recordings, operated his own acting school, and directed and produced plays. He is also recognized as the first African American to be hired as a screenwriter for a major motion picture studio.

Edwards' television appearances served as more than entertainment, but his appearances in dignified settings and his casting as a real person, not a type, served to uplift the race during a precarious period in the history of Black America. Indeed, he seemed cognizant and respectful of his position as a symbol of his race and, early on, spoke out about issues of race in America.

Information for this volume has been taken from media materials, archive collections, books, newspapers, periodicals, and government documents. Citations for material which could be attributed to many sources are kept to a minimum, and all sources are listed in the bibliography.

Copies of productions in which Edwards appeared were obtained from various sources, including cable television, DVD, VHS cassette, and 16 mm film. Today, versions of many films and older television programs have been altered or edited of important scenes. The reasons are many and include time constraints and the deletion of material that today might be deemed objectionable. Though care has been taken to recognize that productions have been altered and to obtain *true* versions for this study, original versions are not available for every production.

Indeed, this discussion of Edwards' work has certain limitations, among them the difficulty of finding recordings of his performances that have not been horribly altered, and the need to rely on the memories of those who knew him.

Though his career was relatively brief, having been cut short by his early death, he left behind a fascinating record of stage, film, radio, and television credits. Since his death in 1970, James Edwards' contribution is often relegated to a brief mention about his appearance in *Home of the Brave*. It is hoped that his book will elevate him to his due place in the history of Black America and to the history of American film.

1. Inner Rage

On August 15, 1945, the Empire of Japan tendered its unconditional surrender to America and her allies, and the long, bloody, and most devastating war in the history of the world was declared over. In the coming months, the harbors, airports, and train stations of cities and towns across the United States celebrated the end of the war and the return of American fighting men and women. A year or so earlier, while still on active duty, Lieutenant James Edwards, U.S. Army, was severely injured in a car accident. His recovery period was long, and he endured a number of surgeries required to rebuild his face and vocal cords. He was confined to a hospital for months as surgeons "patched him up, rebuilding one ear, his mouth and parts of his face." For a time he was compelled to cover his face with a mask to hide the slowly healing scars. Laden with anxiety about his circumstance, and depressed that he might be permanently scarred, Edwards accepted a psychiatrist's suggestion that he engage in some kind sort of therapy. Using his G.I. Bill, he enrolled at Northwestern University and took classes in public speaking and acting.[1]

The experience kindled something inside him. He learned that he was pretty good at acting; someone even remarked that he should be on the stage. Against all odds, he took the bold step of deciding that he would pursue acting, not as a diversion or hobby, but as a career. He gave up the chance to return to his government job and instead honed his skills as a performer, appearing in Northwestern University's theatre production of Thornton Wilder's 1952 play, *The Skin of Our Teeth*, which ran May 23 through 26, 1945. He played the role of "Chair Pusher" and his fellow cast members included Jean Hagen, Cloris Leachman and Paul Lynde. Later, in July 1945, he played the part of "Cal" in the Lillian Hellman drama, *The Little Foxes*.[2]

In 1946, recovered and discharged from the Army, Edwards became affiliated with the Skyloft Players, a little Chicago theatre group founded by Langston Hughes and managed by Helen Spaulding, a Black Chicago educator, actor, director, and Northwestern University product. It was with Skyloft that Edwards made his debut of sorts as a professional actor, in what he described as his first play, when he appeared as Prince Sirki (Death) in *Death Takes a Holiday*. He later earned a part in the Skyloft production of an original play called *Downdraft* which garnered the Players, and Edwards, much positive notice. "I now realize that I found myself as an actor," Edwards revealed, speaking of this period. Indeed, in a relatively short time, he earned a reputation for himself as a serious performer.[3] The *Chicago Defender* wrote:

> Jimmy first clicked as an actor ... when acclaimed by local theatre patrons from his unusual acting talent in amateur theatre circles. He received high acclaim with the former Skyloft Players for his portrayal of His Serene Highness ... in *Death Takes a Holiday*.... Later he scored a hit for the Players ... which brought the second place prize to the Sky loft [*sic*].[4]

"If I hadn't been in the Army," Edwards said in 1949, "I guess I never would have become an actor."[5]

After the war, some playwrights were compelled to create works that explored social and cultural problems such as America's legacy of racial hatred. Of particular interest to a few writers was the relevant predicament of Black veterans who had fought a war to free others from bigotry and totalitarianism, only to return home and be treated as second class citizens. The late Ossie Davis, seminal actor of stage, screen, and television, discussed the period in his biography:

> In those days, Broadway had a conscience ... the war against racism in Europe was over; the good guys had won by the skin of their teeth, and were determined that now was the time to attack racism in American, head on.[6]

In 1946, a Broadway producer "casting among Chicago amateurs for possible new faces" selected Edwards to come to New York and audition for a role in the Robert Ardrey play *Jeb*. *Jeb* is the story of a handicapped Black veteran, the recipient of a Bronze Star and Purple Heart, who returns to his home in the South expecting to gain employment in a job traditionally reserved for Whites. Edwards did not earn the part; the lead would go Davis, then another aspiring young actor. Unfortunately for Davis and the show's backers, *Jeb* failed miserably and closed in less than a month's time. Another play exploring a similar theme that opened during the period was *On Whitman Avenue* by Maxine Woods. Set in a city in the north, it starred Canada Lee and focused primarily on the attitudes of Whites when a returning Black veteran wishes to rent an apartment in an all–White neighborhood. Like *Jeb, Whitman Avenue* did not capture the imagination of theatre-goers or dollars at the box office.[7]

While touring with a singing group, Edwards received a wire asking him to return to New York to audition for *Deep Are the Roots*. Edwards earned a spot as understudy in the James Gow–Arnaud d'Usseau Broadway play which would become a huge hit.

Both Gow and d'Usseau had backgrounds in journalism: Gow was a film and theatre critic and d'Usseau was a correspondent for United Press International. Both served during the war in the Army Signal Corps where Gow wrote Army training films. Both were film writers who met when they collaborated on an RKO production. Their first play, *Tomorrow the World*, opened on Broadway at the Ethel Barrymore Theatre in 1943. The successful drama ran for more than a year.[8]

Deep Are the Roots is a drama about a Black man named Brett Charles who returns home to the South after having served as a decorated Army officer during the war. Brett is the son of the housekeeper of a Senator and his family. The play explores the social machinations of a postwar Southern family, racism, lynching, and the doomed romance between Brett and Generva, the youngest daughter of a Southern Senator whom Brett has known all his life.

The play's daring theme stunned audiences unaccustomed to even the slightest hint of a possible romance occurring between a Black man and White woman being depicted on a stage. The subject was strictly taboo. While the play would suffer its share of unkind remarks, protests, complaints about its touchy subject matter, and accusations of being propagandistic, the New York mounting was highly successful and the show ran for nearly 500 performances. Why did *Deep* become such a hit while the other plays exploring similar subjects failed? One scholar explained:

> The other major plays ... let their emotions run away with them and jumped from scene to scene in spasms of righteous indignation, pounding their points home with hysterical fist and brickbat. *Deep Are the Roots* by concentrating its heat, packed a much harder wallop.... And it has aroused the healthy controversy such a theme should inspire.[9]

The characters include Brett, a man who is upstanding, educated, polite, and without guile; his mother Bella Charles, a staid, traditional, loyal Negro servant; and Honey, a silly young Black housekeeper who spitefully gets Brett into deep trouble. Senator Ellsworth Langdon is old, rich, and a bit of a curmudgeon, but honorable and a bastion of Southern tradition and custom. The authors describe the oldest daughter Alice as "a Southern woman of good will and liberal disposition." She wants to build a better school for the Negro children, and pulled strings to get Brett into graduate school. Alice's sister Generva is portrayed as "a young southern girl, virginal as any heroine of a Confederate romance ... unbesmirched by prejudice or evil."[10]

Deep Are the Roots is set in the days of Jim Crow train cars, when Whites did not shake hands with Blacks, when Blacks were compelled to move from the sidewalk when a White person approached, and when Blacks required permission to travel, generally from the White person who was responsible for them, most often their employer.

Brett grew up in this environment but spent time in combat overseas where he was housed with an English family who treated him with kindness. While on active duty he discovered a world very different from his hometown. And there were other issues that affected the psyche of Brett. Indeed, at one point Langdon muses about what killing White people (the enemy) during the war has done to Brett's Black soul. Even he realized that Brett's experiences in combat had caused a profound change in his attitude. Brett's mother, too, is chagrined at how Brett has changed. But most of all, she warns him about his attentions for Generva. As children, they played together. She wanted to be at the train station to greet him upon his return but was cautioned, "One does not go to the station to meet a colored man." Later, when Brett and Generva steal away for a moonlight walk, the news quickly gets around town. His mother rails against his being "hot-blooded and foolish" and warns him that if he plans to pursue her, "Better you died in one of them foxholes."[11]

Brett returns from the war with plans of his own, plans not in keeping in what the Langdons expected from him. He goes about town as he pleases, in uniform, and without permission from the Langdons, and then develops an interest in Generva, all of which cause tumult in the Langdon household. When Honey the housemaid implicates him in the theft of a watch, Brett is jailed and could be lynched. Indeed, as the play progresses we see that the characters do not act as the people we believe them to be. Langdon is not so honorable but turns into a race-baiting ogre. Generva is not so liberal after all; she is the one who believed that Brett was a thief and called the police. Even the dim-witted Honey has a change of heart and gives back the money Langdon gave her to lie. Bella, Langdon's loyal darkie, has no problem telling him off and leaving his employ after he has her son wrongfully jailed. The authors note, "This play is about prejudice, as you will see, and the cruel and irrational things that prejudice leads people to do."[12]

One evening, Gordon Heath, who played the role of Brett in the Broadway mounting, arrived late for a performance and Edwards played the part. Heath wrote in his autobiography:

> Jimmy Edwards, my understudy, was tying Brett's uniform tie in my dressing room. I watched the performance from out front. All things considered, he and the play made a solid impression. I felt he had more thrust than I and was closer to Brett's inner rage than I ever would be.[13]

Two off–Broadway companies were formed: One played forty-four weeks in Chicago before heading to the West Coast, and the other played East Coast cities such as Philadelphia. In 1947 Edwards served as understudy to Henry Scott in the Chicago production before joining the West Coast touring company, at one time working as both lead actor and stage manager. The cast consisted of Betsy Blair (wife of performer Gene Kelly) as Generva; Robert Warwick as the Senator; Rose Hobart as Generva's older sister; and Jessie Grayson as Belle, the housekeeper and Brett's mother. The play was directed by John Berry.

The Los Angeles production, which opened on January 15, 1948, at the Belasco Theatre, was produced by Ray Spencer and received the support of "Negro and White sponsors ... Catholic, Jewish and Protestant groups, from labor organizations and banks, from the right, the left and the middle."[14] The area chapter of the NAACP endorsed *Deep Are the Roots* as "highly educational and thought provoking and helpful in bringing about a better racial understanding,"[15] while Henry Blankfort writing for the *Los Angeles Tribune* described *Deep* thusly:

> [A] fine courageous play, superbly staged and acted.... This is piece of theatre, in my opinion, that combines expertly exciting entertainment and a meaningful and forceful stated message that is as important as it is powerful.[16]

With some help from the selling of discounted tickets, *Deep Are the Roots* broke box-office records and played to full houses, with the final performance standing room only. Playwright Patterson Green told the *Valley Jewish News*, "The play moves stirringly on its own momentum. Warm, prolonged applause indicates that Los Angeles will like it as well as New

York liked it." Rumors circulated that filmmakers had begun bidding for film rights.[17]

Having taken up acting only two years prior, Edwards now appeared in one of the most talked-about and successful plays of the period. His acting talent, described as "sensitive and skillful," no doubt added to his increasing stature. The *Los Angeles Fortnight* heaped applause on John Berry's direction and on Edwards' acting.[18]

However, in a bittersweet twist of fate for the *Deep Are the Roots* troupe, life imitated art as the cast found itself mired in the kind of situation that the play itself addressed. Following the success of its Los Angeles run, the company commenced a tour of the West Coast, with a planned extended tour of San Francisco.

But that city was ill-prepared for the sudden appearance of Black citizens who arrived there during the war years in search of employment at places such as the Hunters Point shipyard. Racism and systematic discrimination infected housing, education, public transportation, and labor. Neighbors banded together to keep Black (and Jewish) families from moving in, using a practice called restrictive covenants; Labor unions refused to admit Blacks.

Edwards, who along with stage manager David Sarvis and publicity manager Don Wheeldin, arrived at the Hotel Cecil on Post Street in San Francisco about 6:30 in evening on March 22, 1948, only to be informed that, as a family hotel, "they did not cater to Negroes." Wheeldin had wired the hotel earlier to confirm that reservations were in order. When the party arrived, the hotel clerk asked if the other guests were colored, and then preceded to deny them a room.[19]

The NAACP initiated a case against the Cecil (and against the Summerton Hotel on Geary Street). Cecil Poole, an African American war veteran and up-and-coming young attorney, represented the NAACP. The cast sued for $10,000 but Poole was more interested in mandated change than a cash award that he believed he would never see. (Keep in mind that $10,000 was a considerable amount of money in 1948.) In the end, the case was settled out of court and San Francisco Hotels would no longer discriminate against anyone on the basis of race.[20]

Edwards' comments about this incident, if he made comments, were apparently not widely publicized in the newspapers that would soon cover his every activity. Moreover, he would have little time to lament the situation. He career was taking off. He was cast in the part of a doomed boxer in an episode of the popular radio drama *The Adventures of Ellery Queen*;

later he performed in the *Lux Theatre* radio presentation of *Body and Soul,* starring John Garfield, with Edwards playing the part made famous by actor Canada Lee in the 1947 picture. And soon Edwards would make his debut in a Hollywood picture. The incident at the San Francisco hotel was untoward, heartrending, and not doubt hurtful to all involved. But Edwards was no stranger to racial bias.

2. The Greatest Break of His Life

Indiana native James Edwards was the eldest of four brothers and four sisters. His mother was Annie Mae Johnson, a domestic and Baptist minister; his father, James Valley Edwards, was a laborer and an instructor at the nearby Baptist Institute. They were married in August 1917 and James Edwards was born on March 18, 1918. The family moved from Muncie to Hammond in Lake County when Edwards was about five years old. The family moved again to Anderson, where Edwards attended Washington School and graduated from Anderson High School in 1936.[1]

The Edwards family was "staunch, spiritual and dedicated to education," notes one article on Edwards's life, with the children raised according to "American principles." Black parents knew that education was the key to being able to make something of oneself and the Edwards family was no different: Schooling was paramount. Edwards' siblings would become athletes, educators, members of the medical profession, entertainers, and business owners. Indeed, his mother would earn a degree in Theology in 1948 and, as part of her ministry, travel to Africa. Edwards' brother Chase, a track star, broke Jesse Owens' record for the 100 meters and coached the French Olympic track team during the 1950s. Brother Fred operated his own nightclub.[2]

Though the Edwards family appears to have thrived, like most families, they were not immune to life's challenges. In 1940, a notice of divorce appeared in the *Hammond Times*; unlike similar announcements, the suit between Mr. and Mrs. Edwards offered no details, beyond her request for $500 alimony. (Mr. Edwards remained in the area after the divorce; after hitting stardom, James paid him visits.) Still, it seems safe to assert that the Edwards family managed to weather their tribulations.[3]

Edwards seemed to be ordained for great achievement. In fact, his name appeared in newspapers long before he became a movie star. As a student at Anderson High he participated in school talent shows where he sang and performed a tap dance routine with another student. He was an instrumentalist in the school band and a student athlete; his name appears among a group of Anderson boys who competed at the annual sectional track and field qualifications in May 1936. No doubt enticed by the unparalleled fame of fighter and American hero Joe Louis Barrow, Edwards, too, took up boxing.[4]

"Edwards is an East Hammond colored boy who has taken all of his tourney fights by Kayo route," the *Hammond Times* noted. On April 19, 1938, Edwards, fighting in the 147-pound weight class, beat his opponent in a Calumet District Amateur Boxing Tournament sponsored by the Hammond-area American Legion Post 168. The tournament featured nineteen bouts and along with six other boys, Edwards represented Hammond in the novice division.

At the finals on April 20, at the Hammond Civic Auditorium, Edwards once again triumphed. "The Hammond colored boys ... and Jimmy Edwards, gained the acclaim of the crowd and the esteem of their victims," noted the *Hammond Times*. Edwards scored two first-round knockouts in three bouts, earning a comparison to Louis.[5]

Edwards pursued his dream to become a prizefighter for nearly ten years and was successful, becoming a Chicago Golden Gloves alternate. He turned pro and joined a stable of young boxers who traveled the East and Midwest, earning a salary of one dollar per day and a bonus for each match. One match was particularly brutal; Edwards was "beaten to a pulp," he reveals, and with some cajoling from his mother, he decided to forget boxing and turn his attentions to completing his education.[6]

Edwards enrolled at Indiana University but remained only briefly. He was disgusted, he revealed, by his encounters with race bias and segregation. Instead, he earned a degree in psychology at the Presbyterian-run Knoxville College in Tennessee. At Knoxville, he received an athletic scholarship and become a letterman. At the time, Knoxville was known for its teacher training programs and some sources hint that he considered a career in education. Becoming an actor, however, was the farthest thing from his mind. Edwards told the *Anderson Daily Bulletin*,

> When I was coming up, acting was unheard of—for blacks—except for Stepin Fetchit.... There was no chance and many of my friends thought me out of my mind.... But I decided I wanted to do it.[7]

After graduation from Knoxville, Edwards worked in the department of industrial personnel at the Calumet Steel Mill. He also worked for two years as a District representative for the War Production Board. At one time, he was a CIO organizer.

On December 7, 1941, with the Japanese bombing of the American naval base at Pearl Harbor, Hawaii, the stage was set for America's involvement in the second European War. The calls for isolationism ended and young men and women around the country enlisted in the United States military. At this time, even though racial bias was prohibited, the military made clear its lack of interest in enlisting Black men. There were no Black Marines and in the Navy, Black seamen were generally relegated to jobs as laborers or mess men. By 1943, however, as the war dragged on and the need for men in uniform increased, both James and his brother Charles were inducted into the Army.

By 1948, Edwards had been out of the Army for about two years. He had been acting for only about the same amount of time but had already earned a name for himself with his Chicago performances with the Skyloft Players and particularly for his appearance in the hit Broadway play *Deep Are the Roots*. Indeed, many actor hopefuls struggled for years just to be recognized, but Edwards' career careened upward.

In 1949, Edwards made his debut as a film actor as the servant of a murderous husband in the Paramount noir murder story, *Manhandled*. The picture, released in April, featured Dan Duryea, Sterling Hayden, Irene Hervey, and Dorothy Lamour. Edwards' name does not appear in the credits of this film, but then, neither do the names of many other bit players, including Maidie Norman, with whom Edwards would later work on radio and television.

In March of that same year Edwards saw the premiere of the Robert Wise production *The Set-Up* featuring Edwards in a small but intriguing role. *The Set-Up* was released by RKO Pictures (then owned by the elusive, eccentric millionaire, Howard Hughes) and directed by Wise, who would go on to create such notable films as *West Side Story* (1961), *Two for the Seesaw* (1962), *The Sound of Music* (1965), and *The Sand Pebbles* (1966). The picture stars Robert Ryan, fresh from his portrayal of an anti–Semitic killer in the 1947 Edward Dmytryk film *Crossfire*, and was based on Joseph Moncure March's long poem about a washed-up Black fighter. Edwards plays a boxer named Luther Hawkins, who, unlike the middle-aged and all but washed-up Stoker (Ryan), is young, strong, keen, and has a good chance of making it as a champion. We see him early in the

2. The Greatest Break of His Life

Edwards, a former fighter in real life, portrays prizefighter Luther Hawkins in the motion picture *The Set-Up* (1949). He is flanked here by Robert Ryan and Wallace Ford, whom Edwards credits with offering him guidance on the art of screen acting.

72-minute drama throwing punches to the air and announcing to everyone within earshot, "I feel good tonight!"[8]

Many scenes of the picture, which takes place in real time, are set in the crowded, dismal locker room where a stable of fighters, young, old, punch-drunk and battle-weary, dress and prepare for their bouts with the help of ragtag trainers and corner-men. At one point the coliseum manager appears and warns them to put on a good show since the patrons "paid a lotta dough to see 'em fight."

Midway through the black & white film, we witness a jubilant Hawkins, emerging successfully from his contest, exclaiming with the glee of a young boy, "What'd I tell ya? I knew I could take 'im ... I could feel it."

Edwards' co-stars include Audrey Totter as Stoker's wife, George Tobias, Alan Baxter, Wallace Ford, Percy Helton, Darryl Hickman, and

Kenny O'Morrison. It was Ryan, however, who would most influence Edwards' performance in the film.

In an April 1949 article appearing in *Ebony* magazine, Edwards made clear his appreciation for the advice he received from Ryan (and from Wallace Ford, who played the role of Gus, one of the trainers). Edwards said of Ryan:

> He told me about the differences between stage and screen acting. On the stage you express emotion more or less with complete freedom; on the screen, mostly with the eyes with very little facial contortions.[9]

Edwards revealed how unnerved he became performing in front of fellow cast members, the director and the technical crew. He notes, "Luckily, I went through the first take without blowing a line.... From then on, everything was gravy."[10]

While still appearing in the Los Angeles production of *Deep Are the Roots*, Edwards also performed in two Harry Wagstaff Gribble plays, *The Torch Grows Dim* and *Almost Faithful,* which were mounted at the Beaux Arts Theatre in Los Angeles. His co-stars in *Torch* included Gene Walker, Allen Derrick, Richard H. Farmer, Henry Corden, Jon Gusick, and Rosalyn Hayes.[11]

The Torch Grows Dim garnered little buzz and closed quickly. At the last performance, less than one dozen patrons filled the seats (the cast was fifteen actors).

One evening, after seeing Edwards' performance of *The Torch Grows Dim*, a stranger, a tall, lanky, blonde man, approached Edwards and complimented him on his skill as an actor. He gave Edwards a business card and requested his attendance at a meeting at 10 A.M. the following Monday. Edwards gave the stranger's request little consideration. He blew off the meeting. The man was Stanley Kramer. With his plain talk, earnest look, plaid shirts, and Plymouth coupe, Kramer probably did not exude the aura of anyone of importance. Kramer, too, was a veteran of the war, assigned to a Signal Corps company in New York where he edited Army newsreels. He was born in 1913 in New York's formidable Hell's Kitchen, where his bedroom, notes one biographer, consisted of a tiny roped-off space next to his mother's door. His mother held the family together, sans his absentee father's help, by working at the New York office of Paramount Pictures. He received his degree in business at NYU in 1933 and left New York for Hollywood where he pursued a job as a screenwriter. He found employment as a junior writer (and occasional laborer) at Twentieth Century–Fox. Later, he did research for Metro-Goldwyn-Mayer, progressing to a job as a scenario editor of two-reelers. On the side he wrote radio plays. At one time he served as an assistant to producer Albert Lewin and as associate producer to David Loew for the films *So Ends Our Night* (1941) and *The Moon and Sixpence* (1942). After the war, Kramer, dissatisfied with "Hollywood set-ups," decided to launch his own production company. He convinced a bank to put up sixty percent of the money needed for his first film, *So This Is New York*, by convincing the loan officer that all the individuals connected with the project "had a great deal of talent." He had also received the financial support of Robert Stillman, the son of a wealthy retired garment manufacturer who was interested in investing his money in the pictures. *So This Is New York* was a failure, but the deal Kramer cut called for financing for two pictures. With cash in hand he produced his second picture, *Champion*, starring Kirk Douglas. The classic boxing tale fared well and Kramer began work on his next project, based on an unsuccessful stageplay called *Home of the Brave*.[12] Edwards did not make the Monday morning appointment with Kramer. His manager telephoned him, asking the reasons why he skipped the meeting. He told Edwards to get down there or he would "come and drag him down."[13]

At the meeting, Edwards learned that the man he met was the producer of the hit film *Champion*. He told Edwards that he needed just the right person to star in his next picture. He "looked at Edwards, carefully studying him." Kramer, who preferred intuition to a formal audition process, learned of Edwards through his uncle, Earl Kramer, who was Edwards' manager at the time.[14]

"Look, you are the man for the lead in this picture," he told Edwards.[15]

No doubt when he initially dismissed Kramer's summons, Edwards didn't realize that their association would be life-changing. Little could he know, he had just been given the greatest break of his life.

3. A *Brave* Picture

In 1946, a recently discharged Army sergeant named Arthur Laurents basked in the triumph of watching his first stage play, *Home of the Brave,* open at the Belasco Theatre in New York. Laurents, who never experienced overseas combat during the war, blended fiction and personal experience for his hard-hitting dramatization of the trials and tribulations of a Jewish Army recruit, on duty in the South Pacific, who must come to grips with his resentments and sensitivity to anti–Semitism.

"When I was writing this government propaganda program, I used to make up stories," Laurents said in an interview. "That led to *Home of the Brave*.... I wrote that play in nine days while I was also writing Army stuff."[1]

Unfortunately for Laurents and his backers, *Home of the Brave* was not well received and closed after sixty-nine performances. Laurents, on the reason why audiences perhaps rejected his play, said:

> Innocently and unintentionally, I clouded my theme by using epithets ... never before seen or heard on the Broadway stage.... *Home of the Brave* emerged for too many as simply an angry play about anti–Semitism.[2]

Still, the play received the New York Drama Critics Circle Award; it toured London (retitled *The Way Back*); and Random House published the playscript. "*Home of the Brave* hadn't succeeded, but it hadn't failed either," Laurents said in a 1997 interview.[3]

Enter Stanley Kramer, another war veteran and the head of his own independent film production company, Screen Plays, Inc., which he located in an office on Sunset Boulevard. The staff of Screen Plays consisted of Kramer, a publicist named George Glass, writer Carl Foreman, and film director Mark Robson. Foreman, a Chicagoan, was born in 1914 and, like James Edwards, enrolled in classes at Northwestern University. During his time in the Army, he worked with Hollywood director Frank Capra's crew, which produced some of the most compelling documentary images of World War II. His first credit as a screenwriter was for the 1941 Monogram production of *Spooks Run Wild*. Robson was a Canadian-born film editor, producer, and director who earned positive praise for his work on Kramer's well-received production *Champion* (1949).

With a bit of front money from retired businessman Robert Stillman, Kramer sought already established properties such as popular novels, short stories, and hit stageplays for his material. He was well aware, he claimed, of "how the action of a stageplay is limited to a small space"; nonetheless, he sought out properties that he believed could be easily adapted to film. He purchased *Champion* and *The Big Town* from writer Ring Lardner for $17,500 apiece. *Champion* would become a huge hit. Kramer purchased *Home of the Brave* from Laurents for $50,000.[4] The screenplay was adapted for film by Foreman, who drew from his years living in Chicago and his observation of the city's treatment of Black citizens. He told *Ebony*:

> All of us were tense and excited when we got the green light to go ahead. We hoped we could be good enough to do justice to the story and we worked as we never did before in our lifetimes. This was breaking new ground, pioneering — and we had to be truthful and courageous. We didn't pull any punches.[5]

Foreman's script includes one major alteration of Laurents' story. Since earlier films such as *Gentleman's Agreement* and *Crossfire* (both released 1947) had exploited the subject of anti–Semitism, Kramer told Laurents, "Jews had been done." Therefore, in the motion picture version of *Brave*, the tortured Jewish soldier is changed to a Black man and the theme and lines of dialogue altered to reflect the problem of racial prejudice against Black Americans.[6]

In *Ebony* magazine, Kramer offered another reason why he switched from anti–Semitism to race hatred against Blacks:

> It would be three times as dynamic because if the story of a Jew forced to feel different was gripping on stage, then in motion pictures, the story of a Negro would be much more so, because the audience could see the difference in terms of color[.][7]

Edwards was cast as Peter Moss, a young Army private who is paralyzed after an attack, not from a wound endured in battle but from the rigors of racism that have haunted him for most of his life. After experiencing the traumatic loss of his friend and comrade, Finch, Moss suddenly finds he cannot walk. His paralysis is not physical but psychosomatic. Moss's story is told in flashback to the Army psychiatrist whose job it is to rehabilitate him.

As the film opens, four soldiers discuss whether they will accept a potentially dangerous assignment or back out while they still can. Their task is to map an enemy-infested Pacific island in preparation for an Allied invasion. In the midst of their debate, Pvt. Moss, a combat engineer, reports for duty, and to everyone's surprise, Moss is Black. Finch is delighted. As it happens, Moss was his high-school buddy and the two men enjoy a friendly reunion. Not everyone is so pleased. T.J. makes clears his utter displeasure with the idea of working with a *boogie*. He protests Moss' inclusion in the mission, reminding the others: "Why do you think the Army kept 'em out in the first place?"[8]

Major Robinson is nicknamed the "boy major" because he is only 26 years old. He slips away and calls his commander by telephone to explain, "He's colored, sir."

A crotchety, no-nonsense colonel asks, "Well, what color is he?"

He then informs Robinson that he doesn't care what color Moss is; further, that Moss is a capable engineer and good soldier (the major agrees). Most importantly, there is no alternative; other eligible men are either indisposed or not available. (Whether the general is truly color-blind or just simply desperate is not clear.)

T.J. serves as the villain of the story. He is a mean-spirited bigot who generally can't get along with anyone. He subscribes to common racist stereotypes about Blacks and questions their suitability for service in the armed forces. He makes no bones about using insulting language whenever he pleases. In one scene, he attempts to joke with Moss, and pats him playfully on the arm. In his own derisively crude manner he pretends to compliment Moss, and when he notes the disapproval in the eyes of Moss and

Edwards in his breakout role as the tortured Pvt. Moss in Stanley Kramer's *Home of the Brave* (1949).

the other men, he pretends he doesn't understand what he could have possibly said wrong.

Once the clamor over Moss is resolved, the five-man squad proceeds to their destination, an uncharted island infested with biting insects, overgrown foliage, and the unseen Japanese enemy. The men commence the work at hand, engaging playfully in soldier talk about women and bad Army food. Their uniforms are sweat-soaked and perspiration trickles from every face; they feign indifference to the danger that surrounds them, a danger heightened by the raucous screech of tropical birds.

The squad meets with enemy fire and the men flee. Sgt. Mingo takes a bullet but is ambulatory. However, before they can return to the raft and make their escape, they must retrieve the all-important maps left behind during the attack. While doing so, Finch is badly wounded and, for the good of the mission, has to be left behind. Moss wants to stay with his friend, but Finch insists he goes on. Moss insists. Finch, angry, yells at Moss and almost calls him a *nigger* but says *nitwit* instead. Moss is shocked. Now, he must struggle with the anguish of losing his best friend, and his bitterness at Finch's ugly words. Indeed, he decides that Finch is just like the others, the people who "make those cracks." Earlier, Moss revealed some of the experiences he had at school:

> When I was six, my first week at school, a bunch of kids got around me, whites, and said, "Hey, is your father a monkey?" I was dumb. I smiled and said, "No." They wiped the smile off my face. They beat it off. I had to get beat up a couple more times before I learned that if you're colored, you stink.

Later, Finch manages to crawl back to the makeshift camp. Moss is alone, as the others have gone to the raft. He is jubilant that his friend has returned. But his joy quickly turns to grief when Finch succumbs to his wounds and dies while cradled in Moss' arms. The other men return to retrieve Moss and the maps. Amongst deadly gunfire, Moss suddenly finds he can't walk. Though he has not been wounded, he must be carried to the raft.

At a field hospital, Moss is attended by an Army psychiatrist who, using a method called narcosynthesis, hopes to cure Moss of the hypersensitivity to the racism that affects him. "You've got to be cured," the doctor repeats again and again. The entire story, the mission, the racist taunts of T.J., the men's narrow escape from the island, and Finch's tragic death are related to the psychiatrist in flashback. The doctor convinces Moss that he needn't be ashamed for being glad that Finch was killed and not him.

Moss lies helplessly in bed, sobbing and perspiring, while the imposing figure of the psychiatrist looms over him with a Godlike presence. Moss tries to explain his feelings about being Black: "You're not like other people. You're different. You're alone. You're something strange...." When Moss refuses to try to make his legs work again, the doctor resorts to the same familiar, ugly words that help to put Moss in his predicament in the first place: "Get up and walk, you dirty nigger!"

Moss, stunned and fuming, staggers up from his bed. He can walk again. He falls into the doctor's arms in tearful thankfulness.

Today a dénouement such as this one would most likely elicit little more than boos and derisive laughter. However, in 1949, the travails of Peter Moss resonated with audiences of all races who were willing to overlook the rather contrived plot device. Donald Spoto, who wrote a biography of Kramer, noted, "[The film] has an awkward sincerity, which is probably hard for most viewers to respect today, because the conventions of dialogue, acting and setting now seem dated. But in 1949, *Home of the Brave* was a revolutionary expose of a real social evil."[9]

"I told Mr. Kramer I'd play the part just for three meals a day and a place to sleep. Money was unimportant," Edwards told *Negro Digest*. Edwards would be paid, $750 per week for approximately five weeks of work. The small all-male cast consisted of actors who were largely unknown, including: Lloyd Bridges as Finch, Frank Lovejoy as Sgt. Mingo, Douglas Dick as Major Robinson, Jeff Corey as the psychiatrist, and Steve Brodie as the bigot, T.J.[10]

Native Californian Lloyd Bridges was born in 1913 to a father who owned a nickelodeon. He began his acting career in the 1930s appearing in two-reel comedies. By the war years he earned speaking parts in such features as the 1943 Columbia Pictures war story *Sahara*, starring Humphrey Bogart. Frank Lovejoy was born in New York in 1912 and debuted on Broadway in 1934 in the play *Judgment Day*. *Home of the Brave* was only his second picture. Born 1920 in West Virginia, Douglas Dick had four film roles under his belt, including a part in Alfred Hitchcock's 1948 production of *Rope*. New Yorker Jeff Corey, born in 1914, began acting in a Shakespearean repertory before amassing dozens of film credits as a character actor in such productions as *My Friend Flicka* (1943) and *Miracle on 34th Street* (1947). Kansan Steve Brodie was born in 1919 and had appeared, mostly uncredited, as a bit player in dozens of films before his role in *Brave*.

The secrecy involved in the production of *Brave* is the stuff of Hol-

3. A Brave *Picture*

Edwards, pictured with *Home of the Brave* co-stars Lloyd Bridges and Frank Lovejoy.

lywood legend. The film's cast was all but sequestered on their closed sound stage, taking their lunch and breaks together. "The company practically slept on the set," Robson told Hedda Hopper. When questioned, Kramer lied about his intentions. The production was shot under the working title *High Noon*.[11] Both the cast and crew were sworn to secrecy. Kramer recalled, "All the actors ... came in through the rear entrance of the set, had lunch there. Everything was very quiet so no one would know what we were really doing."[12]

In regard to his desire for strict confidentiality, Kramer revealed, "We had to expect opposition from every corner." He knew that any announcement of the picture's true theme would draw demands from many people, from Black organizations to Southern theatre owners, to anti–Negro pressure groups. Therefore, Kramer claimed that he wished to avoid the "pressures, suggestions of those not connected with its [*Home of the Brave*] making."[13]

Secondly, Kramer was aware that there other productions in progress with a similar theme. Some say that his only motive was to release the first film to explore America's race issue. Kramer admitted, "A desire to get my picture into the theatres ahead of them may have influenced my decision to keep *Home of the Brave* secret, but the fear of stirring up racists was the primary reason."[14]

In fact, from Kramer's purchase of the play, to the casting of Edwards as Pvt. Moss, the project's existence was reported in both the Black and mainstream press. Still, no one really knew what to expect.

Home of the Brave was conceived and released in a period of perhaps three months. The budget for the production was approximately $600,000; the shooting was completed in thirty days for $525,000. Robson described his technique to keep shooting time down as "conference-rehearsal": an intensive, shot-for-shot rehearsal for the cast, crew, and designers. Further, Kramer revealed that at one point they used three units, shooting simultaneously, "to make time."[15]

In May 1949, *Home of the Brave* debuted at the Victoria Theatre in New York, but not before a protracted sequence of pre-screenings and preparation. A special booklet was developed and distributed to set forth various policies pertaining to the film. George Glass, Kramer's publicist, traversed the country to convince theatres to book the film. *Variety* reported on the nearly 100 screenings and private showings of the film that had been arranged for the benefit of various individuals and organizations. The purpose was to avoid controversy, to "build word of mouth," and, of course, garner publicity. Glass hired a squadron of "vet picture flaks" to circulate amongst Black groups and labor organizations. The *Home of the Brave* campaign, reported *Variety*, would be "one of the biggest ever staged by a film company." Eddie Burbridge, writing for the *Los Angeles Sentinel*, described how at a screening at the Carthay Circle Theatre on San Vicente Boulevard in Los Angeles "before a notable audience of press representatives," some of the audience members screamed and cheered at the very sight of Edwards when he appeared in various scenes. Glass, satisfied with the enormous amount of generated buzz, jokingly referred to himself as a "promotional genius."[16]

Home of the Brave became one of the most talked-about films of 1949. In his biography, Kramer described how people stood and cheered and remained in the theatre after the film ended. Others lingered in the aisles to discuss the film with other members of the audience. Many were stunned by the film's power and message or shocked that such a picture had been made at all. "Don't be discouraged by the lines and the SRO signs," urged *Color* magazine, "just be sure you see [*Home of the Brave*]."[17]

Home of the Brave was nominated for Best Picture by such organizations as the New York Film Critics Award and the Associated Press Poll. Edwards and Kramer would become the subject of essays, feature stories, and photo spreads that appeared in publications in the United States and abroad, including such mainstream periodicals as *The Commonweal, Life,* and *The Saturday Evening Post.*

Assessments of the picture were, of course, not universally positive; some were downright unflattering. To be sure, the film is far from a cinematic masterpiece. First, the scenario presented was implausible due to the Army's practice of racial segregation during World War II. (Kramer conceded the unlikelihood of such "race mixing" actually occurring, but noted, "I figured I might be forgiven for jumping the gun[.]") The main set resembled a sound stage full of fake foliage, which one critic described as "broccoli-like." Even the bird calls were apparently phony. An article in the *New York Herald Tribune* revealed that a man named Herbert Tweedy performed "twelve calls correctly corresponding to those of birds indigenous to Pacific islands." While the stirring score by composer/arranger Dmitri Tiomkin added immeasurably to the solemn atmosphere and tension, the fact that the story was all but lifted from a script intended for the stage sometimes caused the film to stall and feel out of rhythm.[18]

"I doubt that the scars of race prejudice can be healed as neatly and briskly as *Home of the Brave* would have us to believe," noted the film critic for *The New Yorker*.[19] *Time* magazine tendered its complaints about the film's theme:

> [L]ike most movies with a weighty message, *Home* pays a heavy price for treating human beings as if they were clearly defined symbols in a propaganda tract.... [T]he arguments against discrimination get badly mixed up with the abracadabra of psychiatry.[20]

Even baseball star Jackie Robinson weighed in, complaining to the *San Rafael (CA) Independent Journal*, "I liked *Home of the Brave* except for the scene where Edwards broke down and felt sorry for himself because he was a Negro. I don't think many people feel that way[.]"[21]

It is interesting to note that few reviews of *Home of the Brave* can be found in papers of the Deep South where it was banned in many cities. Also noteworthy is the number of critics, possibly offended by or resentful of the picture, who damned it with faint praise by offering little more than a synopsis of the plot—steering clear of offering commendation or condemnation and omitting any assessment or even mention of the film's message, power, or impact. Some took umbrage at the fact that *Brave* was a *message* picture. Probably one of the more notably negative assessments of the picture was delivered by Manny Farber of *The Nation*:

> The irrelevantly titled *Home of the Brave* is a war film which starts with some good shattering shots ... but suddenly changes into idle, muddy psychiatric double-talk and a tepid display of the Negro problem.[22]

But many of the individuals who tendered their comments on the film, from local rags to major monthlies, were fulsome in their praise of Kramer's newest offering. A critic for the *Clearfield (PA) Progress* wrote: "*Home of the Brave* is one of those pictures it's difficult to be lukewarm about.... These actors, plus eloquent background music and overall two-fisted treatment make the Arthur Laurent play into an excellent movie."[23] Even *Time* magazine, along with laying on criticism, extolled its praises of *Home of the Brave:*

> [F]or all its faults, the film has novelty, emotional wallop and the excitement that comes from wrestling with a real problem ... even when it fumbles the statement of its message, the film retains a sort of rough-&-ready strength.[24]

The *Motion Picture Herald* called the film "superb," noting:

> Beautifully acted by the small male cast, the film is an achievement in direction.... It is hard hitting and tense; the dialogue is crisp; there are touches of subtle humor; the camera work and musical score are top shelf, and its moments of pathos will choke up the most calloused.[25]

A review for the *Annapolis (MD) Capital* said,

> Arthur Laurents' unusual drama ... has been made into a screenplay of exceptional power and distinction.... [I]t is the most exciting screen entertainment of the year.... [I]t is a mighty big, important and thrilling production, telling a scorching story that will thrill everyone who is lucky enough to see it.[26]

The *San Mateo (CA) Times* wrote:

> For the second time this season, Stanley Kramer has made an important contribution to the American screen.... [A] drama of significance is arrived.... [H]ere is a picture that not only forces its onlookers to think and study and evaluate and become introspective, but one that is fine entertainment ... it should not be missed.[27]

The critic for *Variety*, who referred to Edwards as "the colored boy," noted:

> This comparatively inexpensive picture hits hard and with utter credibility.... [O]nce customers are inside the theatre *Home* will have started a

progression of comment that should win an accolade for the producer for having the courage to produce such a pic. And for doing it so well.[28]

The Commonweal offered this opinion:

> I now urge those audiences as well as others to go to a new picture called *Home of the Brave*.... [It] is done in first-rate cinema and manages, as a true work of art should, to be entertaining and at the same time put over its message without sounding like a sermon on tolerance.[29]

Bosley Crowther, writing for the *New York Times*, which ran a six-photograph feature on the picture, lauded Edwards' performance and describes the film as, "a drama of force and consequence — a film of emotional impact as well as a strong intellectual appeal."[30]

Clearly, much of the postwar film-going audience was not put off by the film's shortcomings. African Americans, in particular, were too engrossed with the hard-hitting story and the appearance of Edwards in the leading role to quibble about the corny set design and counterfeit ending. In sum, a failed stage play, quickly adapted for the screen, produced by a little-known filmmaker, shot in a hurry and on the cheap with no-name actors, was an unequivocal and resounding hit.

4. "Hollywood's Boldest Stroke for Democracy"

Home of the Brave was landmark in its depiction of the ugliness of racial bigotry. Critical acclaim aside, however, the film offered no solution to the problem. Edwards told the *Christian Science Monitor*, "I don't believe any human being can tell what the solution is today.... This picture isn't the last word on the subject; it is the first word."[1]

While no clear-thinking person would believe that any one motion picture could ameliorate what was then called "the Negro problem," given the response to the picture, it is clear that citizens of various races saw *Home of the Brave* as an educational tool that might serve as a catalyst for positive change. One *Washington Post* editorial writer declared, "Certainly, the educational impact of these films [*Home of the Brave, Pinky, Lost Boundaries*] has been wholly positive." Indeed, hundreds of letters poured into the editorial offices of the Black and mainstream press touting the edifying effects of *Home of the Brave*.[2] The Baltimore (MD) *Afro-American*, in a two-page, photo-laden feature, declared that the picture "pulled no punches and hits hard against racial hatred." The article, which described the film as "sensational," printed selections from the script, noting:

> There are many more conversations in *Home of the Brave* like this which will make you say "amen" and there are some scenes, especially those in the thick of battle, when white GIs are still worrying about color that will make you grit your teeth. But one thing is sure, *Home of the Brave* has a lesson to teach[.][3]

Brave was a significant film on three fronts. First, of particular note is the opportune timing of the film's release in May 1949. Just ten months earlier, President Harry Truman issued Executive Order 9980 establishing the Committee on Equality and Opportunity in the Armed Forces, a directive that would begin the long and painful process of integrating America's military services. During the second European War, even as Army officials reluctantly began to accept the fact that racial segregation was a wasteful and inefficient use of personnel and equipment, the topic remained a thorny one. With his issuance of the Executive Order, Truman applied the first stroke toward ending segregation and racial bias in the military services. In a discussion of the film, the Baltimore (MD) *Afro-American* posed this question: "What happens when a colored solider is asked to defend his country on the one hand, and then is tortured by his fellow Americans who are fighting a common enemy?"[4] Kramer would be the first filmmaker to explore the volatile topic, not of integration per se, but of racial prejudice in the military and the effect that bigotry had on the morale and productivity of the armed forces. *Home of the Brave* addressed the implications of integration, opening up for conscious consideration the need to dismantle prejudice and discrimination in America's military.

Home of the Brave was significant on a second front: For decades, the vicious lampooning of Black life and popular culture was a standard element of illustrations, marketing, advertising, radio, and narrative film. Images of the docile, toothless Sambo, the foolish and dandified Zip Coon, contented slaves, mindless but devoted servants, and Black pickaninny children who lived in trees, played to the expectations of the audience, many who believed these depictions truly represented Black people. After World War II, Black Americans, many of whom had fought in the war against totalitarianism, refused to acquiesce to the insulting depictions which had been a mainstay of Hollywood pictures. Postwar Black citizens were engaged in a daunting struggle to lift up the race and prevail over the limitations imposed upon them. They earned advanced degrees, ran businesses, and gained employment in government, business, and the professions. At the same time, Black leadership tendered their demands that Hollywood depict Negro citizens in an improved light. Still, while the more demeaning images slowly disappeared, producers seemed reluctant to cast Black actors in roles other than as servants. Writer and poet Langston Hughes ruefully described the standard direction for Black actors playing chauffeurs:

> Upon opening the car door for one's white employer in any film, the director would command: "Jump to ground. Remove cap. Open car door. Step back and bow. Come up smiling. Now bow again. Now straighten up and grin.[5]

Black citizens saw *Home of the Brave* as a signal that Hollywood had finally put the worn-out, derisive Negro film types to rest. *Brave* depicted a Black man as an everyday individual, an authentic person and not an anomaly. Moss was not a coward or comic with so-called Negro dialect spilling from his lips, nor was he someone's manservant: He was an American soldier. Eddie Burbridge, columnist for the *Los Angeles Sentinel*, wrote,

> The writer sees in Edwards' acting a cheering aspect for future roles of a similar nature for Negro actors ... pulling him out of the old Uncle Tom, maid, butler, stable boy and other menial roles which the general public, both Negro and white, are getting sick and tired of seeing.[6]

Edwards described *Home of the Brave* as the "daring vehicle of a producer who decided to explode the myth that Negroes couldn't play straight dramatic roles."[7]

Thirdly, though discrimination infected nearly all facets of American life, the Negro problem was considered a taboo subject not to be broached candidly. Prejudice against Black citizens was an unpleasant fact, but was not a popular topic of discussion for most beyond a contingent of brave journalists and fearless leaders. *Home of the Brave* was the first Hollywood film to present an honest and forceful rendering of the serious issue of race prejudice in America. Incorporating some of the harshest and most explicit language that had ever emanated from a motion picture screen, *Brave* tackled the important issue in a fashion that contrasted the soft-touch exploration of social problems deployed in the average film. Bosley Crowther of *The New York Times* wrote, "The urgent and delicate subject of anti–Negro prejudice, often remarked but never fully discussed ... is finally advanced with thorough candor[.]"[8]

The critic for *Motion Picture Herald* said:

> *Home of the Brave* is indeed a brave picture in the sense that it deals with the sensitive subject of racial intolerance.... [I]t is in fact startling to hear many of the expressions, which are employed usually by the prejudiced, coming from the screen.[9]

"Run, do not walk, to the nearest subway and see *Home of the Brave*," urged Bill Chase of the *New York Age*. "For at last, Hollywood has come of age ... with Stanley Kramer's ingenious and adult treatment of the anti–Negro question, which, until now, has been a mere suggestion here and there."[10]

"Once in a while," wrote a critic for the *Cedar Rapids (IA) Gazette*, "...a movie comes along that seems to call for an editorial rather than a review.... Here is a picture that you can't look at dispassionately.... A picture that hits hard and fast ... a picture that makes no bones about the Negro prejudice in America, that even uses the word 'nigger' when it does the most good."[11] The film critic for the *Abilene (TX) Reporter* opined, "*Home of the Brave* already has excited film fans over the nation, rating high praise from some and criticism from others. Many consider Hollywood courageous to have filmed a picture based on a subject 'taboo' for many years."[12] And the *Madison (WI) Capital Times* noted:

> *Home of the Brave* is, in its way, a work of art, an example of acting and a penetrating lesson in tolerance.... [S]ome of its sequences will choke up the most calloused moviegoer.... It is something new and venturesome in our censor-ridden society as it deals, tellingly, with anti–Negro prejudices and the forces that deny citizenship to 10% of our people.[13]

Crowther also said in his review, "Mr. Kramer's picture comes directly and honestly to grips with the evil of racial defamation, which is one of the cruelest disturbers in our land. It faithfully shows the shattering damage which racial bias can do to one man.... [T]he impression upon the national audience will be most interesting to gauge."[14]

"The producers of *Home of the Brave* thought there might be resentment among colored people at the use of the word *nigger* in the picture," Edwards told the *Monitor*. "But it was intensely satisfying to me to find that not a single criticism came from those on whom we previewed the picture on that score."[15]

Indeed, screenings of *Brave* were accompanied by controversy and the fear of race riots. The film saw its share of censorship, protests, and picket lines; Kramer described the countless demonstrations that accompanied screenings of the film. But no screening of *Brave* was ever reported as the cause of violence. Some officials of Southern states banned the film in fear of racial unrest that never materialized. In Houston, Texas, Black citizens turned out in droves for the segregated midnight screenings of *Brave*, while in Dallas, at the Majestic Theatre, Black residents filled the Blacks-only balcony seats. *Time* magazine notes, "The sky did not fall, but a Dallas box-office record did.... [N]either city had seen any ugly incidents nor received any customer complaints. Word-of-mouth in Dallas was overwhelmingly favorable, and the local critics greeted the film with applause." The story of Peter Moss became the theme of church sermons, not riots.[16]

In Washington, D.C., the film's showing prompted citizens to protest the discriminatory practices of the Trans-Lux Theatre chain with its outright banning of Negroes. Black and White citizens wrote letters of complaint and Black patrons attempted to purchase tickets, knowing they would be turned away. The theatre was picketed by various organizations. "Truly, I felt ashamed," remarked an editorial writer to the *Washington Post*, "and I can only hope that somehow its [*Home of the Brave*] story will make enough others ashamed, so that Washington will open their doors to Negroes[.]"[17]

When the National Press Club in Washington, D.C., invited its members to attend a special screening, *Time* magazine pointed out the irony: "What the invitation did not need to say was that only whites will be welcome; the Press Club bars Negroes from its club rooms and from membership."[18]

Also worth mention is the controversy generated by the Memphis, Tennessee, censor, Lloyd T. Binford, who was notorious for his conservative, heavy-handed banning of films from Memphis movies screens. During his nearly 30-year term, he arbitrarily banned any picture that didn't fit his tastes, whether he had actually seen the film or not. He even banned *Our Gang* shorts because of the series' multi-racial casting. Therefore, it came as a surprise to some when he gave *Home of the Brave* the green light. Binford no doubt realized that even he could not ebb the film's notoriety and that a ban would do little more than to deny Memphis theatres their profits.[19]

Edwards had described *Home of the* Brave as the first word in the dialogue toward change, adding, "But many, many thousands of such words, millions perhaps, all driving toward the same goal, will sooner or later roll over this tradition and wipe it out." Indeed, for Americans of every race, *Home of the Brave* was more than simply an entertaining film, it was groundbreaking, and as described by the *Chicago Defender*, "Hollywood's boldest stroke for democracy."[20]

5. James Edwards Had Arrived

Edwards spent approximately three years in the U.S. Army but the details of his enlistment and his subsequent assignments are difficult to confirm. His military record and those of thousands of other veterans were lost during a 1973 fire at the National Personnel Records Center in St. Louis, Missouri; eighty percent of the records of persons discharged from the Army between 1912 and 1960 were destroyed. Edwards was enlisted, possibly in 1943. At this time the military services, grappling with a dwindling number of enlistees, and bowing to the fervent protests of African American citizens and their leaders, consented to the drafting of Black men for military service. A 1940 selective service act had prohibited discriminatory practices in the draft, but Black man were nonetheless routinely rejected on the basis that they were deemed unsuitable and further, that there were not enough separate facilities to house them. By 1943, as the world teetered toward catastrophe, the military was forced to bend from its discriminatory policies.[1]

Edwards began as a private in the 92nd Infantry Division U.S. Army, the only all–Black division infantry division that saw combat in Europe during the Second World War. The unit's components included among others, the 365th, 370th, and 371st Infantry Regiments, the 597th, 598th, 599th and 600th Field Artillery Battalions and the 317th Engineer Combat Battalion, as well as a medical battalion, signal, and quartermaster company. As was standard practice, this all–Black unit was commanded by White officers, including the infamously bigoted Major Gen. Edward M. Almond, who did not believe that integration would increase combat effectiveness and who once described his Negro troops as lazy, undependable, and good at avoiding work.[2]

Edwards was assigned to the Quartermaster Corps for a time, and was then selected for Officer's Training School, perhaps without his consent. The military hierarchy, again responding to demands of America's Black leadership for a fair shake, began the training of Black men as commissioned officers. Edwards earned a commission as a 2nd Lieutenant, and later exchanged his gold bars for the rank of 1st Lieutenant.

The next problem for the segregated Army was where to assign the new Black officers, who were, of course, limited to serve only with all–Black units. Eventually, the number of Black officers exceeded the places they could be assigned. Many were forced to languish in make-work projects, a further cause of dissension and low morale within the ranks.

At some point, Edwards was assigned to the unit's signal company. Perhaps because of his degree in psychology and his experience with personnel issues, he was tasked to amass data on the behavior of Negro troops under pressure. Whether this was an example of a make-work assignment or not, for Edwards it would be a perfect training ground for his future work as an actor.[3]

While the personnel records of many Black soldiers are lost to history, well documented is the record of the racially segregated American military: the plight of Black soldiers stationed in racist Jim Crow communities; the separate but not quite equal facilities; the bigoted White Southern officers who were assigned as commanders of all–Black companies; the Black soldiers who were unfairly court-martialed because they dared venture into a local segregated eating establishment; the mysterious and unsolved murders and mutilations of Black soldiers; the fatal racial conflicts; the complaints of Black units who were constantly uprooted and shuttled from location to location because of the objections of Whites living in nearby towns; and the bias in career fields and promotions. Indeed, the tales of Negro airmen, soldiers, sailors, and Marines who suffered through mental and physical abuse and insults not only from the military hierarchy and fellow soldiers, but from the local communities in which they were stationed, can be found in memoirs and letters, and in brutal accounts found in newspaper articles written by the reporters of the African American press. Edwards would have been very lucky to escape his share of tribulations. One biographer notes that during Edwards' extended hospital stay, his roommate, a North Carolinian, refused to speak to him. Indeed, Edwards told the *Christian Science Monitor* that there were few sides of racial prejudice that he had not personally experienced. One might conclude that he had been in training for the role of Moss for most of his life.[4]

Even as he was showered with accolades and called a hero and the symbol of his race, Edwards understood that what people most appreciated about *Home of the Brave* was the impact and power of the film's weighty message. This does not imply, of course, that he was undeserving of the applause heaped upon him for his outstanding portrayal of an anguished soldier. The part of Peter Moss was an emotionally and physically challenging role for any actor, and it was novice Edwards' third picture with a speaking role.

As Moss, he portrayed a Negro who was aware, painfully aware, of his second-class status. Overly sensitized, Moss recoils at every real or perceived racial slight; he seethes with umbrage, wallows in self-pity, and allows the years of bitterness and resentment to spill from lips full of derisive sarcasm. Finally, he succumbs to the physical and psychological consequences of years of abuse. In Edwards' deft hands, the character Moss feels disarmingly authentic.

In one notable scene, Moss loses his bearing and flies into a rage; he recalls how his family was threatened, and how he was beaten up by a bunch of white kids. By then, he declares ruefully, at the age of ten years, he was "used to it." Edwards delivers these lines with finesse. Moss' anguish is ever so genuine and heartfelt, that it is not hard to imagine that Edwards had drawn upon his own personal experiences.

Edwards' review clippings for *Home of the Brave* were nearly universally positive. "James Edwards as the Negro is superb," wrote *Motion Picture Herald*. Indeed, from the major dailies to the smallest Midwestern hometown weekly, film critics sang their praises of Edwards. *Variety* wrote, "James Edwards plays the Negro; he gives an always believable performance." Edwards' hometown paper, the *Chicago Defender*, declared, "If a person likes good acting, he will like Jimmy Edwards."[5] For the Cedar Rapids (IA) *Gazette*, a critic wrote:

> And standing out above all the rest is the performance by James Edwards, the young Negro who has the principal role. He is always exactly right — from the quiet moments in which he must take insults to the searing moment when his buddy dies in his arms."[6]

The *Monthly Film Bulletin* concluded:

> Just as *Champion* was partially mitigated by a powerful central performance, so *Home of the Brave* at moments gains authentic quality from the playing of James Edwards as the Negro; he brings dignity and passion to the character.[7]

The *New York Age* said that Edwards "turns in a top, well-controlled performance in a role that might easily have been over-played." The *San Mateo (CA) Times* described Edwards as "magnificent," and the Clearfield (PA) *Press* said, "James Edwards ... gives a sensitive and powerful portrayal[.]"[8]

Brave was released during a thorny period in the history of the civil rights struggle in America. The lynching of African Americans continued almost unchallenged; public water fountains and restrooms were separate for each race; personal relationships between Black men and White women, such as portrayed in plays such as *Deep Are the Roots*, were illegal in many states; Black life and culture was defiled in popular entertainments; publicly funded schools were segregated along racial lines; and in government, housing, education, professional sports, business, and other institutions, discrimination against Black Americans was the accepted norm. The Black man was considered a second-class citizen, a threat and a monster, yet Edwards' performance in a film that depicted a taboo subject, the Negro problem, was seen as exemplary, so much so that the film critics could not help but applaud his efforts in a sometimes effusive manner.

Indeed, for Edwards the critical acclaim and positive notoriety of *Brave* would be life-changing. Three years prior, when asked to come to New York to audition, he had to borrow the fare from friends. He revealed to *Negro Digest*:

> I got to New York with ten cents in my pocket. I walked all the way from LaGuardia Airport, over the Tri-Borough Bridge to 125th Street and then downtown to a friend's apartment. I was carrying three bags and was hot, hungry, and tired.[9]

Upon his return to the city just two years later, he was welcomed with ceremony normally reserved for heads of state. A barrage of reporters, newsreel photographers, the Mayor's Committee, and a brass band greeted the new star at the airport. A motorcade of motorcycle policeman and "50 cars packed with Harlem's most prominent citizens" escorted him to his hotel as their sirens screamed to New Yorkers that a prominent visitor had come to town. In Harlem, during a parade in his honor, Edwards was received by Hugo Rogers, borough president, who gave Edwards the keys to the city. An entourage consisting of sixteen Cadillacs, the 369th Infantry Regiment Band, and elements of the New York National Guard led Edwards' party to the Theresa Hotel. Indeed, a minor clamor erupted as local politicians and organizers of the event who were not offered seats in the same car as Edwards acted like spoiled children and made clear their discontent. Edwards lunched at Sardi's and made a speech, declaring that he was "proud to be a part of the struggle for racial equality."[10]

"Mr. Edwards was a good representative of the best of negro artists and artistry," declared Jane White, aspiring actress and daughter of Walter White, chair of NAACP. Edwards proclaimed his "responsibility as a man who is proud to be a part of the over-all struggle" and assured the crowd, "I accept this responsibility as a person and as an artist."[11]

Edwards was no doubt thrilled and pleased when on May 31, 1949, *Brave* premiered at the Woods Theatre in Chicago, his adopted hometown. He made personal appearances there on May 31 and June 1, and later that week, he appeared at Chicago's South Center Department Store. He also visited high schools and received honors from Chicago's civic organizations.[12]

Edwards was now a movie idol; fan clubs sprang up and his activities were covered in the mainstream and African American press. Riding the tide, he basked in the celebrity and éclat of his new-found fame as the handsome and unmarried lead of a wildly successful motion picture that everyone was talking about.

An article appearing in the May 1951 edition of *Our World* followed him to Bermuda where he enjoyed sun, golf, tennis, tours, "pink-tinted sand," and "warm invigorating winds." He appeared in a lengthy photo-filled travelogue, nattily attired and donning in his preferred yachting cap. In one shot, his arms encircle the waist of a shapely bathing beauty. On his face is a toothy, open-mouthed smile.[13]

James Edwards, the regular guy from Indiana as he liked to refer to himself, had arrived.

6. "Triple-Threat Edwards"

In 1949, neophyte movie star James Edwards appeared in the casts of three motion pictures playing at the same time. For this feat, the Baltimore (MD) *Afro-American* assigned him the moniker "Triple-Threat Edwards."[1]

In the film *Manhandled*, Edwards had made his film debut with a small speaking part. According to *Variety*'s "Boxoffice Survey" for late May 1949, the film was doing just "average." Edwards also appeared in *The Set-Up* in a meaty role as a boxer. *The Set-Up*, noted *Variety*, was "proving a strong entry."[2]

At the same time, *Home of the Brave* made box-office history, breaking attendance records. *Brave* brought in $21,000 in one week in Houston, unprecedented in 1949. "There's not much exciting among the new pictures except *Home of the Brave*," *Variety* noted. For the week of June 1, the trade paper reported, "*Home of the Brave* ... is setting new all-time high in Chicago this week and still going great guns in third N.Y. stanza." In the same issue of the paper, a display advertisement announced, "*Home of the Brave* has Broken the All-Time House Record Set by *Red River* at the Woods Theatre, Chicago." By June 8, *Variety* wrote that *Brave* was "off to a smash weekend" and did "rousing trade" in Chicago, New York, Los Angeles and San Francisco. Even during the summer slump, *Brave* continued to draw."[3]

With the success and the popularity afforded him by his performance, James Edwards took his place as a bona fide movie star, icon, spokesperson, and public figure. His activities were detailed in periodicals tailored to the tastes of African Americans (*Our World, Hue, Color, Tan Confessions,* and *Sepia*), and news of his projects was published in mainstream newspapers across the country. He hobnobbed with such Hollywood notables as Van Johnson and Richard Widmark; he dined at Sardi's;

and throngs of female fans who competed for his attention at speaking engagements. He seemed to be everywhere: from cocktails at the El Grotto, the swingingest nightclub on the Southside of Chicago, to parties at the popular club Morocco in Los Angeles where he socialized with his friend, the flamboyant singer and musician Dorothy Donegan.

He came to feature prominently among what some called the "New Negro" in Hollywood film, including Ossie Davis, the tall stage sensation with the commanding voice, and Ruby Dee, whose talent matched that of her husband; Dorothy Dandridge, talented, posh, and alluringly beautiful (she would be the first African American woman whose face would grace the covers of *Life* magazine); Harry Belafonte, the suave, sexy singer with the creamy complexion; and Sidney Poitier, infinitely gifted as an actor and on his way to stardom with the success of his performance in the Oscar-nominated 20th Century–Fox production *No Way Out* (1950).

Edwards embraced the accoutrements of success: nice clothing (he was a snappy dresser) and a new car, awarded him by "the Buick folks." In 1952, he appeared in print advertisements for Lord Calvert Whisky in their "Men of Vision" advertising campaign featuring outstanding men in their field. He attended the best parties that Black Los Angeles had to offer. Some were hosted by Lillian Cumber, a journalist and talent agent known as "the bronze tattler," and others presided over by Lillie and Dan Montgomery, whom Edwards called his "California family." Edwards bragged, "I've lunched at Romanoff's, had caviar at Gourmet's. I've inhaled the rare vintage wines, and I believe I have the proper savior faire." (Just a few years prior, Edwards had arrived in New York for his first audition with 10¢ in his pocket, dressed in a purple zoot suit, yellow coat, yellow feather in his hat, and a long gold chain dangling from a pocket.)[4]

But socializing and schmoozing encompassed only a small part of Edwards' life at this time. According to an article that appeared in the *Pittsburgh Courier*, the handsome new star of *Home of the Brave* was "very, very busy." Sans new offers for pictures, Edwards kept himself in the public eye and capitalized on his celebrity. Indeed, by his own admission, he pursued "a hectic three years of theatrical ups and downs, work on new movies ... radio stints and barnstorming over the country." Among other ventures, he worked in the old medium of radio, ventured into the new medium of television, wrote magazine articles, explored his options as a director and producer, made recordings, appeared in live theatre, and maintained a grueling schedule of speaking engagements, personal appearances, and part-time jobs.[5]

With an opening day cocktail party in August 1949, Edwards established the James Edwards School of Dramatics. "Jimmy is putting forth every effort in making this school one of the best in the country," wrote Gertrude Gipson, columnist for California's premier Black newspaper, the *California Eagle*. Edwards joined a staff of four to teach classes in "dramatic technique."[6]

In October 1949, as *Home of the Brave* continued to make box-office history, and as the original cast (including Hilda Simms and Frederick O'Neal) toured London, Edwards appeared in performances of the Philip Yordan play *Anna Lucasta* during its Chicago engagement at the Regal Theatre. Later, in Los Angeles, Edwards was "thrilled and happy" to receive an honorary commission as a captain in the U.S. National Guard in recognition of his "outstanding contribution" in his field; it was given to him by the 6th Engineers Combat Division during a hospital fund drive. "Become necessary," Edwards said, "I will defend the liberties for which it stands." By the end of 1949, in their annual polls, Black newspapers across the country proclaimed Edwards one of America's outstanding entertainers of that year.[7]

Edwards was an engaging and polished orator and he exploited this ability at personal appearances at department stores, schools, beauty pageants, and charitable and fundraising events.

Our World magazine wrote:

> Edwards' ability as a speaker delights the civic groups before which he appears willingly. Men like the "regular guy" in Jimmy.... All these things, plus his looks and personality, have combined to make him a sort of racial symbol.[8]

In Spring 1950, he commenced an NAACP-sponsored goodwill tour of the South, where he spent time "listening to the problems of Negro farmers, teachers and youth." He made the rounds, receiving honors and accolades for himself, and standing in for Stanley Kramer to accept awards for *Brave* from organizations such as the Anti-Defamation League. In April 1950, along established stars Cab Calloway, Ethel Waters, and W.C. Handy, Edwards was honored as an outstanding personality at a "Salute to Show Business" ceremony.[9]

Edwards had a fair singing voice and he exploited this talent in a number of venues. The *California Eagle* declared that he "caused quite a sensation" while performing at the Club Elsino in Detroit in the Spring of 1950. Some contend that he contemplated a stint with the Charioteers, one of the most popular quartettes of the period, well-known for their rendition of popular spirituals.

That same year, Edwards performed in a revue at the Apollo Theater in Harlem. He then used his own money to produce a vaudeville act that was set to make an 88-city tour — a venture that was unsuccessful and nearly broke him, financially and for a time, emotionally. However, by 1951, a display ad promoted Edwards' appearance in the Paul Peters play *Nat Turner*, which was mounted at the People's Drama Theatre. Edwards took over the lead role from Juano Hernandez, who went to Hollywood for a picture.[10]

Not surprisingly, columnists hinted at Edwards' purported romantic alliances, including one with Jane White, the aspiring actress daughter of Walter White, chair of the NAACP. Walter Winchell claimed that Edwards maintained a long-distance romance with Lena Horne (who unbeknownst to Winchell was already secretly married to musician Lenny Hayden). He, too, was also linked with various projects. The *Los Angeles Sentinel* announced in August 1949 that he would play the lead role of the Negro doctor in the 20th Century–Fox production *No Way Out*. The part, however, went to Sidney Poitier. At a lecture at Queens College in New York in January 1950, Edwards revealed that he had indeed vied for the role in the film, and that his agents were informed that Darryl F. Zanuck preferred instead to "cast a new face."[11]

Color magazine announced that Edwards was signed to appear in another Kramer production, this one about paraplegic war veterans, called *The Courage of Ten*. Kramer did produce such a picture, ultimately called *The Men*, but it starred a brilliant newcomer named Marlon Brando. Edwards was paired with Lena Horne in a film project to be called *The Big Fall*. There is no evidence that this production ever made it beyond the discussion stage. In his newspaper column, Ed Sullivan announced that Edwards would join Helen Hayes in *The Wisteria Trees*, Josh Logan's stage adaptation of Chekhov's *The Cherry Orchard*. Ossie Davis, instead, was cast in this play. Frank Sinatra apparently considered Edwards for the lead in a picture on the life of Sugar Ray Robinson, and Louella Parsons wrote that Zolton Korda talked to Edwards about playing the lead in *Cry the Beloved Country*, a role that eventually went to Sidney Poitier.

Though much of what was written about him was inaccurate, it nonetheless served to keep him firmly in the public eye. Edwards wrote that a Hollywood press agent told him, "As long as you don't rape old women or choke little babies, you can have no bad publicity. Just make sure your name is read often and spelled correctly." He added, "I, for one, know that actors have to be very sensitive to public opinion. You can believe me when I say I've had many a sleepless night because of some untrue reports."[12]

Still, Edwards' film career remained stalled. He endured nearly two years with no picture offers and seemed to be on "leave of absence" from Hollywood since his much-heralded movie debut, wrote his hometown paper, the *Chicago Defender*. Why? Because of Hollywood's burgeoning postwar economic problems? Anti-Communist blacklisting/greylisting? Or because the film industry was unequipped or unwilling to make pictures featuring serious Black male actors in roles that were not stereotyped? Perhaps Edwards delayed his own progress by refusing to accept typed roles. Whatever the reasons, not until perhaps early 1951 did Edwards begin work on another picture.[13]

"So you want to be a movie star," mused columnist Dorothy Kilgallen. "James Edwards, the young actor who won plaudits as the soldier in *Home of the Brave* ... he's never had another film offer."[14]

7. Soldier Stories

In late 1950, Edwards was cast as army medic Cpl. Thompson in the combat film *The Steel Helmet*. The picture debuted in January, 1951, six months after the start of major hostilities in Asia, and is regarded as the first Hollywood feature film to depict the Korean Conflict.

The scenario was written by Samuel Fuller, after he made a deal with Robert Lippert of Lippert Productions to allow him to direct the film. Fuller, a World War II veteran, was born in Massachusetts. His many occupations, including copyboy for a newspaper, crime reporter, crime writer, and fiction writer of such works as *Burn, Baby, Burn*, and *The Big Red One*, served as his apprenticeship for a career in filmmaking where he would work as a director, producer, script writer, photographer, and actor. *The Steel Helmet*, like a number of his films, was based on his experiences in World War II when he was a rifleman with the 16th Infantry Division, U.S. Army.

Fuller told *Ebony* magazine that Edwards' character in *The Steel Helmet*, Thompson, was based on his acquaintance with a boxer named Turkey Thompson, whose wife Eunice worked for Fuller's family as a domestic, and who assisted Fuller with writing the scenes for the Negro character.[1]

In some ways, this Fuller classic is much like any other combat feature film: A group of battle-weary grunts struggle to kill the enemy and keep themselves alive. In the competent hands of Fuller, however, *The Steel Helmet* differentiates itself by providing a striking contrast to the soft touch of the archetypal Hollywood war pic of the period, the latter usually featuring a fine-looking, well-groomed leading man, handsome leading lady, and battle scenes sprinkled with only the tiniest bit of blood, gore or grit. Bosley Crowther of *The New York Times* wrote that the picture eschews "romantic war clichés" for a "distinctly melancholy and dismal view of the business at hand."[2]

Edwards as Cpl. Thompson, with Sgt. Zack (Gene Evans) and Shortround (William Chun) in Samuel Fuller's 1951 Korean War classic *The Steel Helmet*.

The leading role, Sgt. Zack, is played by Gene Evans. Evans was born in Arizona in 1922 and while living in California he appeared in summer stock. During his World War II stint in the Army, he performed with a troupe of GIs. After the war he pursued acting as a profession and made his Hollywood debut in the 1947 Western *Under Colorado Skies*.

As the story opens, we see Zack belly down in the muck, crawling away from the corpses of his squad mates. His captors, who are now also dead, have tied his hands behind him. A young South Korean boy appears and uses a knife to free Zack. As much as he tries, Zack can't rid himself of the boy and so relents to his new pal, naming him "Short Round." Ambling through a foggy wooded area, man and boy chance upon Thompson, a medic. Zack tells him that his men were captured, bound, and executed by Reds and that only he survived. The bullet hole in his helmet attests to the truth of his story. Thompson is the only survivor of *his* captured squad. The enemy kept him around to tend to the medical needs of their men. Thompson talks about his experiences as a veteran of the

Second World War when he was a truck driver with the legendary Red Ball Express — the truck convoy system responsible for hauling critical supplies to the Allied armies in the European theater after the Allied invasion of Normandy. After returning home, Thompson hoped to study to become a surgeon, he explains, only to end up back in the Army. But at least this time, he notes, he was doing more than driving a truck.

The three make their way through the woods and come upon another squad of American troops commanded by Lt. Driscoll, a somewhat inept and apparently inexperienced officer. (Driscoll is played by Steve Brodie who appeared as the bigot T.J. in *Home of the Brave*.) The ragtag band of men also includes a Nisei sargeant played by Richard Loo. Loo, a Hawaiian, spent most of years in Hollywood typecast as characters of Asian descent.

The men of *The Steel Helmet* are ill-groomed, grimy, perspiration-soaked, their uniforms soiled, and their faces covered by unkempt beards; in sum — an unappealing bunch. In one scene, they chance upon a patch of melons and stuff their faces like animals, using their sleeves as napkins and allowing the juice to drip from their whiskered chins. Sgt. Zack is perhaps the most obnoxious of all. While he is the most experienced, and the men need his knowhow to survive, he is also mean, profane, and callous.

The group holes up in a Buddhist temple. Unbeknownst to the men, a North Korean officer is also hiding in the temple. He is taken prisoner after he tries to kill them with a grenade that doesn't detonate. The officer, played by Harry Fong, is glib, unlikable, and arrogant, and the men treat him in kind for his attitude.

Edwards' part as Thompson is well-developed and he appears liberally throughout the film, delivering many of his lines with a cigarette dangling from his lips. In one oft-cited scene, Thompson is tasked to tend the wounded North Korean officer. The camera frames them in a medium shot, focusing on the dirtied, angry, sweat-soaked face of the North Korean who chides Thompson unmercifully.

> OFFICER: I don't understand you. You can't eat with them unless there's a war on and even then it's difficult, isn't that so?
> THOMPSON: That's right.
> OFFICER: You pay for ticket but you even have to sit in the back of a public bus.
> THOMPSON: That's right. A hundred years ago I couldn't even ride a bus. Maybe in fifty years, [I'll] sit in the middle, maybe even up front of the bus. Some things you can't rush, buster.... Why don't you get wise to yourself.[1]

The officer calls him stupid and spits in his direction. In retaliation, Thompson brusquely rips the dressing from his chest. Apparently, the fact that there *were* no city buses 100 years ago was lost on everyone working on the film, but for postwar audiences, the Booker T. Washington–like repartee perhaps rang true. In fact, Fuller claimed that he inserted the scene purposefully, in the hope of swaying the opinions of Negro citizens, whom he believed were being unduly influenced by Communist ideology.[4]

Near the end, in a long and engaging sequence, the squad is nearly overrun by the enemy. In a Lewis Milestone–like panning shot, we watch a sea of fresh and well-equipped enemy soldiers cascade from the side of a hill. Interspersed in this sequence are brief clips of actual combat footage borrowed from the Department of Defense. Soon, Thompson has no choice but to throw off his corpsman insignia and man a machine gun. He drops to the floor onto his rump, knees up, the gun between his legs, and commences to fire off rounds, as the recoil all but lifts him from the floor.

The Steel Helmet premiered in Los Angeles and New York in January 1951, but only after some concessions were made to Joseph Breen, head of the new Production Code Administration, which among other things objected to the use of the word "gook" and to the violence taking place in a Buddhist temple.

The Washington Post described the film as "considerably better than you might expect.... [T]he appeal ... clearly lies in its ability to capitalize on the immediate." For 1951 readers of this review, "the immediate" included the fact that as they sat in a darkened theatre watching the film, the Korean Conflict raged on some 6,000 miles away. Keep in mind that people of the time did not have access to instant and detailed news of the war from 24-hour cable news networks, RSS news feeds, blogs, or video news diaries. They relied on radio newsreels and brief reports from network news. Films like *The Steel Helmet* afforded them an immediate, albeit fictionalized picture of what was going on in Korea.[5]

The fact that the picture was filmed on sets is occasionally all too apparent and some critics made light of the artificiality of some scenes and the fact that this low-budget production was filmed in just ten days, with the exterior scenes shot at Griffith Park in California. In interviews, Fuller admits that he wished to be the first to capitalize on the growing hostilities in Korea. A review of the film printed in the *San Antonio* (TX) *Light* was sprinkled with words like "highly improbable," "absurd," and "rather ludicrous" but the critic rated the film as "no better or worse than average." The critic for the *Statesville (NC) Record* regarded it as "one of the finest motion pictures, certainly the finest war picture ever made.[6] The *Charleston (SC) Gazette* wrote, "Startling, moving and almost shocking in its approach, *The Steel Helmet* brings the war from a remote headline status to the full reality that Americans are dying in Korea[.]"[7]

Most reviews noted Edwards' appearance in the film and mentioned his role in *Home of the Brave*. "James Edwards does a job of smooth and dignified performing as the Negro medical man," wrote Crowther for the *New York Times*.[8]

Ebony magazine focused its attention on Edwards' appearance, pointing out how he was cast as simply another GI. His participation in the film represented a kind of first. Not only did he play a central character in the first film produced about the Korean conflict, but lost not on Negro filmgoers was the fact that he appeared in one of the earliest films produced after the integration of the military to feature a Black soldier, not as the subject of a racial issue but as a normal part of the action. Edwards, apparently pleased with his role in the picture, told *Ebony*, "It's by far the best thing I've had since I first hit Hollywood."[9]

Interestingly, the story of *The Steel Helmet* does not quite end here. First, the film not only drew the attention of film critics and filmgoers but the scrutiny of the FBI. Indeed, Edwards' appearance in the film was noted by agency operatives assigned to investigate Communist influence in the film industry. Fuller claimed that while *The Daily Worker* and *People's World* called him a "Fascist war-mongerer whose film was personally financed by General Douglas MacArthur," the film was scrutinized by FBI informants for its supposed Communist ideology. The *Steel Helmet* was banned in Iran but no explanation was provided except that the country had seen Communist demonstrations erupt during screenings in Teheran. Then, visiting correspondents from the Russian newspaper, *Pravda*, saw the film and declared that Hollywood turned out little more than "poisonous propaganda" for war.[10]

"That fine Negro actor, James Edwards, who was so good in *Home of the Brave*," wrote columnist Louella Parsons, "has been signed by Mark Robson for *Lights Out*."[11] Newspapers across the country noted with interest Edwards' casting as a blinded soldier in this film which was released as *Bright Victory*. *Bright Victory* is the story of Joe Morgan (ably portrayed by Arthur Kennedy), an Army soldier who loses his vision after venturing into a German booby trap and being shot by what he describes as "Kraut snipers."

Morgan is a Southerner hailing from Seminole, Florida. Released from a contingency hospital in Iran, he boards an evacuation plane for the United States. Throughout the aircraft, Black faces dot the assembly of wounded men. Some are on crutches and the nurse treats everyone with compassion.

Morgan's eyes are heavily bandaged. A young Negro soldier dressed in pajamas, robe, and a metal neck brace expresses his excitement at going home. He is from Atlanta, Georgia, and his accent makes clear his Southern roots. Morgan, delighted to meet another Southerner, asks the soldier to sit down and inquires whether he has ever been to a certain nightspot in Atlanta. The soldier recollects the club Morgan describes. "I waited tables there once," he answers with excitement in his voice. The smile quickly fades from Morgan's face, as he realizes the man must be a Negro. He doesn't want to continue the conversation, and asks a nurse to sit by him instead. The Black soldier realizes what has occurred and walks away with his face downcast.

At the hospital, Morgan struggles to come to grips with the fact that he will never be able to see again. His world is shattered and he considers suicide. *Bright Victory,* which offers a careful documentation of his recovery and rehabilitation, is as much a propaganda piece for the rights of the disabled as a document on the plight of injured veterans. The setting for *Bright Victory* was a real rehabilitation facility, the United States Army Hospital in Valley Forge, Pennsylvania. Here, the men live several to a room with their domain consisting of a single posted bed and a locker. All have lost their sight during the war and are in various stages of rehabilitation. Most appear to be upbeat. They take on the challenges of having to relearn how to shave and tie a necktie. They wear watches with crystals that pop up so that the arms can be palpated. They are taught to use a cane. Some cover their useless eyes with dark sunglasses as they go out on dates and supervised outings. Few complain about being saddled with such a traumatic and permanent injury. Even Morgan, after he attempts to slash his wrists with a razor, pulls himself together and gets into the routine, albeit after some counseling from his doctor and cajoling from his roommates. Black soldiers have also become victims of blindness. Their faces are evident in shots of group training sessions and outdoor activities. Edwards plays the character Larry Nevins. We first see him in a classroom filled with other blind soldiers who listen to a physician explain the challenges they will face.

Later, in a hospital hallway, Nevins and Morgan bump into each other and the two become fast friends. We see them rough-housing in the swimming pool. An *Ebony* article promoting the picture claimed that Edwards could not swim but bravely jumped into the pool anyway. In truth, Edwards, a superb athlete and letterman, was a good swimmer.

The men go on supervised outings to a local bar and club. After one such outing, one of the men mentions that a new group of patients will arrive the next day. "I hear some of them are niggers," Morgan blurts out callously. "I never knew they let niggers in this war. Did you?"

Some of the other men are taken aback by Morgan's coarse words, especially Nevins, who unbeknownst to Morgan is Black.

"I've been here seven weeks now," Nevins responds before walking away with dejection written across his face.

Morgan doesn't apologize for his statement. He says nothing to Nevins and the sequence ends abruptly.

Morgan continues with his therapy and training and develops a close relationship with a woman. He is also, incidentally, being ostracized by the other men for never trying to make amends to Nevins. "They act as if I killed someone," he complains to his therapist.

Morgan's therapist counters, "Are you gonna ask them [referring to everyone] what race or religion they are before you like them or not?"

After being released from the hospital, Morgan heads for his parents' home in Florida. Both his mother and father appear to be supportive enough, but it is evident that his fiancée, a Southern belle from a rich family, played by Peggy Dow, is not emotionally equipped to deal with a permanently disabled husband. Her manner contrasts with that of Morgan's female friend in Pennsylvania, played by Julie Adams, who is mature and sympathetic.

Joe's apparent change of heart regarding his feeling towards Blacks, too, becomes an issue. In one scene, his mother, played by Nana Bryant, says, "What the war has done to our nigras!" She can't believe that after all she has done for their maid Ella Mae (for instance, giving her hand-me-down clothing) the woman would leave for a war job in the North. As soon as the war is over, Mother declares, "They'll be back." Joe is disturbed by his mother's attitude. He loses his temper, accusing her of pretending that the Civil War had ever been fought and lost. In the next scene, over whiskeys at a local bar, Joe and his father discuss how prejudice is handed down from generation to generation. His father, played by Will Geer, is not positioned as a liberal even though he does not object to his wife's point of view.

Peggy Dow, Richard Egan, Edwards, Arthur Kennedy, and Murray Hamilton in *Bright Victory* (1951).

By the end of the story, Morgan has come to grips with his situation. He makes plans to move away from Seminole, deciding against taking handouts from his family or his wealthy ex–in-laws to be. On a train back to Pennsylvania, he hears a familiar voice. It is Larry Nevins. At Morgan's insistence, Nevins reluctantly sits with him.

    MORGAN: We're still friends, aren't we?
    NEVINS: If you wanna be.

Their friendship is presumably renewed.

Bright Victory is a unique film in some respects. It depicts the aftermath of World War II from the very personal viewpoint of a particular man whose Southern-bred attitude about race is quickly and dramatically shattered when he loses his vision. Like *Home of the Brave*, the film posed a clear challenge to the very core of racial bigotry, but in a manner much more subtle. *Bright Victory*'s "message" is clear without being overly preachy or didactic. Exploring the senselessness of race prejudice through the eyes of a man who is suddenly blinded is an apt plot device. Morgan can no longer discern the color of the skin of the people he meets. His training as a child, when he wasn't allowed to play with Black children, is thus effectively rendered obsolete. Twice he strikes up friendships with Black men. The film's quiet moral is very effective. A review in *Ebony* illustrates this point in hopeful words: "By its routine inclusion of the scenes about discrimination, [*Bright Victory*] sets a new standard for Hollywood which has in the past hesitated to include bits about bias in ordinary pictures about everyday life."

Bright Victory was produced after the federally mandated integration of the armed forces. Therefore, the producers had some motivation to depict the recovery of blinded Black soldiers as well as White. Blacks, too, had performed with bravery during the war and had the permanent injuries to prove it. Though no great importance was placed on promoting the various ethnic backgrounds of the men, the film offered a decidedly balanced view of the war's traumatic aftermath.

The film occasionally reverts to notes of falseness and some aspects of the story are decidedly blurred. For example, Nevins' reactions to Morgan's racist outburst are suppressed. As mentioned, the scene ends quickly and Nevins disappears for the next several sequences of the film. Nevins' anger and hurt is thus submerged and left unexplored. Secondly, we learn nothing about Nevins' personal life. Still, these shortcomings do not ruin the engaging nature of the story.

Bright Victory was released by Universal on July 31, 1951. The reviews were not all positive; some critics felt that the racial tolerance angle was an unnecessary distraction. Manny Farber made this observation for *The Nation*:

> [T]his mixture of *The Best Years of Our Lives* and *The Men* is so unimaginatively perfect and so well-barbered by its cutters that is it a little like being caught on a fast assembly line.[12]

Bosley Crowther of the *New York Times*, in an otherwise complimentary review, complained about music, noting that director Robson "has leaned a little too heavily on Hearts and Flowers—or music of a similar soulful nature.... It rather disturbs the senses, in view of the general fine restraint of the film." And *Time* magazine wrote, "Not content with solving the problems of its blind hero so easily, *Bright Victory* is even more superficial in an over-tricky subplot that as glibly poses and solves the Negro problem."[13]

Dorr of the *Washington Post* wrote, "[*Bright Victory*] is good for you ... because it reminds you that as a human being, you possess a degree of courage and grit that will carry you through seemingly insurmountable difficulties." Indeed this rather small, 90-minute black-and-white picture won acclaim and a host of awards. At the Festival de Cannes in May 1951, it was nominated for Best Picture, Best Actor, and Best Screenplay. The film ultimately won a Golden Globe for Best Screenplay. *Bright Victory* was also Oscar-nominated for Best Actor and Best Sound. Dorr made a special point to commend all the supporting actors: "[E]very actor gives a convincing performance, if not great.... Richard Egan [and] James Edwards ... are really fine[.]" The film critic for *The Commonweal* described himself as being "at a loss" for words to describe his enjoyment of the film, noting, "[I]t is a tremendously moving and very entertaining cinematically in spite of its serious material."[14]

In *Ebony* magazine, *Bright Victory* was promoted with an article accompanied with six photographs. The film's director Mark Robson, a veteran of *Home of the Brave* and *Champion* (1949), said of Edwards:

> Edwards has the key role in the film for it is through him that the white soldier grows to understand himself.... And the picture's comment and meaning is made through the character portrayed by Edwards. Jimmy did a wonderful and expert job throughout.[15]

When the picture premiered at the Abilene, promoted as Abilene, Texas,' only all-colored theatre, Edwards received top billing in newspaper advertisements and was described as, "Hollywood's Newest Negro Star."[16]

Bright Victory was based on the 1945 Baynard Kendrick novel *Lights Out*. Kendrick, who was a veteran of the First World War, became interested in the plight of blinded soldiers during his stint with the 1st Canadian Battalion. The rights to Kendrick's story (and the subsequent film project) passed from hand to hand and collected dust for years before Robson took on the project. Kendrick, who had, "grievous misgivings" about how his story would translate to film, was ecstatic about the picture.[17]

Robson had worked previously both with Edwards and with the film's lead, Arthur Kennedy, who appeared in *Champion*. "For the important role of the Negro veteran," Robson wrote in an article for the *New York Times*, "we had long since settled on James Edwards."[18]

The screenplay for *Bright Victory* was penned by Robert Buckner, author of scripts for the films *Santa Fe Trail* (1940), *Dive Bomber* (1941) and *Yankee Doodle Dandy* (1942), and episodes of *Burke's Law* and *Bonanza*. The film features an early appearance by star-to-be Rock Hudson, who is seen in the first sequence. Bernie Hamilton, an up-and-coming African American actor who would appear with Edwards in television programs, also played a small speaking part. Other cast members include Richard Egan, Jim Backus, and John Hudson.

Edwards told the *Chicago Defender*, "This picture is so significant ... so full of meaning ... that it will prove to be an important picture of our era."[19]

8. Reading, Writing, and Radio

James Edwards exploited his talent as a practiced and outstanding orator in the field of recording. For Decca Records, he made spoken-word recordings, to a choir background, of such spiritual mainstays as the Lord's Prayer, the Sermon on the Mount, the 23rd Psalm, and the Ten Commandments, all done as part of the label's "Faith Series." The Syracuse, New York, *Post Standard* reported that he planned to record poetry, including Walt Whitman's *Leaves of Grass*. "His ambition," notes the paper, "is to become the first great Negro star to win fame as a dramatic reader."[1]

In 1954, Edwards, in addition to acting in a motion picture, on television and in live theater, surprised many as he took on another pursuit: writing. His efforts were publicized in May of that year in the *New York Times*:

> James Edwards is not complaining about the fact that good dramatic roles for Negro performers ... don't come along frequently.... He has decided to take direct action by writing some scripts himself.[2]

It is not surprising that Edwards, an imaginative actor and fluent speaker, was drawn to the craft of Hollywood screenwriting. In the *Times* article, he said that his hope was to "make producers more conscious of the Negro's role in American life, past and present."[3]

Edwards' potential apparently evoked interest from the major studios. In 1956, two years after announcing his new occupation, he signed as a screenwriter with Universal-International. "Mr. Pratt [studio head James Pratt] told me I was being hired not as an experiment," Edwards said. "That's the way I want it."[4]

In 1957, Edwards' pursuit of screenwriting credits garnered a great deal of press when a story appeared in newspapers across the country announcing that he was giving up his acting career for writing. Moreover, the story claimed that Edwards "appears to be the first Negro to find success as a screen writer." "As far as I know, two others have tried it," Edwards was quoted as saying. *Jet* magazine said that Edwards "will abandon his acting career and devote full time to screen writing"; the Danville (VA) *Bee* printed an article titled "Hollywood Has First Negro Movie Writer; Former Actor."[5]

Edwards said, "Sure I like to act, but I've got to think of security. There just aren't enough good roles that come along for a Negro actor." Indeed, on more than one occasion Edwards spoke freely about how his career as a professional actor had affected him financially. In 1953 he revealed that he had earned "less money since becoming an actor than before...."[6]

> What I'm about to say may break all precedents, but I have no front to maintain. I've been working in the movies for five years and, during this time, my total net earnings have amounted to approximately $16,000. Divide that figure by five and you'll see that I've earned less than the average working man.[7]

Four years later he told the press:

> [T]here aren't enough roles to keep me going. In the acting business, you take four or five years to get off the ground. So even when you do hit it well and establish some success you've got all that catching up to do.... So it was catch-up, catch-up all the time.[8]

Edwards was not the only serious Black actor struggling to pay the bills. In 1962, testifying before the House Committee on Education and Labor headed by New York representative Adam Clayton Powell, Jr., Sidney Poitier spoke out about the lack of opportunities for Black performers in the entertainment industry: "It is virtually impossible for Negro actors to earn a steady livelihood in the American theatre, movies, or broadcasting." Ossie Davis explained, "[T]he small-job opportunities open to Negroes were minimal."[9]

Edwards' writing projects included a dramatization of the story of Frank Giraud, a Black man taken captive by Sioux after his parents were killed. He eventually became a blood brother to Chief Crazy Horse and made his living as a Pony Express rider and as a scout for the U.S. Army. The working title of this project was "Silent Thunder."[10]

With James Altieri, he developed a concept based on a true story titled *The Boy from Korea*. Sounding much like a sequel to Universal's Korean War story *Battle Hymn* (1956), in which Edwards co-starred, *The Boy from Korea* concerns a Korean war orphan who ends up at Boy's Town. In the first draft of his step outline, dated May 25, 1956, Edwards notes that he had revised it to reflect suggestions given him in a meeting with Albert J. Cohen. Cohen was a story editor, producer, and screenwriter who had worked for Republic Pictures and later Universal Studies. Though the project made it to the point of casting, the fate of *The Boy from Korea* is unknown.[11]

In late August 1956, Edwards joined forces with Robert Gordon, director of *The Joe Louis Story*, after Gordon formed Robert Gordon Productions, an independent production company. Gordon revealed to the press that he hoped to produce both feature films and made-for-television movies, particularly, "offbeat entertainment" and "stories the major studios seldom tackle." Edwards and writer Holland Byrd partnered to develop a script called *Devil's Harvest*, an outdoor drama set in 1870s Missouri. The screenplay was purchased by Robert Gordon Productions. It was to be the second picture produced by the company. Edwards also worked on a comedic stage play about a Black man raised in Scotland who comes to Harlem to live, and developed a Western for Universal-International with the working title of *Beyond the Pass*.[12]

Joining forces with prolific Hollywood writer John McGreevey, Edwards continued to develop the teleplay "Silent Thunder," which was produced by Robert Gordon Productions and aired in late November 1958 on CBS TV's *Westinghouse-Desilu Playhouse*. By this time, Edwards had developed his concept into a 123-page, somewhat typical Western yarn about a mute Apache named Little Horse and an Indian hater named Les. However, the credit as screenwriter went to McGreevey, not Edwards, who received a mention for the story idea. *Silent Thunder* starred Earl Holliman, Wallace Ford (Edwards' co-star from *The Set-Up*) and John Drew Barrymore who co-starred with Edwards in *Night of the Quarter Moon*.[13]

How did Edwards fare as a Hollywood writer? His scripts available for study (completed well before the era of personal computers, electronic spell checkers, or screenwriting software) demonstrate average writing skills and good story ideas. Though he would continue his pursuit until the end of his life, his alliance with Universal Pictures apparently lasted only a few years. (In an article about tokenism in Hollywood in 1961, the *Los Angeles Sentinel* wrote of Edwards' *former* position with Universal.[14])

The number of scripts Edwards completed, how many were produced, and the fate of the never-produced works is near impossible to determine. The sequence of events from paper to screen might well encompass years of what is sometimes referred to as development hell. Even then, a script might remain unproduced for years or decades. More importantly, when a given picture was finally released, the name of the original writer might well be expunged and the script attributed to someone else, leaving the writer with no credits and little or no income from his/her work. And Edwards would have learned other unfortunate truths about writing for Hollywood. As a writer he had little control over the fate of this work; he held few rights on ownership; and had little or no say over changes to the material. Add to this the fact that not until 1965 was the Writers Guild able to negotiate some payment to writers of feature films shown on television. These were just some of the frustrations Edwards would have encountered. Indeed, the issue of being properly credited and compensated has been a long and difficult struggle for Hollywood writers who, at the time of this writing, are fighting for rights with regard to emerging technologies.[15]

It is easy to imagine Edwards, outspoken but perhaps naïve, a newcomer to Hollywood, and a Black man with his own strongly held ideas about what made for a good story, encountering a host of roadblocks as he attempted to negotiate Hollywood's mired, all–White, old-boy system. In 1970, a writer for the *Chicago Defender* divulged the details of a conversation he had with Edwards:

> He told me about a TV script which was accepted by a lesser figure connected with a TV company. But when the director or producer saw the script, he turned thumbs down.... This man could give no reasonable answer for his refusal. Finally, the lesser figure asked point blank: "Is it because Jimmy Edwards is a Negro and you don't like him?" The bigot said, "Yes."[16]

The article alluded to Edwards' resentment at having his scripts ignored or rejected, he believed, only because he was Black. "His life was sometimes turbulent," the article claims.[17]

How many performances Edwards made on local and network radio during the 1940s and 1950s in unknown. Some directories of radio credits do not mention any of his performances. Others list only his roles on *The Adventures of Ellery Queen* and the *Lux Theatre*. Edwards' radio credits are likely much more extensive and include guest appearances and performances on local radio stations located in and around the Los Angeles area.

As commercial network radio began its slow decline in the late 1940s, race radio stations sprang up in place of poorly performing mainstream stations. Race radio stations were designed to cater to the tastes of the Black community with programs on cooking, religion, jazz, and entertainment. Bill Sampson was one of only two California-based African American disk jockeys. In 1949 he announced plans to produce an evening show to be broadcast from Jack's Basket Room Nightclub. Edwards was to act as co-host. Edwards was also associated with the radio drama "Nocturnal Meeting," a program written by Ray McIver for WERD radio station in Atlanta, Georgia. WERD, operated by J. B. Blayton, Sr., was the first Black-owned radio station in the United States. With his stretched schedule, it is difficult to see how Edwards could have devoted much time to these pursuits.

In 1953, Edwards played the part of Roger Chapman in an episode of the NBC radio production of *Confession*. This pseudo-documentary crime drama, which featured stories about crime and punishment, ran on Sunday evenings during the summer. Based the old adage that crime does not pay, the program opened with *Dragnet*-like commentary from the director of the California Department of Corrections. A hapless criminal would offer his confession. Then, actors would dramatize the events that led to the prisoner's downfall. Edwards' co-stars included Maidie Norman, Jester Hairston, and Jay Loft Lynn.

More notably, in 1950 Edwards performed in an unusual episode of the radio comedy *The Halls of Ivy*, which starred Ronald Colman and his wife Benita Hume Colman. Each episode presented the incidents, events, people, and problems of the fictitious Ivy College, with the Colmans cast as its president, Mr. Todd Hunter Hall, and Mrs. Hall. An erudite, sophisticated program, its scripts often peppered with reverse clichés and literate humor, *Halls of Ivy* presented a striking contrast to the average radio comedy replete with vaudeville-style shtick and corny jokes. Edwards performed in an episode called "The Leslie Hoff Painting." Racial prejudice was the theme of the story, which was described by critics as one of the best of the show's two-year run.

As the story opens, a reporter from the *Ivy News* visits the Halls to question them about a beautiful portrait of a young man painted by one of their alumni, Leslie Hoff. The painting has aroused interest and praise in their small community after the artist was given an award from a national art foundation for his efforts. After some humorous dithering, the Halls must reluctantly admit that they don't know Leslie Hoff and can't recall having met him. During the same conversation, we learn from the reporter that Ivy College is weathering a period of financial troubles but someone wants to provide the college with an endowment.

President Hall asks the reporter to come back the next day. He then receives a phone call informing him that the mysterious donor wishes to meet with him. While Mrs. Hall contacts Leslie Hoff, President Hall contacts the donor. Both will meet with the Halls later that afternoon.

The donor arrives first; her name is Mrs. Marshall. She, too, saw and admired the portrait. As it turns out, it is a painting of her son who was killed in the war. Indeed, she is so moved by the work that she has decided to establish the endowment in her son's name Gene Marshall. She has never met Leslie Hoff, whom she only knows is an Ivy graduate but agrees, "I believe that the young man who painted this portrait really knew my son."[18] Unfortunately, there are conditions: "My money must absolutely not be used to provide scholarships for [*she pauses*], certain races or creeds ... if you know what I mean."

President Hall cannot accept the money, and explains to Mrs. Marshall the principle behind which the school was established, that of "personal freedom and individual integrity." Ivy College, he explains, is not for sale. Their conversation becomes contentious and in the midst of this, Leslie Hoff arrives. In the foyer, Mrs. Hall explains to him that Gene Marshall's mother is in the next room. Hoff is reluctant to meet her at first, but relents. Mrs. Marshall is staggered. "You! You are Leslie Hoff!"

To Mrs. Marshall's surprise, Leslie Hoff (Edwards) happens to be of a "certain race." In a voice that is soft, emotive, and kindly, Hoff describes the short relationship he had with Gene Marshall, which consisted of a very long night in a foxhole during the war. Knowing that they might not make it through the night, each "laid their cards on the table":

> He was proud of his great-grandfather who fought in the Civil War. I was proud of mine who was freed by it.

He painted the portrait from his memory, Hoff explains, recalling the dim moonlit night and the look on his subject's face on the last evening of his life. "I sat and watched him, his face half-hidden in shadows, only the nose and eyes lighted by the enemy flares.... I'll never forget how he looked." In the end, Mrs. Marshall softens her attitude and leaves President Hall with a check, no strings attached.

Given the rather fluffy nature of most episodes of *The Halls of Ivy*, this story's treatment of race, as well as its reference to the tragedy of war, made for a program that was poignant and moving. "The Leslie Hoff Story" was written by Cameron Blake and Don Quinn.

In the program tag, Edwards is credited for his fine performance in *Home of the Brave*. Also noted is his appearance in the soon-to-be released picture *Lights Out*, which was retitled *Bright Victory*. The *Chicago Defender* described the story as a "slap against intolerance" and called the program "one of the most powerful pleas on behalf of racial intolerance ever to be heard on the air."[19]

9. "I Am Arrogant and Shall Remain So"

Edwards did not shirk when it came to voicing his opinion on various subjects. And his bluntness and straight-talking manner sometimes made the news. He made clear his disdain of typed Black roles, lashed out against the *Amos 'n' Andy* television show, and went as far as to complain about the dearth of opportunities for African Americans in Hollywood. In 1953, he wrote in *Our World* magazine, "It worries me when I find that — except for actors — Negroes are almost totally excluded from the motion picture industry."[1]

Edwards' comments would be perceived by some as arrogant. Indeed, at this time in America, Black citizens were expected to keep their place and avoid being seen as uppity. Edwards risked much by complaining openly about injustice as there were various tactics that could be employed to silence a Black man who spoke out of turn. Edwards defended himself:

> You may have also heard that I'm conceited and arrogant. If arrogance means I look down my nose and think my fellow man inferior this isn't true. For I have always attempted to do just the opposite. But if arrogance means that I try at all times to maintain a pride and dignity that would exemplify favorably my person and my people — I say, yes, I am arrogant and shall remain so.[2]

Truth be told, Edwards, along with other new-wrought Black postwar talent (some of whom had fought in the war against totalitarianism and bigotry), were decidedly less conciliatory and patient, and more vociferous and candid than their predecessors, some of the old Negro types of the ready grin and slightly stooped shoulders who knew better than to step over the line. Performers like Sidney Poitier, Harry Belafonte, Ruby Dee, and Ossie Davis were of a different breed, exuding assertiveness, intellect, and political savvy. They were unafraid to speak out against racism, discrimination and America's Negro problem, even at their own peril.

But what did Edwards and his fellow Black actors have to complain about? Plenty.

To begin with, they had cause to complain about the lack of roles for serious Black actors. In 1952, African American actor William Walker was appointed to the board of the Screen Actors Guild which formed the Negro Employment Committee. Walker said of the lack of opportunities for Black performers in Hollywood:

> [W]e must correct this situation ... by enlarging his [the Negro artist's] scope and participation in all types of roles and in all forms of American entertainment — just as in American life, the Negro's role now extends from the kitchen to the United Nations.[3]

After Sidney Poitier's appearance in his breakout film *No Way Out* (1950), Poitier spoke candidly about how he was all but ignored by Hollywood and took on odd jobs and various business ventures to support himself and his family.[4]

Postwar Black actors also had cause to complain about the persistent typecasting by filmmakers who attended to bigoted perceptions of the Black race. Poitier's scathing remarks about typed roles appeared in the *New York Times*:

> Hollywood as a rule still doesn't want to portray us as anything but butlers, chauffeurs, gardeners or maids. They just don't want to make us part of contemporary American life. As an actor, if I have the ability, all I ask is opportunity. When it's denied because of my color then I can't help feeling resentful.[5]

"[T]he majority of colored actors are of the Uncle Tom, minstrel show, shuffling dancer type," declared Alfred Werker, director of the 1950 film *Lost Boundaries*. Werker said he could not use many Black actors in his film about a Black man passing for White because, as he put it, "the majority of colored actors can't present such roles effectively." He could not, he claimed, find enough Black actors who could exude the refinement and intelligence required for the parts.[6]

Black performers, too, complained about working conditions, especially when film shooting took place in locations where people of color were subject to the indignities of Jim Crow ordinances and in some cases were denied access to the same accommodations offered their White counterparts. For example, in the shooting of the Civil War era film *Band of*

Angels, actors were compelled to queue for lunch in separate lines and be housed in separate hotels due to Louisiana's strict system of racial segregation.

Black postwar performers also had cause to complain about their experiences as victims of outright bigotry and hatred. Nat Cole was harassed and threatened when he moved his family into a White neighborhood in Los Angeles. In her biography, Pearl Bailey recounts a 1952 incident when she was cornered backstage by a White man she had never met, who called her a name and then proceeded to kick and beat her with his fists until she feared her end.[7]

Then there was the issue of motion pictures and television programs containing appearances by Black performers being subject to the whims of local censors, particularly if the characters depicted were not in the realm of a Black stereotype. Like *Home of the Brave* and *The Joe Louis Story*, the Stanley Kramer production *The Defiant Ones* (1958), starring Sidney Poitier and Tony Curtis as prisoners on the run, was banned in many cities in the South. The same fate awaited the film *The World, the Flesh and the Devil* (1959), featuring Harry Belafonte and White actors Inger Stevens and Mel Ferrer as the last three people left on Earth. Southern-style censorship, too, often pre-empted the airing of television shows featuring Blacks not presented in stereotypical roles. Fearful advertisers steered clear of Nat Cole's show, causing its eventual demise.

Another contributor to the woes of Black actors in postwar Hollywood was the fact that by the time Edwards and Poitier came to the forefront, the Golden Age of Hollywood was over and the industry was mired in a host of troubles. "The next time you feel like kicking the cat because business gets you down," noted *Business Week* in 1949, "think of the movie industry. Its troubles are almost in a class with Job's."[8]

Shifting economic imperatives, changes in government regulation of theatres, changes in foreign film distribution, the Cold War, expensive technological advancements, a drastic decline in revenues, anti-trust actions, the Cold War, changes in race relations, Communist witch-hunts — these are just a few of the prominent issues that affected the overall structure and performance of the Hollywood film industry after the war. Too, the *New York Times* reported on "the bewildering apathy" of the film-going public for even the most finely produced and elaborately pitched features and the loss of star power by some of the biggest names in Hollywood.[9]

Few Negro actors, beyond long-established comedians, would be offered a rich, long-term contract with any major Hollywood film. Athlete cum actor Woodrow "Woody" Strode wrote in his biography:

> I had four pictures in release with the biggest actors in the world. By then I had a whole career going. But I was never under contract to any studios; they weren't signing black actors. Only our comedians, the song-and-dance men had contracts.[10]

In truth, even the larger studios were hard-pressed to sign an actor of any race to a lengthy contract during this period of substantially shrinking profit margins. The old system of maintaining a stable of stars on payroll was becoming a part of history. Edwards had made lots of money for Stanley Kramer, but for the average independent producer, signing players to contracts was not an astute strategy. "My company is interested only in making pictures," Kramer told the *New York Times*. "We're not in the agency business."[11]

Like the country as a whole, postwar Hollywood was very slow to react to the changing status of Black Americans. World War II was the catalyst for some of the most significant changes in race relations in nearly a century. And while the postwar years saw opportunities for Black performers improve ever so slightly, employment in front of and behind the camera remained limited, compelling Edwards and other members of the Black film community to speak with candor about their dissatisfaction with racial exclusion, bigotry, and bias in Hollywood.

10. "Mad Behavior"

In her biography, performer Diahann Carroll called Edwards "one of the most seductive men I have ever met." Indeed, she described in some detail the curious pseudo-romantic friendship that the two maintained for several years—one that she claims did not include sex. Carroll revealed that she was infatuated with Edwards, and eager for his attention; because of this, she readily overlooked his "obvious flaws." She reveals, "to my nineteen-year-old thinking, James Edwards was a god. He was handsome. He was talented. He was famous." She also described Edwards as drunken, rude, violent, nearly out-of-control, and all but consumed by his lack of success in Hollywood. While he maintained a nonsexual friendship with Carroll, he reported to her the details of his supposed host of conquests, including, in her words, "the wives of producers he met with the next day." Edwards, at the time, was married to Leola Mosley. He maintained two homes, one on each coast. It is interesting to note that references to his life with Mosley seem to be absent from the entertainment columns that covered his career and activities.[1]

Edwards didn't mind being considered a handsome ladies' man. A photo that appeared in an issue of *Our World* showed Edwards being kissed simultaneously by two women—one on each cheek. One was the wife of singer Billy Eckstein. In another shot he posed with his arms wrapped around the shapely waistline of a swimsuit-clad beauty. Edwards exuded sex appeal, and the gaggles of autograph-seeking female fans who showed up at airports and hotels to meet him sometimes became rowdy and on at least on one occasion tore his clothing.[2] In 1953, before he was married, Edwards revealed:

> For years it has been bandied about that I'm a playboy.... It has been said that I'm a ladies' man. I'm a bachelor and I've never been married. But let it be known that I think there is nothing as wonderful as women.[3]

Some sources linked him with Jane White, aspiring actress and the daughter of NAACP chairman Walter White. Walter Winchell supposed that he carried on a long-distance liaison with Lena Horne, who was already secretly married to Lenny Hayden. Unfortunately for Edwards, problems with two particular women resulted in some humiliatingly bad press.

In September 1949, *The Chicago Defender* reported that a suit had been filed against Edwards by Donna Rayburn, described as a "white housewife," who claimed that she had an affair with the actor and was beaten up by him after a party. According to the *Defender*, which splashed the incident across its front page complete with a 72-point type banner, Rayburn said that she had received "permanent injuries," was having "troubled dreams," and now lived "in terror and fear for her life." She filed a $57,000 suit against Edwards, which his friends claimed was little more than a "shakedown."[4] He defended himself with a statement that appeared in *The Los Angeles Sentinel*:

> With regards to the story ... I hardly know what to say. I am shocked and surprised that my friends have made an incident out of a slight misunderstanding.... I am sure that Mrs. Rayburn and the others will agree that this whole matter has been greatly exaggerated.[5]

Edwards also hinted that it was only because the victim and her husband had many associates in the entertainment field, that details of the "little incident" were widely reported out of spite and had perhaps been overstated. "[T]hey are great people," Edwards said of the Rayburns, "[and] as soon as we get together I am certain that the whole thing will be straightened out."[6]

Appearing on the cover of the March 1951 edition of *Ebony* magazine, attired in a bikini, is Rosalind "Roz" Cunningham. *Ebony* described Cunningham as a student of ballet who had been in Los Angeles for about five years, and who made her living as a model and dancer. Her ambition: "to get into the movies." That same edition featured a story about Edwards and his part in *The Steel Helmet*.[7]

In September 1949, the *Los Angeles Sentinel* reported Edwards' fight with her at a party. She had reportedly retaliated: "A neat right cross connected with the jaw of James Edwards," the paper reported. The story reads as a lovers' tiff gone violent. Edwards appeared at a Los Angeles party only to find Cunningham. He apparently disapproved of her appearance at the same party since he was escorting another woman. In a bedroom, the two had words and Edwards took his anger out on a piece of furniture. Possibly defending herself against violence directed toward her, she reacted, as described in the *Los Angeles Sentinel*, "by whipping a stinging roundhouse right to Edwards' jaw." "She hit me! She hit me! She can't do that to me," Edwards reportedly exclaimed.[8]

Cunningham would later deny the entire story. "I wish to have it known that this story is not true in any particular," she told the *Sentinel*. "[I]'ve been friendly with Mr. Edwards. Personally, I think he's one of the finest persons I've ever known."[9]

Most telling, however, is the *Sentinel*'s photograph of the party-goers. Edwards' usual boyish grin is replaced by a sober expression.

Keep in mind that these incidents occurred during a time when such scandal was not only embarrassing but potentially detrimental to one's career. The major studios invested large sums of money in the careful crafting and maintenance of the reputation of their stars. Edwards had no contract with a studio but was appearing in three films and could ill afford to get bad press which included allegations of assault and a relationship with a White married woman. Even if the allegations were false, he might well see the end of his career. Edwards, no doubt chastened, told the *Eagle*, "Just can't figure the whole thing out."[10]

The idea that one's alcohol consumption should be carefully controlled was a concept not widely touted before, say, 1970. Sammy Davis, Jr., a championship drinker and carouser with a penchant for porn movie actresses, was said to have had a prosthetic eye designed bloodshot-red to match his good eye after a night of hard drinking. Actor Ossie Davis remarked that his hangovers "were verbalized with just a touch of iambic pentameter."[11] By most accounts, Edwards, too, drank heavily and was not always able to control his behavior. Edwards revealed in 1953:

> It has been said that I drink excessively. To this I can only answer, "Yes!" I like to drink now and then as does any man. But I doubt very much that I've been plastered more times than any "Joe Doe" who finds drinking a pleasant social pastime.[12]

"I felt better drinking vodka [than water]," Edwards commented on his 1951 trip to Bermuda: In addition to a wardrobe of summer clothing, he packed three bottles of vodka for a ten-day trip and boasted that he had "vodkanized" the island. "He always smelled of alcohol," Carroll said of the times she spent with him, "he drank constantly from morning until night." Former athlete and actor Woodrow "Woody" Strode, who appeared with Edwards in *Tarzan's Fight for Life* and *Pork Chop Hill*, said of him, "He drank heavily, couldn't control it[.]"[13]

Carroll also recalls those occasions when Edwards flew into what she describes as "alcoholic rages." During these spells, he would exhibit erratic behavior and would rant about "personal beefs against supposed enemies." Carroll described her fear that he might explode at any moment: picking fights, berating waiters at restaurants, and causing embarrassment for all involved.[14]

Since his early success as a stage actor, Edwards seemed to prefer a hectic schedule which sometimes included working on a number of projects at once. In the years following *Home of the Brave*, he opened an acting school, began work as a screenwriter, then announced his intention to be the first Black man to direct a motion picture for a major studio. He directed, produced, and acted in stage plays, then announced his interest in writing an adaption of *Othello* and becoming a producer. He organized a vaudeville show that was to go on an 88-city tour. He recorded spoken word records, and announced his desire to become the first Black man to make it as a dramatic reader; he associated himself with locally produced radio and television programs, and even talked about creating a summer stock company. In truth, like any celebrity, not everything printed about Edwards was accurate. Still, taking on half of these projects would be more than sufficient for most. Diahann Carroll remarked how she would listen to him as he would "carry on about how he was meeting producers and developing projects and negotiating for the lead in this or that."[15]

Edwards' purported mood swings, sexual indiscretions, high capacity for activity, constant involvement in various projects and activities, and his apparent belief that he was being persecuted (a trait described by both Woody Strode and Diahann Carroll) resemble a chapter from a medical encyclopedia. Today he might well be diagnosed as suffering from some kind of mood disorder. In Edwards' time, problems related to one's mental health were stigmatized and not talked about openly. Moreover, Hollywood has always had more than its fair share of drunken, moody actors who manage to get into trouble. It is unclear whether Edwards sought help or even recognized that perhaps he might benefit from professional help.

Cocky, defiant, manic, odd, raging, alcoholic, sullen, out-of-control, misogynistic: The James Edwards described by some of his associates exhibited all these traits. Somehow he must have maintained his professional reputation or his ability to get parts would have been greatly curtailed. He continued to find parts, working multiple times with various individuals in the industry, including producers Stanley Kramer and Aaron Spelling and director Franklin Schaffner. Was there another side to the actor and individual James Edwards? In a 1953 article for *Our World*, Edwards wrote:

> Hollywood, its stars and actors have always been fair game for critics.... And whatever you may have heard, most of its stars are just hardworking, intelligent people working at the craft they love...Actors aren't loose and without morals. The majority enjoy home life and attend church just as you do.[16]

"Warm hearted, lovable, unaffected"—this was a description of Edwards written by Lillian Smith for the *New York Amsterdam News* in 1949. Edwards met her at an informal gathering in New York, where Edwards sang and later revealed to her his desire to "see Negro women take their rightful place as beauties of the cinema world."

In addition, as if being tall, handsome, gifted and bright were not enough, Edwards presented himself as a regular guy, enamoring his many fans, both male and female. Smith wrote:

> The 100 citizens who had come by motorcade to La Guardia Field to welcome him, took one look at his friendly, boyish smile, felt the firm clasp of his hand, heard his softly spoken, sincere words of greeting, and succumbed—every man, woman and child.[17]

Edwards endeavored to prosper in the highly competitive business of acting. Still, he seemed openhanded and accommodating with his fellow performers.

Woody Strode was chosen for film roles not because of his acting skill but to exploit his magnificent physique. By his own admission, his skills as an actor were minimal and he conceded that most of the time he was "over his head." "I was lucky. I had good advice," Strode notes. Strode appeared with Edwards in two films. And in his biography, he credits Edwards for coaching him and supporting him. It was Edwards who suggested, then coached Strode for his role in the 1959 production *Pork Chop Hill*.

He also coached Carroll, young and still wet behind the ears, before she appeared before the intimidating director Otto Preminger to audition for the part of Carmen in the 1954 film, *Carmen Jones*. Carroll wrote, "He was very helpful, urging me to go over my lines with him."[18]

"I have heard that Jimmy was an egotist. I have heard that he was selfish and conceited," wrote Milton C. Lamb Jr., for the *Woodlawn (CA) Booster*. Lamb wrote in 1970, "Some of these traits are necessary for this crazy business of acting. The James Edwards I knew was a man of charity and concern for others. Wish to God there were more like him."[19]

11. Scandalize My Name

For the Hollywood community, the postwar days of the Congressional investigation of the Communist influence on the motion picture business was a period fraught with anxiety, disquiet, viciousness, and resentment. Jobs were already scarce as the film industry wandered through a financial meltdown; for many performers, including established stars, the indignity of being labeled a Communist or a Communist sympathizer reduced already meager employment opportunities. The Red Scare commenced a time of suffering for artists of all races but for Black performers, who had just seen some doors open to them, the timing could not have been worse. In 1950, *California Eagle* warned:

> FREE LAWSON, TRUMBO, DENNIS FAST, OR THIS YEAR OF FREEDOM MAY BE YOUR LAST. WRITE THE PRESIDENT![1]

This advice referred to the travails of the infamous Hollywood Ten, the writers, directors, and producers imprisoned for being uncooperative witnesses in the hunt for the Communist influences in the film industry.[2]

From Lena Horne to Harry Belafonte, faces old and new and of every stripe saw their careers adversely affected by allegations, finger-pointing, and fear. Many would not survive. Canada Lee, one of Black America's esteemed performers, managed to carve out a respectable career for himself with performances on the stage in such plays as *The Tempest* (1945–56), *The Duchess of Malfi* (1946), *On Whitman Avenue* (1946), and *Set My People Free* (1948). He played the character Danny in the original cast of the Black-cast Broadway production of *Anna Lucasta*. Lee was applauded for his dignified appearances in the 1944 Hitchcock production *Lifeboat* and in the 1947 United Artists boxing tale *Body and Soul*. He was also a militant champion of civil rights, a man who refused to play typed roles and who joined forced with Paul Robeson to demand that Black performers be afforded better opportunities in the entertainment industry, charging for example, that the commercial radio industry made "cannibals, menials, thieves and liars" out of Black people. Even though he denied being a Communist, he was blacklisted and eventually found it impossible to get work, sending him into a deep depression. Some contend that the stress and depression he suffered during the period was a cause of his early demise in May 1952.[3]

Many individuals were singled out because of their memberships in organizations such as HICCASP (Hollywood Independent Citizens Committee of Arts, Sciences & Professions) and the Negro Actors Guild, both of which were considered to be under the influence of Communists. Among its other activities, notes an FBI report on the Guild, one goal of the organization was to "get more Negroes into motion pictures." The Committee for the Negro in the Arts, a 1953 FBI memorandum claims, "continues to serve the interest of the CP (Communist Party) and propagandize alleged acts of racial discrimination in the employment of Negroes in the arts field." The National Negro Labor Council was established to fight racism and discrimination in labor and but in the 1950s was seen by the FBI as being little more than a Communist mouthpiece. Innocent individuals with current or past ties to these and similar groups often found themselves under suspicion.[4]

Most unfortunate is the fact that performers were sometimes pilloried because they chose to speak out against discrimination and racism. Whether an individual was a Communist or simply a champion for civil rights was of little consequence to the unnamed FBI informants who infiltrated organizations and then filed the reports on Hollywood figures from perhaps 1946 and continuing into the 1960s. Ruby Dee and Ossie Davis both came under scrutiny for their rights activities. Dee recalls:

> I had been warned that speaking out could cost me jobs and adversely affect my career. Ugly things were beginning to happen to free-thinking people in the business, especially in Hollywood; well-known writers and actors were refused work, and lost access to a livelihood.[5]

Still other Black performers came under suspicion because of their personal and/or professional ties with the outspoken performer and social activist Paul Robeson. "Black actors who wanted to continue working in the movies soon realized that denouncing Paul Robeson before HUAC (House Un-American Activities Committee) was a virtual guarantee of work," noted one writer. But not all would succumb.[6]

Soon after his leap into stardom, Edwards, too, joined the mass of actors, performers, and film industry professionals caught up in the investigation of Hollywood conducted by the House Un-American Activities Committee, headed by the infamous Senator Joseph McCarthy.

In 1950, Edwards revealed that he had been visited by FBI agents whom he described as "three well-dressed and well-poised gentleman who had Harvard-Princeton-Yale written all over them." The purpose of their visit was to convince him to appear before the House Un-American Activities Committee and publicly disavow Robeson. They spoke with Edwards "man-to-man," he recalled, and reminded him of his duty as a citizen. According to Edwards, his answer was a firm, "No."[7]

How much was Edwards' career affected by the HUAC investigation, the Red Scare, and his principles? In his biography of Sidney Poitier, Aram Goudsouzian claims that Universal-International originally considered casting Edwards as the lead in the film *Red Ball Express*, but since he had declined to testify before HUAC and repudiate Robeson, the studio instead cast Poitier, who never assumed Edwards' "position of defiance."[8] And though his name did not appear within the pages of *Red Channels: The Report of the Communist Influence in Radio and Television*, a nondescript-looking book published in 1951 by American Business Associates containing the names of entertainment industry folk with supposed Communist ties, Edwards was most assuredly on the personal or in-house blacklists and graylists of various producers and studio and network executives. He was a Negro movie star who had appeared in one of the most powerful motion pictures about America's race problems ever produced; he was intelligent, college-educated, articulate, blunt, and unflinching in his denunciation of racial intolerance; he was a popular personality in the entertainment world who rubbed elbows with individuals of all races. His outspokenness about racial discrimination and his refusal to testify against Paul Robeson no doubt put him in a precarious position and negatively affected his career, although to what degree it is now not possible to know. How many producers were too frightened to cast him for fear of coming under scrutiny themselves? How many times was he rejected for a part only because of his politics? Which projects with which he was associated were scrapped because of the climate of fear and finger-pointing? Was graylisting less detrimental that outright blacklisting? In an essay on the Hollywood graylist, one author commented in *The Nation*:

> Every relationship in the industry is affected by people's awareness of the gray list. No one is sure where he stands or whom he can trust. Fear determines the proper warmth with which to greet an old friend, the proper

line to take on a story, with whom it is wise to be seen having lunch. A social boycott reinforces the graylisting of workers.[9]

Edwards' FBI file, destroyed in 1993, was unavailable for this study; the extent of FBI snooping on his personal affairs is presumably lost. Not lost, however, are the details about some of Edwards' professional activities and the activities of his associates and co-stars which can be found amongst the thousands of pages of carefully detailed records and memoranda contained in the FBI report on the Communist Influence in Motion Pictures, also known as COMPIC. For example, FBI informants noted Edwards' inclusion in the cast of *The Steel Helmet* which was considered a suspect film. It must be noted that in more cases than not, many pages of this declassified report have been released with vital information blacked out. Not blacked out was Edwards' venture into screenwriting. One FBI memorandum reports:

> On page eight of the June 6, 1954, edition of *The Worker* it is reported that "James Edwards, young Negro star of *Home of the Brave*, starts work soon on an independent movie of his own story *Silent Thunder*, about a Negro in the last century who was brought up by Sioux Indians and won fame as an Indian scout for the U.S. Army and Pony Express rider."[10]

Particularly noteworthy, however, is the number of individuals associated with *Home of the Brave* who, for one reason or another, became mired in the HUAC investigations, including Stanley Kramer, Lloyd Bridges, Jeff Corey, George Glass, and Carl Foreman. Corey, who played the doctor who works to cure Moss and considered himself "a good and responsible American citizen," said in a published interview:

> When they asked me to come and testify before the committee, I took the Fifth Amendment, and when I began to read my war records, they said that Darren McDonald was in the armed service and he betrayed the country, so then they assumed that I also betrayed the country.... But that's how narrow-minded they were.[11]

Kramer was not identified by the Committee as a Communist and even went so far as to threaten to sue an organization for hinting that he was a Communist. For a time he was forced to limit or curtail his long association with Carl Foreman after Foreman appeared before HUAC in 1951 as an unsatisfactory witness. Moreover, Kramer's activities remained under suspicion; his name appears repeatedly in the FBI reports because of his production of pictures like *The Defiant Ones*, and because he admitted on a television program that he had employed individuals who had been blacklisted.[12]

Bridges, an FBI report claims, admitted his past membership in the Communist Party. He refused, however, to offer the names of anyone else he knew and thus remained under suspicion. George Glass, the self-proclaimed promotional genius behind *Home of the Brave*, was identified by an informant as having joined the Communist Party in 1945 and holding several meetings in his home. Glass claimed that he had attended a party discussion but "had no intention of joining the CP ... and never did."[13]

The Steel Helmet, in which Edwards co-starred, received a mention in a suspect newspaper. This alone could put a film and its cast and crew under the watchful eye of the FBI, which noted how the picture had been reviewed by such left-leaning publications as *The Daily Worker* and *The People's World*. Fuller contends that his inclusion of the scene where the American soldier brutally assassinates an unarmed enemy POW caused some to paint him as a Communist sympathizer.[14]

In 1946, Edwards was hired as an understudy in the hit Broadway play *Deep Are the Roots*. The play, a triumphant success, garnered approval and commendation in many circles. Still, its controversial theme did not escape the scrutiny of those of believed it to be subversive and in 1953, playwright Arnaud D'Usseau was summoned before Congress to defend himself and his play in a fiery squabble with Senator Joseph P. McCarthy. McCarthy warned D'Usseau that he "was not there to give a speech" and threatened to have him removed from the room and cited for contempt of Congress. Betsy Blair, Edwards' co-star in the West Coast company of the play, also came under scrutiny for her membership in various suspect organizations. It didn't help that she called on the Screen Actors Guild to use "its power to oppose discrimination." The resolution she proposed to attack racial inequality was established in 1946.[15]

In an FBI memoranda, Will Geer (*Bright Victory*) is described as a "sponsor of Communist fronts." He was eventually subpoenaed to appear before the Eighty-Second Congress House Un-American Activities Committee. Humphrey Bogart, with whom Edwards appeared in *The Caine Mutiny*, came under suspicion for his activities as did the director of the film Edward Dymytrk, whose travails as one of the Hollywood Ten have been well-documented. Jose Ferrer, another *Caine Mutiny* cast member, was labeled in FBI reports as being affiliated with several Communist front groups, as was Lewis Milestone, director of the film *Pork Chop Hill* (1959). Ben Maddow, a scriptwriter, had to ghost-write the film *Men at War* (1957), another Edwards film, because he was officially blacklisted and therefore unemployable.[16]

Singer and performer Nat "King" Cole, who appeared with Edwards in *Night of the Quarter Moon*, was cited in a 1955 FBI letter:

> A confidential informant of known reliability advised in August, 1949, that "King" Cole was a member of the Music Division of the Southern California Chapter of the Arts, Science, and Professions Council ... cited as a Communist front[.][17]

Because of his affiliations, Cole's activities were closely scrutinized, and his travels across the country and overseas were summarized in detail, as were the activities of Sammy Davis, Jr., who Edwards worked with on *Zane Grey Theatre* and the 1959 film version of *Anna Lucasta*. Lena Horne, who never acted with Edwards in a film or television show but who appeared with him in a photo spread for *Our World* magazine in 1951, and who was erroneously linked with him romantically, was listed in *Red Channels* for her affiliations with such groups as the International Film and Radio Guild (she served on the board in 1946). The IFRG, which was organized to promote the interests of minority performers and to fight against negative racial stereotypes in entertainment, was seen by FBI watchdogs as little more than a Communist mouthpiece.

While he tested as the leading character Joe, Edwards did not earn the role in the highly anticipated 20th Century–Fox musical *Carmen Jones*. Edwards told Diahann Carroll that he passed up the part in *Carmen Jones* for something better, when in truth he might well have not passed muster with Fox's legal department. Director Otto Preminger (who was not blacklisted) wrote in his autobiography:

> [W]hen I made a deal with Fox for the distribution of my independent film, *Carmen Jones*, Fox insisted on one condition: I had to submit the names of everyone I intended to hire, everyone, to their legal department, which would have the right to veto without giving any reason.[18]

The part of Joe, ironically, went to Harry Belafonte, an outspoken critic of racial discrimination who would endure the legacy of the Hollywood blacklist for many years. Belafonte recalled in a 2000 interview, "Yes, there was a backlash against almost anyone who took up the cause of free speech, anyone who took up the cause of human rights, civil rights."[19]

At late as 1960, Hilda Simms, star of the *Anna Lucasta* stage production and Edwards' co-star in *The Joe Louis Story* (1953), was told by the Department of Defense that her services were not needed for a 14-week Armed Services entertainment tour because her name was linked with subversive activities.[20]

The purges and blacklists of suspected Hollywood performers occurred just at the time when Black performers enjoyed slightly improved conditions in the entertainment industry. Films like *Home of the Brave*, *Bright Victory*, and *The Joe Louis* Story served to open the doors to Black performers who earned a measure of universal acceptance in roles that cast them as ordinary people. The blacklist and the air of suspicion greatly curtailed any progress on this front as producers were afraid to cast a Black actor in anything but a typed role, or to broach any subject matter or casting that might arouse suspicion. Indeed, some producers found it easier to eliminate Black characters altogether.

To make matters worse, the period of Hollywood blacklisting coincides with the birth of commercial television. For Black Hollywood performers, the opportunities for work on this new medium quickly evaporated. Actor William Marshall appeared with Edwards in a photograph in the December 1953 edition of *Our World* magazine. Earlier that year, Marshall had been cast in the lead of the locally produced television crime drama *Harlem Detective*. Marshall associated himself with Paul Robeson, and when his name appeared in an anti–Communist publication, the show was cancelled. The terrifically talented and boldly beautiful pianist-singer-performer Hazel Scott hosted her own locally produced television show. Her fate was sealed and her show was cancelled when she was accused of being a Communist sympathizer and appeared in front of HUAC of her own accord, but refused to be bullied.

For the Hollywood community, the period of the Red Scare could be likened to a horrific and destructive storm. And along with his fellow actors of all races, Edwards could do little but sit and wait for the squall to pass.

12. "It Wasn't a Damn Bit Funny"

In 1951, the ever-blunt James Edwards added fuel to fire when he spoke out about one of early television's most controversial shows, *Amos 'n' Andy*. Well before its premiere on CBS in June, *Amos 'n' Andy* generated a wellspring of discourse and debate both negative and cautiously hopeful. The comedy originated on radio in the late 1920s and became one of the longest running and most popular series in radio history. Creators Charles Correll and Freeman Gosden were White men who played the Black characters Amos and Andy by employing so-called Negro dialect and vernacular.

Nearly thirty years later, as commercial radio began its decline, the *Amos 'n' Andy Show* transitioned to television with veteran African Americans actor Alvin Childress as Amos Jones and Spencer Williams, Jr., as Andy Brown. Other cast members include Tim Moore, Johnny Lee, Ernestine Wade, Nick Stewart, and Amanda and Lillian Randolph.

The first episode of *Amos 'n' Andy* aired to mixed reviews. Some in the Black community were simply glad to see a television show featuring a Negro cast. Moreover, the show was funny, the acting superb, and the production values high. Nevertheless, to many of America's Black citizens, the program's portrayal of Black life and culture was crude and offensive. Indeed, the over-the-top antics of Kingfish Stevens, a scheming smoothie; Calhoun, an underhanded lawyer that no one trusted; Lightnin,' a slow-moving janitor; Sapphire Stevens, a nosy, loud-mouth; Mama, a domineering mother-in-law; and the infamous Madame Queen were described on the front page of the Baltimore (MD) *Afro American* as "thriftless, lazy, semi-literates living by their wits," and the show as "a modernization of the old time minstrels."[1]

Many postwar Black citizens hoped that the medium of television would be free of the old ethnic stereotypes promulgated on film and in other forms of popular culture, so they were mortified and embarrassed by the images of Black people as depicted on *Amos 'n' Andy*.

Edwards boldly inserted himself into the middle of the fray. He blasted the program in no uncertain terms with his comments printed in the *New York Age*:

> For the sake of the 142 jobs which Negroes hold down with [the] *Amos 'n' Andy* show, 15 million more Negroes are being pushed back 25 years by perpetuating this stereotype on television. The money involved (and there's a great deal) can't hope to undo the harm that the continuation of *Amos 'n' Andy* will effect. We don't have to take it, not today.[2]

The NAACP led the way in denouncing the *Amos 'n' Andy Show*. The civil rights organization called the show "gross libel on the colored American and a distortion of the truth." They sent a telegram to the program's sponsors, requesting that they withdraw sponsorship, noting:

> In picturing colored people as immoral, semi-literate, lazy, stupid, scheming and dishonest, the caricature thus circulates, perpetuates and extends a harmful stereotype which went out with the old-time minstrel show.[3]

Why did the program become the subject of so much contention? First, still fresh in the minds of many was the acrimony that had erupted one year prior over the debut of the ABC sitcom *Beulah*. The concept was developed from the radio program of the same name; Amanda Randolph starred as the lovable servant of the Henderson family. When the program transitioned to television, many in the Black community dismissed the show as demeaning. Even the *New York Times* reproved *Beulah*'s outdated concept:

> *Beulah*, the story of one of those southern jewels who turns out corn bread and greens and generally manages the household, made the transition to television ... but on the whole the opening installment suffered from a trite story and was regrettably stereotyped in concept.[4]

After veteran performer Ethel Waters left the cast, she was followed by Hattie McDaniel, Louise Beavers and Amanda Randolph in the part of Beulah the maid. Then, actor Bud Harris complained to the *Chicago Defender* about the course that the show took:

> People have been writing me asking why I left the show.... The writers for this show are sending scripts that require Bill Jackson, Beulah's boyfriend, to eat chicken, use dialect, fight and things that are really degrading to my race. This I refused to do.[5]

12. "It Wasn't a Damn Bit Funny"

Moreover, the rough-edged characters of *Amos 'n' Andy* and the lovable but ignorant servants of *Beulah* were the only representatives of the race found regularly on primetime network television. A scant few Black actors like Edwards managed to earn roles on dramatic anthologies. No African American characters appeared recurrently in a dramatic series, there were few Black cowboys to be found in the ever-popular Western; except for variety specials, Black faces on television were uncommon. According to *Chicago Defender*,

> The gripe of fans over the country today is why won't television and the motion picture industry give us merit programs which will DEPICT the "otherside" of Negro life in contrast to the Southern, lazy drawling dialect of *Beulah* and *Amos 'n' Andy*?[6]

Edwards declared, "I'd starve first.... I'd rather dig mines than say one 'yassah' on the screen." One columnist chided him, noting that not all Black actors could afford to be as choosy as he was about what acting jobs they would accept. But Edwards held his ground and concluded with his prediction that the *Amos 'n' Andy Show* would soon be off the air (the show lasted three years before going into syndication). "I've seen *Amos 'n' Andy*.... Fifteen million Negroes laughed, but it wasn't funny ... it wasn't a damn bit funny."[7]

13. *The Joe Louis Story*

"Films Go Biographical" was the title of a photographic spread that appeared in *The New York Times* in January 1953. Hollywood began a cycle of biopics that year, including a feature called *Melba* (Horizon Pictures) which chronicled the life of opera singer Nellie Melba; *Young Bess* (MGM), a dramatization of the life of Elizabeth I of England; *Houdini* (Paramount), the story of the great magician; and *The President's Lady* (20th Century–Fox), on the life of Rachel Jackson, wife of President Andrew Jackson.[1]

The article also highlighted the release of the low-budget but highly anticipated and widely promoted feature *The Joe Louis Story*, a dramatization of the life of African American boxing champ Joe Louis Barrow, aka the Brown Bomber, perhaps the first African American to achieve the status of national hero. In 1953 he was still a very popular figure and for many Americans he was not only a sports hero but also an icon with movie star–like standing. This black and white picture was directed by Robert Gordon and produced and mostly scripted by Stirling Silliphant, a former publicist. *The Joe Louis Story* was distributed by United Artists.

Silliphant met with Louis and acquired the rights to his life story. He hired Robert Sylvester to write a screenplay but was unhappy with Sylvester's treatment and wrote many of the scenes himself. Louis' real story, that is, his poor beginnings as the grandson of slaves in racist 1920s Alabama and the story of his sharecropper father who was committed to an asylum, was submerged for a more pleasant image of a largely carefree Black middle-class family life in Detroit, Michigan, where the family eventually moved.

The Joe Louis Story was shot on location in early 1953 at Madison Square Garden, Yankee Stadium, a Harlem nightclub, and a Baptist church in Brooklyn. "The shooting," wrote A. H. Weiler for the *New York Times*,

13. The Joe Louis Story

"will be in short, a local operation except for a two-day side trip to Detroit."[2]

The story of Joe Louis is told through the eyes of a journalist, Tad McGeehan, played by Paul Stewart. The cast also features Hilda Simms as Louis' first wife. Simms, who had achieved recognition from her appearance as Anna in the highly successful Black-cast Broadway production of the Philip Yordan play *Anna Lucasta*, had been touring Europe as a performer before returning home to play the role. Also appearing is Dotts Johnson and Buddy Thorpe, son of Jim Thorpe, who portrays German fighter Max Schmeling. Ossie Davis also makes a brief speaking appearance. Twenty-four-year-old Coley Wallace, who was a real prizefighter and Golden Gloves champion, plays the part of Joe Louis. Though far from a polished actor, his youthful demeanor, sincerity, and training as a boxer lent an authentic and agreeable air to the film. Wallace stood 6'2" and weighed 200 pounds; in build and countenance he greatly resembled the real Louis.

Edwards earned the role of Jack "Chappie" Blackburn, Louis' trainer. There are some interesting connections between the lives of Edwards and Louis, and the lives of Edwards and Blackburn.

Joe Louis was born on May 14, 1913; he and Edwards were just a few years apart in age. Edwards idolized Louis to the point where he, too, took up boxing. Like Louis, he pursued this endeavor for a time without his mother's consent. It is not difficult to imagine a high school-aged Edwards being attracted to the fame, notoriety, and adulation that was heaped upon Louis, a Black man who made good in 1930s America.

Blackburn, like Edwards, was born in Indiana. Legend has it that his boxing career began when he was paid to spar with legendary heavyweight fighter Jack Johnson and bloodied the champion's nose. Blackburn was successful as a fighter but was never able to secure a championship-caliber match. His career was further hampered when he spent five years in jail for shooting a man for talking about his common-law wife. He was a notorious drinker and a no-nonsense type who often carried a gun. Like Edwards, he died in his fifties of a heart attack.[3]

At a nightclub opening in April 1953, Edwards mugged for the camera with his head clean-shaven. Edwards was shaved bald and had to be heavily made-up to transform himself into Blackburn. In the photo, Bill Kenny of the famed musical group, The Ink Spots, playfully pats his hairless dome.[4]

Playing the role of the surly Blackburn, Edwards is steely-eyed, exact-

James Edwards, as Jack "Chappie" Blackburn, reprimands a recalcitrant Joe Louis (Coley Wallace) in the Sterling Silliphant production *The Joe Louis Story* (1953).

ing, no-nonsense, and unsmiling. He delivers his lines in his trademark quiet, down-home manner, his speech tinged at times with a slight Midwestern accent. Blackburn cajoles, instructs, and drills a young and sometime recalcitrant Joe Louis into a champion-level fighter. He is by Louis' side when he chooses a manager and meets the woman who would become his wife. In other words, Chappie would become like a father, and Edwards' interpretation of the role is honest-to-goodness and unassuming. Too, he appears as a realistic corner man; his real-life boxing experience was clearly a plus.

The Joe Louis Story was shot on a shoestring, with bleak, boring sets, bad sound, and stodgy, didactic dialogue. It wasn't that producer Silliphant was tightfisted, he simply had no money for a lavish production. The production of the film was nearly shut down when financing dried up. "Unless more money, and lots of it, is turned up pretty soon," the *Chicago Defender* declared, "the contemplated production will fall flat." Investor Walter Chrysler reportedly withdrew his investment of $100,000, followed quickly by the film's other backers. The reasons centered on the issue of Southern exhibitors, who considered the film, with its predominantly Black cast of players, to be a "race movie." They also objected to the scenes of Blacks and Whites commiserating together as equals. When word got out about the film's subject matter, and backers heard veiled warnings that it would never get any Southern bookings, some became, the *Chicago Defender* noted, "leery of the film's success." They backed out, taking their money with them. Silliphant told the *Pittsburgh Courier* that financial problems nearly scrapped the entire production. "People I hardly knew would warn me that such a picture wouldn't get any bookings, in 'white' houses in many areas."[5]

Chrysler was convinced to change his mind and reinvested in the film. But the premiere was again delayed by Louis himself, who demanded some last-minute changes which required retakes and a subsequent reediting of the film. Well aware of how much importance was placed on the final production of his story, he requested that the film be free of stereotyped depictions and so-called Negro dialect.[6]

Problems aside (and there are many in the uneven script), *The Joe Louis Story* is an enjoyable and engaging film if for no other reason than the fact that footage of the real Louis' fights is interspersed throughout the film. The *New York Times* described the inclusion of Louis's bouts with Max Schmeling, James Braddock, and Max Baer as "surprisingly thrilling."[7]

Accompanied by much fanfare, *The Joe Louis Story* premiered at the Holiday Theater in New York in November 1953. In Chicago, women attended the Chicago opening draped in silk dresses and fur stoles. On October 14, *The Joe Louis Story* opened in Detroit and Mayor Albert E. Cobb proclaimed it "Joe Louis Day." A critic described the premiere:

The huge screen had just gone dark as *The Joe Louis Story* came to an end. The first reaction was a stunned sort of silence — then a terrific burst of applause from the SRO audience in Detroit's Broadway Capitol Theatre.[8]

Reviews of *Joe Louis Story* ranged from middling to glowing. The *Oakland Tribune* wrote, "No major fault could be found with the picture as a whole ... nothing to detract from enjoyment of the show." "*The Joe Louis Story* is no knockout," declared *Stars and Stripes*, "It might better be described as a light tap on the chin."[9]

Edwards could only be pleased about the attention the film got and the publicity he received for his performance. His face is featured prominently in publicity stills which appeared in local as well as national newspapers such as the *Washington Post*. Further, he received good reviews for his performance.

"James Edwards is austerely competent as the martinet-like but compassionate trainer, Chappie Blackburn," wrote Weiler for the *New York Times*.[10]

The sports editor for the *Oakland (CA) Tribune* made a point of mentioning Edwards' performance:

> A few words of praise for the performance of James Edwards.... Edwards *was* Jack Blackburn, in appearance and action. The studio makeup man didn't give Edwards the long facial scar which endowed Blackburn's face with a sinister cast, but otherwise the likeness was perfect.[11]

However, for Edwards, *The Joe Louis Story* was noteworthy for reasons beyond the positive reception it received. Sitting in the audience at the Chicago opening of the film at the Bratton-Gavilian Theatre was a woman named Leola Mosley. Edwards, the ladies' man, was ready to tie the knot. The *Chicago Defender* offered no details about Mosley beyond the fact of her engagement to Edwards. The couple would be married the next month in California.[12]

Today, *The Joe Louis Story*, apparently now public domain, most often fills air time on local access cable stations, with the backstory, publicity and hoopla that this small picture generated more than fifty years ago, lost to the viewers who chance upon it.

14. Some of His Best Work

In 1951, popular young star James Edwards made his debut in the new medium of television: That January, he appeared as a guest on *Toast of the Town* (precursor to *The Ed Sullivan Show*). This installment of the legendary CBS variety show also featured Sugar Ray Robinson, Anna Maria Alberghetti, and the requisite stage acts.

Edwards also exploited his talents on locally produced programming originating from the Los Angeles area. The *Los Angeles Sentinel* announced his association with the program *Spotlight Wednesday*, "telecast from the bandstand and floor of the 5-4 Ballroom at the corner of 54th and Broadway." Edwards was chosen to act as emcee and to appear as a performer. He was associated with "the nation's first all–Negro produced and starring video program," KCOP's *Swing Street*, where he was to act as emcee with singer Dinah Washington. This Sunday night variety program was also produced at the 5-4 Ballroom. Edwards' name was also connected with the program *Ebony Showcase*, which originated from the Ebony Showcase Theatre and was telecast on KTTV in Los Angeles. It is unknown how much Edwards was ultimately involved in these endeavors.[1]

But Edwards did not limit his television appearances to variety shows. In 1954 he made his debut on early American television's most popular genres, the dramatic anthology.

Only viewers of a certain age can still recall Fred Coe's *Philco Playhouse* production of *Marty*; *Studio One's* production of the seminal play *Patterns*; Loretta Young's swirling entrance for each episode of *The Loretta Young Show*; and *Playhouse 90*'s adaptation of the classic Rod Serling drama *Requiem for a Heavyweight*. There were many other programs, many long forgotten, such as *Decision, Ellery Queen, Tales of Tomorrow* (which featured science fiction melodrama), *Shirley Temple Storybook* (one-hour dramas aimed at children), and *Medallion Theatre*. Some programs featured famous and soon-to-be-famous actors such as Rod Steiger, Paul Newman, Joanne Woodward, George C. Scott, and Jack Lemmon, who performed in dramas conceived by up-and-coming writers named J.P. Miller, Horton Foote, Paddy Chayevsky, Arthur Penn, and Reginald Rose.

In the beginning the programs were produced in New York and were broadcast live, in real time, like a stage play (in fact, many scenarios were adapted from stage plays). Later, some of the programs moved to Hollywood sound sets where they were filmed.

Black performers appeared only sporadically in dramatic anthology programs. In 1950, Canada Lee performed in the *Chevrolet Tele-Theatre* production of the boxing tale "The Final Bell." In 1955, Hilda Simms was cast with Sidney Poitier in the *Philco Television Playhouse* production "A Man Is Ten Feet Tall." Also in 1955, Ossie Davis appeared in the controversial *Kraft Television Theatre* production of Eugene O'Neill's *The Emperor Jones*. Harry Belafonte and Ethel Waters starred in a 1955 *General Electric Theatre* presentation of "Winner by Decision." Bernie Hamilton, who appeared with Edwards in the *Ramar* television series, appeared as the character Sullivan in a *Climax* episode called "The Volcano Seat." And in 1957, NBC presented the *Hallmark Hall of Fame* presentation of Marc Connelly's Pulitzer Prize–winning play *The Green Pastures*. The cast, numbering more than fifty, featured Eddie "Rochester" Anderson, Dots Johnson, William Warfield, Avon Long, Mantan Moreland, Rosetta LeNoire, and Frederick O'Neal. In 1960, Ossie Davis appeared in the *Playhouse 90* production of "John Brown's Raid." Edwards is recognized as one of few serious Black actors who landed more than a single acting job in early television's dramatic anthology programs.

DuPont Cavalcade of America

In 1955, Edwards appeared in a biography of African American educator, civil rights leader, and Nobel Peace Prize winner Ralph Bunche.

In an attempt to make the public forget its reputation for war profiteering, and to counter its image as the merchant of death, in 1935 the E.I. Dupont Company began sponsorship of a radio program, *The DuPont Cavalcade of America*. The CBS radio program promoted itself with the slogan, "Better things for better living ... through chemistry." Weekly shows featured stories about war heroes, inventors, and famous Americans in history. The program attracted a number of top stars: In one episode, veteran actor Robert Montgomery performed as Admiral George Dewey and in another, Charles Laughton played Benjamin Franklin. The selection process for stories was very stringent, and in the early day, scripts about African Americans were generally excluded. Not until 1948 did an episode highlight the life of Black educator and spokesman Booker T. Washington.[2]

In 1952, *Cavalcade* made its television debut in syndication with episodes that featured the stories of historical figures such as Thomas Jefferson, Eli Whitney, and Peter Zenger. Like its radio counterpart, the series maintained strict rules about the personalities and events that could be highlighted on the program. Erik Barnouw wrote of the program, "The series was always idealistic in tone; no iconoclasm permitted.... Absolute taboos included ... for a long time, the Negro."[3]

Ralph Bunche had been a member of President Theodore Roosevelt's so-called Black Cabinet, and under the Truman administration, he was appointed undersecretary to the U.N. Bunche's TV story, called "Toward Tomorrow," would be the first episode of the series that highlighted the accomplishments of a contemporary individual.

The script, written by Joel Murcott, featured actual incidents in Bunche's remarkable life. McHenry Norman was cast as Bunche as a boy and Ruby Goodwin played his grandmother. Other players include Maidie Norman and Bernie Hamilton. Producer Warren Lewis told the *Los Angeles Sentinel* that the casting for the program was "the most difficult he had ever encountered.... Actors in Hollywood were all fighting for parts in the picture."[4]

The Dupont Company previewed the program before a select audience who enjoyed lunch at the Brown Derby. A columnist for the *Los Angeles Sentinel* called it "a thing of beauty...." 'Toward Tomorrow' has all the dignity and finesse we have long wanted to see in a picture with Negro stars."[5]

Edwards appears with Ruby Goodwin in a publicity still published on page 1 of the September 29, 1955, edition of the *Los Angeles Sentinel*. He told the *Eagle* that he considered his performance as Bunche as "some of his best work."[6]

"Toward Tomorrow" also earned the distinction of being appropriated by the United States Information Agency in its program to proselytize American democracy. From 1952 to 1961, the agency produced or purchased and circulated films about carefully selected, popular African American figures such as Duke Ellington, Althea Gibson, and Jesse Owens.

No doubt the agency found the greatly fictionalized 30-minute film about Bunche very useful in its efforts to propagandize to the world, America's good treatment of its Black citizens.

The Fireside Theatre

NBC's 30-minute series *The Fireside Theatre* debuted in 1949. It was one of the earliest of the dramatic anthology programs to be filmed instead of broadcast live and for a time the program was one of the most popular programs on television. In 1954, Edwards appeared in the leading role in an episode called "The Reign of Amelika Jo."

The story, written by John Vandercook, was based on an experience he had while on active duty in the South Pacific during the Second World War, when he found that the natives of a tiny and largely unknown atoll were oddly well-schooled in the ways of Americans. The reason: a mysterious American, a Negro Merchant Marine, had lived among them for a number of years. They called him Amelika Joe. Because of the tiny nation's regard for Joe as their surrogate leader, when the U.S. forces arrived, the island's inhabitants treated them with kindness and gave their complete cooperation.

Vandercook's novelette was published in the March 1948 edition of *The Saturday Evening Post*; the film adaptation was described in *TV-Radio Life*:

> Gene Raymond, host, presents James Edwards in "Amelika Jo."... The story concerns an American sailor who has come to the island 20 years before the war and almost miraculously transformed the natives' way of life. An all–Negro cast is featured.[7]

The program was narrated by Vandercook himself and produced by Frank Wisbar, who wrote or introduced many episodes of the *Fireside Theatre* himself. The cast also included Johnny Lee and Nick Stewart and is remembered as the first American televised dramatic program of its kind to feature a cast consisting only of people of color.

TV Reader's Digest

The ABC anthology program *TV Reader's Digest* was created and produced by Chester Erskine for the Studebaker-Packard Car Corporation.

Some sources note Edwards as having appeared in the episode "Mr. Pak Takes Over," which aired June 13, 1955. The teleplay is based on a story written by Capt. Frederick Haight II which appeared in *Reader's Digest* in March 1953. Other players included Philip Ahn, Kenneth Tobey, and Dan Burton.

The General Electric Theatre

The General Electric Theatre ran on Sunday evenings on CBS from 1953 to 1962. This show, like other anthology programs, featured adaptations of the works of various novelists, playwrights, and mystery and short story writers such as Evelyn Waugh and Henrik Ibsen. Some shows were broadcast live but later, nearly all would be filmed. It was hosted by actor Ronald Reagan; other stars who would appear included Joan Crawford, Tony Curtis, Jimmy Stewart, Cornel Wilde, Jane Wyman, Bette Davis, Jack Benny, and Barbara Stanwyck.

Edwards appeared as Sgt. Davis, in a 1955 production called "D.P." (for Displaced Person). Written by H.F. Walling, "D.P." is the story of an embittered Black soldier whose resentment is softened by his alliance with an Afro-German boy who believes, or perhaps wishes, that Davis is his father. "Beneath the tough exterior," notes the *Los Angeles Sentinel,* "the sergeant feels a resemblance between the boy and his own unhappy childhood."[8]

The part of the boy was played by a Black, German-speaking nine-year-old, Julius Jackson, whom Edwards discovered living right across the street. A publicity still that appears in the *Pittsburgh Courier* shows Edwards buttoning the jacket of the young man. "Edwards did his usual good job," notes the caption, "and Julius was a real find." The cast also included Bernie Hamilton, Lisa Golm, Roy Glenn, and Al Andrews.[9]

Westinghouse-Desilu Playhouse

There would be much more to the Lucille Ball-Desi Arnaz partnership than the zany antics of Lucy Ricardo on the program *I Love Lucy.* With an alliance forged with Westinghouse, the manufacturer of refrigerators, washers, and other appliances, the Desilu Studios moved onto the old RKO lot and began the production of quality anthology programs, including the *Westinghouse-Desilu Playhouse*, which aired a mix of comedy, musicals, and drama. A *Variety* article noted that there would be "no cheapies for Desilu features," only "top quality stuff."[10]

In November 1958, Edwards' "Silent Thunder," aired on CBS. A few years earlier, Edwards told the *New York Times* that he planned to chronicle the story of Frank Giraud, an African American who was raised by the Sioux and became a scout and later a rider for the Pony Express. His first draft of "Silent Thunder," written for Robert Gordon Productions, tells the engaging story of a mute Apache named Little Horse and an Indian hater named Les. The female lead is called Leola, perhaps named after Edwards' wife at the time. As with every such project, Edwards' idea would be developed and rewritten until, by the time it aired, Edwards would receive credit not as screenwriter but as the creator of the original story. The screenwriting credit went to John McGreevey, a prolific writer of episodes of *Studio One, Lassie, Kraft Suspense Theatre, Wagon Train* and many more. "Silent Thunder" was directed by Ted Post.

Alfred Hitchcock Presents

In 1955, Edwards appeared in two episodes of the new CBS program *Alfred Hitchcock Presents*. *Rear Window* (1954), *Dial M for Murder* (1954), *Notorious* (1946), *Spellbound* (1945), *Lifeboat* (1944) — with the success of these films and more, director Alfred Hitchcock had already achieved a substantial measure of notoriety well before the 1955 debut of his television anthology series. This half-hour drama presented original stories penned by such writers as Dorothy L. Sayers, Ray Bradbury, and John Collier, featuring themes that reflected the offbeat, kinky persona of Hitchcock.

Hitchcock hosted the program himself, delighting viewers with his unique brand of banter that often included veiled references, sly witticisms, and wicked political jibes. Contrary to popular belief, Hitchcock was directly involved in the show's production: He chose the actors and stories and directed many of the early episodes himself, including "Breakdown," which featured Joseph Cotten, Raymond Bailey, Forrest Stanley and James Edwards in the part of a prisoner. "Breakdown," which aired November 1955, is considered one of the series' best episodes. The opener to the program teased, "Tonight's story tells about a business tycoon and will give you something to ponder ... if you have ever given an employee the sack, or if you intend to."

In "Breakdown," a hard-hearted businessman named Callew, played by Cotten (who had earlier performed a radio version of the story), holds scant regard for anyone who exhibits any sign of weakness. After an employee he fired tearfully begs for his job back, he muses, "Imagine that, he was crying. I hate that kind of emotion."

Later that same day, Callew is involved in a car collision with a backhoe at a construction site. The workers, made up of a cadre of prisoners, make their escape. Their guards are all killed. Callew is paralyzed. He is in his open-top sedan, the steering wheel wedged under his chin, eyes open, mouth agape, and completely paralyzed. Groups of spectators come and go, commenting on the gruesome scene, and, incidentally, stripping the car of all its valuables. The police and county physician arrive at night, assume Callew is dead, and remove him to a morgue. Only when Callew experiences that "hated" emotion and begins to cry does he alert someone that he is not dead. Not to be overlooked is the fact that in a wonderful Hitchcockian touch, throughout this mini-drama, we can hear Callew's thoughts in voiceover. The effect is eerie.

Edwards plays the part of a prisoner, one of the many individuals who stop to investigate or profit from the situation. His comrade callously strips Frank of his suit. But the unnamed Edwards character is not so sure Callew is really dead. He remarks, "Seems like I kinda seen something shinin' in them eyes...."

Edwards also appeared in an episode called "The Big Switch," based on the short story *Change to Murder* by Cornell Woolrich which appeared in the 1936 edition of *Detective Fiction Weekly*. The cast featured George Mathews, Mark Dana, George E. Stone, and Joseph Downing.

In this episode, Edwards has a small speaking part as Ed the bartender in a club run by a small-time hood named Joe, who makes money on the side by lying to the police and providing alibis for criminals. Joe is a gun enthusiast and it is this passion that causes his accidental death, which ironically falsely implicates the killer for whom he was providing another false alibi.

During the 1949–51 seasons, the 25 top-rated television programs included the anthologies *Texaco Star Theatre, Fireside Theatre, Philco TV Playhouse, Goodyear TV Playhouse,* and *Kraft Television Theatre*. In 1956, NBC's primetime lineup included *Philco TV Playhouse* on Sunday, *Robert Montgomery Presents* on Monday, *Fireside Theatre* and *Armstrong Circle*

Theatre on Tuesday, *Kraft Television Theatre* on Wednesday, and *Ford Theatre* and the *Lux Video Theatre* on Thursday. None of these programs survived the sixties. However, the genre was not completely dead. In 1962, Edwards joined a *Home of the Brave* co-star in an anthology program named for the actor himself. *The Lloyd Bridges Show* (1960–1962) was one of a stable of programs produced by Dick Powell's Four Star Productions. Bridges was cast as Adam Shepherd, an independent journalist who enters the world of his own stories. Edwards provides a proficient performance in an episode called "The Testing Ground." The cast featured Paul Richards as Doc; Frank Aletter as McAfee; Bridges as the commander; and Edwards as Byron. They are astronauts who land on an uncharted planet. Attired in jumpsuit uniforms, the four men cautiously make their way around the dark and haunting terrain. They come to a large rock into which the shape of a cross has been carved. It is clearly not a natural formation but appears to have built by purposeful hands. The men are perplexed and discuss the meaning of the structure. In the meantime, Byron begins taking geological samples and comes to the startling conclusion that the structure is pure diamond.

Suddenly, the aims of the men turn from their mission to help all mankind, to a chance to enrich themselves. They agree to use dynamite to blast the structure to bits. They have put themselves in harm's way, they argue, so why not take this opportunity for a payoff? The diamond cross weighs approximately two tons, Byron approximates, and a pound or two apiece would make each man wealthy beyond imagination. They engage in animated debate. Keyed up at the prospect of instant riches, their demeanors are radically changed. Doc is the only one who fervently believes that the structure is there for a reason and shouldn't be destroyed. Byron challenges him in hot debate:

> We've got our jobs to do! Besides, a small sample wouldn't be a desecration ... we're standing in front of a billion dollars ... knock off the hearts and flowers, Doc!

So adamant is Doc against destroying the structure that a fight breaks out and Doc is accidentally shot. As he succumbs to his wounds, the men slowly come to realize the importance of the structure; indeed, they realize that for them the planet served as a testing ground — a test of their moral fiber.

Though the production values for this episode are meager, the performances are first-rate, as if the all-male cast competed to outdo each other. Edwards was clearly at his best.

Bridges' show lasted only one season. Producer Aaron Spelling said, "Audiences didn't know what to think.... But it was very exciting while it lasted and Lloyd was great."

One of the hallmarks of the early dramatic anthologies was the focus on the pressing and sensitive issues of the day. Unfortunately, it was this spotlight on touchy and sometime taboo themes that help to sound the death knell for such shows, as sponsors quickly learned they could make as much more money and ruffle far fewer feathers by backing more bland fare such as sitcoms.

A scant few of television's early productions of anthology programs can now be found on DVD. Viewed today, some of the programs seem quite awful. But sometimes the writing was brilliant, the stories groundbreaking and the acting impressive. For many, as the anthology faded away, so did television's Golden Age.

15. Negro Products

Even the most ardent of naysayers came to realize that television was more than just another new-fangled whimsy that would soon disappear into the scrapheap of popular culture. Programming schedules, which offered only a handful of shows in 1949, soon featured expanded primetime schedules. By the mid–1950s, there were nearly 500 stations across the United States; almost 40 million Americans owned television sets, and viewers watched an average of five hours per day. The Hollywood film industry, teetering on the brink of financial collapse, negotiated with the television networks for the airing of feature films. Eventual partnerships, such as the ABC–Walt Disney venture, would drastically alter the course of primetime television as motion picture studios began to produce filmed programming such as Westerns and sitcoms like *Father Knows Best*. With lightening speed, the fledgling television industry grew into a major business. And the possibilities afforded by the medium were not lost on the Black population. An article in the magazine *Our World* delineated the hopeful dreams of Negro citizens:

> [N]egroes want to be a vital part.... They want some of the good jobs; they want more and better breaks in shows; they want to be shown to the world differently, and in plain words, they want a fair shake all around.[1]

In 1950, *Ebony* magazine endorsed the new medium's early use of Black talent as a "sure sign that television is free of racial barriers." And the appearance on television of Black performers in dignified settings (mostly singers and entertainers in fifteen-minute locally produced programs) was met with approval from the Black community. Herb Jeffries did a show out of Philadelphia in 1950; singers Mahalia Jackson and Billy Daniels had their own local shows; and on the DuMont network, performers Amanda Randolph and Hazel Scott hosted variety programs. In New

York, WOR-TV ran the crime drama *Harlem Detective* with William Marshall in the leading role. On the West Coast, the locally produced variety shows *Savoy Ballroom*, *Sepia Spotlight*, and *Ebony Showcase*, hosted by stars like Edwards and Dinah Washington, provided music and varied entertainment.[2]

"[T]he biggest thing of all is television," noted the Baltimore *Afro-American*. "[We] will see colored talent on television presented far better than ever presented on radio."[3] As the new medium evolved in sophistication, however, Black performers and technicians found employment opportunities wanting. Bob Howard, Amanda Randolph, and Hazel Scott were soon off the air as cowardly advertisers distanced themselves from subject matter involving Black people. Indeed, within a period of a few years, the once fulgent prognostications about the opportunities for Blacks in the television industry would be considerably dimmed.

In television's early days, the sponsorship of a particular program was often relegated to a single company. Some examples include the *Alcoa* (aluminum) *Theatre*, the *Schlitz* (beer) *Playhouse of Stars*, and the *Lux* (soap) *Show with Rosemary Clooney*. In fact, it was not an unusual practice for the sponsoring company to go as far as to administer the show's production: Material thought too delicate for audience tastes could be modified or deleted. Tobacco companies, for example, could mandate that characters always be seen with a cigarette. One taboo subject for many sponsors were Negroes, and America's so-called Negro problem. In his seminal book *The Sponsor: Notes on a Modern Potentate*, media historian Erik Barnouw discusses the rise of sponsored broadcasting and the unpublished ban on Negro topics, noting, "In the 1950s advertisers readily asserted that they could not afford to have their products known as 'Negro products.'"[4]

In March 1955, the *California Eagle* published a brief article noting Edwards' appearance on an episode of one of early television's most memorable medical dramas, *Medic*. Created by producer-writer James Moser, the program starred Richard Boone in the leading role. *Medic* was not television's first medical drama, but it was certainly one of the most impressive and controversial. Its realistic, hard-hitting, no-nonsense, semi-documentary format would exert a strong influence on the nature of the genre for decades to come.[5]

Edwards was cast in an episode titled "What Is the Color for Courage?" in which he portrays a physician who must decide between going for the money and prestige of a job in the city, or returning to his roots in a small Southern town where his skills are sorely needed. However, viewers of *Medic* would never see this episode. The story's focus on issues of race and class during a formidable time in the history of civil rights caused a number of Southern NBC affiliates to refuse to air the episode, which was shelved.[6]

Performer Nat Cole saw his televised variety show cancelled after only two seasons, not because of criticism or lack of quality, but due to a lack of sponsors. To their credit, executives at NBC worked to improve the quality of the show to compete against other programs such as the infamous *$64,000 Question*. Moreover, they continued production of the show at a significant financial loss, in some cases airing the show with no commercial sponsorship. Big-name stars of all races loaned their talent for minimum fees. Never before had a television variety show featured such a dazzling array of celebrities, including Mel Torme, Sammy Davis, Jr., Count Basie, Ella Fitzgerald, Tony Bennett, and Pearl Bailey. With so much talent and an appealing format that allowed Cole to exploit his amazing talent and affable personality, The *Nat Cole Show* managed to develop an audience. But finding sponsors was another issue. Cole, angry after being informed that, among other things, a Negro show couldn't sell lipstick, later told *Ebony* magazine, "Madison Avenue, the center of the advertising industry, and their big clients didn't want their products associated with Negroes."[7]

In 1954, Brown vs. the Board of Education had ended for all time the concept of separate but equal schools, one for the Black students and another for the White; the Montgomery, Alabama, bus boycott would begin the next year. And in 1957, the same year that President Dwight Eisenhower was forced to send federal troops so that Black children could attend Central High School in Little Rock, Arkansas, the first civil rights bill since 1875 was passed, creating the United States Commission on Civil Rights. Indeed, the postwar civil rights movement with all its viciousness and rancor was in full swing. Timid television producers, advertisers and advertising agencies, and fearful sponsors, thinking of the backlash they might receive from Southern affiliate stations who employed their own brand of censorship, as well as the threat (perceived or real) of organized consumer resistance, caused many to believe it in their best interest to steer clear of appearing too empathetic towards Negro citizens struggling for their rights. Arthur Godfrey received angry mail, threats from Southern viewers, and a dressing-down from Georgia Governor Herman Talmadge for booking a multi-racial musical quartette called The Mariners as regulars on his show. Tennessee Ernie Ford also received the hate mail each time he engaged a Black performer on his popular variety show. Sponsors also withdrew their dollars from broadcasts of dramatic programs when an episode focused on what they deemed was a Negro theme. Talmadge threatened to start a boycott intended to "clean up television before the situation becomes more offensive." As America grappled with integration, racial violence, voting rights, and the hateful rhetoric that emanated from the mouths of Southern politicians, except for a smattering of cameo appearances, the face of American television became increasingly lily-white.[8]

In reaction to the dearth of Black performers on network television shows, in 1955 the Labor and Industry Committee of the New York Branch of the NAACP, in conjunction with the Coordinating Council for Negro Performers, initiated a two-hour blackout in protest of "the almost total exclusion of Negroes performers on television shows." African Americans were invited to turn off their radios and television between the primetime hours of 8:30-10:30 on February 26, 1955, to convince sponsors and stations of the clout of the Black audience. The effect of this action was minimal.[9]

In spite of it all, James Edwards continued his apprenticeship as a television actor, appearing throughout the 1950s on dramatic anthology programs, Westerns, crime dramas, and reality-type programming. He seems to have chosen his roles thoughtfully and for the most part maintained his promise to appear only roles that would uplift, not denigrate the Black race.

Ramar of the Jungle

It didn't take very long for the ever-popular African adventure genre to make its way to television's small screen. In 1953, Edwards appeared in perhaps three episodes of the children's television program *Ramar of the Jungle* (1952-1954). The show starred Jon Hall as Dr. Tom Reynolds (the "natives" call him Ramar, meaning "white medicine man") and Ray Montgomery played Professor Howard Ogden; the two men head a medical research team. With its stock footage of wild animals, chase scenes, and juvenile storylines, this program was no doubt particularly enjoyable watching for wide-eyed, television-addicted fifties children (as well as many adults).

Today, the absurdity of the *Ramar* program is all too apparent: The female natives feature permed hair and painted nails; actors transition from pidgin English to perfect dialect and back again within the same bit of dialogue; the sets are hideously counterfeit; and the storylines preposterous, implausible, far-fetched and silly. In between scenes, stock footage of stampeding elephants, lions at a kill, or alligators tearing apart prey are inserted at random; the time of day or context didn't matter. All this was presented through the eyes of the two White doctors seeking a cure for disease, who would invariably become embroiled in the machinations of the surrounding natives.

The program was produced by Rudolph Flothow, a former B-picture producer for Columbia Pictures. In the 1950s, as the film industry struggled with financial upheaval, he turned to the creation of syndicated programming for television. Flothow's son talked about his father, who was "fascinated with Africa," in a recent book on the history of television:

> Nobody on *Ramar* worried about botanic accuracy. They just wanted a lot of green. They would always throw up these two collapsible straw huts. You never saw any exterior long shots because they didn't want you to see the parked Chevrolet just outside the frame.[10]

Ramar was shot on the Los Angeles estate of an eccentric millionaire who had landscaped his home to resemble a "swampy dreamland." At the very least, while the show was based on the mythical African jungle, the producers apparently made an effort to avoid obvious character typing; the program does not feature the more egregious depictions of ignorant and frightened, bug-eyed African natives afraid of their own shadows–a mainstay of feature films.[11]

In the episode "Savage Challenge," Edwards plays a miscreant medicine man embroiled in tribal political intrigue. He appears dressed in a resplendent costume consisting of a long grass skirt, beaded jewelry, and painted face. Chase scenes offer a glimpse of Edwards' smooth, athletic physique. His lines consist of forged Swahili and, all things considered, he managed to play his role with gusto and dash.

One may question why Edwards, once the bright young rising star, would condescend to appear in such B-level fare. More than fifty years ago, an appearance on *Ramar* could well have been regarded positively by Edwards and his fellow actors who appeared on the show. The role represented work in the new brand medium of television. While the small screen was looked upon with disdain by more established big-studio motion picture stars, some actors regarded television as an exciting opportunity. Secondly, the appearance of so much Black talent on a television show was no doubt considered an event by the Black population. Indeed, the cast of *Ramar* featured a number of recognized Black performers including Juanita Moore, Bernie Hamilton, and veteran actor Rex Ingram, who starred in MGM's *The Green Pastures* (1936), and *Cabin in the Sky* (1943), as well as Nick Stewart, who played the part of the janitor "Lightnin'" on the *Amos 'n' Andy* television show. But perhaps most importantly, for any performer trying to survive the Red Scare and a time of severe economic downturn in the entertainment business, being cast on *Ramar* represented something else: a paycheck. Still, the critics were unkind, with the *New York Times* noting:

> The acting in this obviously hurried, budget-wise production from Hollywood is about what one would expect, only more so. Particularly the native tribesmen. They need more rehearsal.[12]

Flothow would get the last laugh. *Ramar of the Jungle* debuted in New York television in August 1953 and continued in syndication for many years. Episodes of the program were recut and reissued as full-length features providing Edwards a credit for his appearance in the film *Thunder Over Sangoland*. Today *Ramar* has a cult following among some baby boomers, and Flothow is considered to be one of television's most successful producers of syndicated programming.

Navy Log

In 1955, Edwards landed a part in an episode of the semi-documentary program *Navy Log,* which during its 1955-58 run, underwent many alterations as it shifted from CBS to ABC.

During the Eisenhower administration, the history and culture of the United States military services were exploited in a number of television programs produced under the auspices of the Department of Defense. Programs such as *The West Point Story, The Armed Forces Hour, Victory at Sea, Crusade in Europe,* and *Navy Log* served to educate, promote, and dramatize real events.[13]

Navy Log's signature was its opening credits sequence, which featured sailors on a cruiser spelling out the name of the program. Indeed, the show was made with the full cooperation and collaboration of the U.S. Navy and was the first dramatic program series based on Department of Defense records. The show was created by Sam Gallu, a World War II veteran, playwright, television writer, and producer whose credits include the play *Give*

'Em Hell, Harry. Episodes featured dramatizations of rescues, secret missions, and the exploits of real people such as John F. Kennedy, Jr., commander of the legendary PT109. Kennedy, a Senator at the time of the airing of the program on his life, appeared as guest host of the episode. The production values are sharp and it didn't hurt that the Navy provided aircraft, ships, real sailors, footage, advice, and support. Even with all this, the show lacked the panache of the documentary series *Victory at Sea*. But even with low ratings, *Navy Log* remained on the air for nearly three years.[14]

In October 1955, Edwards appeared as Ensign Jesse Brown in a Korean War-themed episode titled "Hiya Pam," about a flier who deliberately scuttles his aircraft to save a pilot buddy who has been shot down. For his efforts, Edwards and costar Douglas Dick, a *Home of the Brave* alum, are featured in a photograph in the magazine *TV Guide*. The picture shows a wounded Brown being comforted by a fellow soldier. The brief review mentions that, unlike *Victory at Sea* and *Crusade in Europe*, the program *Navy Log* focused on the lives of people and that "the actors have been uniformly good, evidencing skill and care on the part of producer and director."[15]

Meet McGraw

In 1958, Edwards joined another *Home of the Brave* alum on the short-lived police drama *Meet McGraw* (1957-58 NBC; 1958 ABC; 1958-59 CBS) starring Frank Lovejoy as McGraw. Edwards appeared in an episode called "The New Orleans Story."

Accused

In 1959 Edwards appeared on the courtroom reality show *Accused* (1958-1959), which aired on ABC. (It is not to be confused with the program *They Stand Accused* which originated from Chicago and ran on the DuMont network.) The cases were real and the judge, Edgar Allen Jones, as well as the bailiff, clerk and reporters, were authentic, not actors. The parts of the defendants and witnesses were played by actors, including such up-and-coming stars as Robert Culp and Pamela Mason. Note Brooks and Marsh, "[R]ealism was the keynote of the series." Produced by Selig Seligman, a former state attorney and later ABC television vice-president, the episodes were carefully researched. Edwards appeared as Bordon Kane, a World War II veteran, in a story about a man who finds and kills a former Nazi prison camp officer, whom Kane believed was responsible for his brother's death during the war.[16]

Peter Gunn

Edwards, working with friend Diahann Carroll, appeared as the character Arnie Kelton in a 1959 episode of *Peter Gunn* (1958-1960, NBC; 1960-1961, ABC) called, "Sing a Song of Murder." The story serves as little more than a half-hour promotional piece for the up-and-coming Carroll who, portraying club singer Dina Wright, sings two full numbers. With its cool jazz opening theme and film noir-like B/W photography, *Peter Gunn* provides entertaining watching even with storylines that today seem corny and contrived.

In "Sing a Song of Murder," Wright's husband Arnie is so consumed with jealously that he kills a man he believed was looking at his wife. After two years in prison, he is now out to kill her. She is so terrified that she stages her own phony death in hopes of throwing him off her trail. Having lost track of her, Kelton calls Gunn (played by Craig Stevens) on the pretense that he is looking for her killer. He tells Gunn: "Maybe I didn't deserve her ... maybe that's why I didn't have her long. I caused it, it was me ... I mean, me being away when she needed me...."[17]

At the end of this rather thin yarn, Kelton is captured during a police set-up. Edwards' part is small in this half-hour program, with the camera firmly focused on Carroll.

Edwards and Carroll had maintained a friendship since 1954 or so. It is interesting to see them working together. Unfortunately, on this program they do not appear together in any scenes, nor do they share any dialogue.

If there were Black people living and working in the same towns as the characters of *Leave It to Beaver*, we never saw them. As America entered the 1960s, appearances by Black performers were largely relegated to guest appearances in variety shows and occasional appearances in dramatic programs such as *Alfred Hitchcock Presents* and *Twilight Zone*. In a 1962 article for the *Washington Post*, Lawrence Laurent described the plight of the Black performer:

> Employment opportunities in television are limited. Singers and dancers get some work on variety programs but a Negro actor almost never gets a call, except to play this role of a Negro. One reason given for this attitude is that network sponsors wish to avoid offending the Confederacy.[18]

Edwards seems to have made no television appearances during the 1960-61 season although unconfirmed is his appearance in an unknown number of episodes of the afternoon soap *The Clear Horizon* (1960-1962, ABC). The program, set in Florida at the Cape Canaveral Space Center, followed the lives of the astronauts-to-be and their families. The program was created by, and some episodes written by, Manya Starr. Even with the heightened interest in the exploration of space at the time of the program's airing, *Clear Horizon* suffered from low ratings in spite of two years of tweaking. Edwards is credited as appearing as Airman Davis.

"Negroes take part in every phase of life in our country today as citizens, as workers, and as the consumers whose buying dollars help pay the costs of television entertainment," declared the American Federation of Labor and the Television Authority in 1951. A decade later, opportunities for Blacks in front of and behind the camera in the television industry remained meager. Not only were there few Black technicians on the rolls of professional organizations such as IATSE (International Alliance of Theatrical Stage Employee), but the ranks of Black performers in the Screen Actors and Screen Extras Guild had shrunk since the end of the war. But soon, the achievements of the civil rights movement and the force of social change would compel the television industry to acknowledge the changing status of Black citizens.[19]

16. "Hollywood: So What!"

Riding the wave of the triumph of *Home of the Brave*, James Edwards reveled in his newfound celebrity. He was the lead of the most talked-about picture of 1949. He was showered with awards, honored with his own parade, and given keys to the city of Harlem. He was called the Bronze Valentino. His continued ascendancy seemed certain. Or was it? In fact, by 1950, Edwards' fortunes made an unexpected downturn.

"Jimmy, since last November, has waded through what shouldn't be 'wished on a dog'—all for his career," *Chicago Defender* wrote in 1950. The article detailed some of Edwards' tribulations:

> [A]fter being the rave of Hollywood, Chicago and New York for his brilliant performance ... the guy lost a fortune trying to carry a vaudeville show across the nation only to disband in Washington, selling everything to pay the debts. This followed a period of disillusionment filled with promises from agents and bitter disappointments. Jimmy almost went into seclusion during readjustment.[1]

Indeed, though busily engaged with the launch of his acting school, speaking engagements, television appearances, and radio performances, Edwards seemed haunted by mishaps.

Even his ten-day tour of the island of Bermuda was accompanied by troubles. On a holiday sponsored by Bermuda Vacations, Edwards went to nightclubs, partied, swapped tennis talk with the governor at a championship playoff, toured the island in a Victorian carriage, sailed St. George's Harbor on a small yacht, visited schools, performed on radio, and even attended a session of the House of Assembly. He wrote, "This was to be my first vacation since before the war.... [It] started off with a bang." However, he was told that any screening of *Home of the Brave* was forbidden. The film had never been shown on the island. "This is tragic," Edwards told a rain-soaked crowd of 300 that had gathered on the steps of the hall to see the film. "[The film] will be shown if it has to be shown in a tent."²

Theatre owners refused to show the film, citing supposed problems with the safety of the film stock, when in reality the reasons were related to the film's incendiary treatment of racial issues. Indeed, public officials from many locales with a significant Black population, from the states of the American South to apartheid South Africa, had refused to allow the film to be seen. Bermuda was no different. Edwards claimed that of the recent films dealing with Negroes, only the 1949 20th Century–Fox production *Pinky* had been approved but the go-ahead was withdrawn before the film could be shown. He had a 16mm copy of *Brave* flown in and, accompanied by Sundel Frank, his manager at the time, and members of the Parliament, he called upon island officials and requested that the film be shown. *Home of the Brave* premiered at the Imperial Hotel lounge for a corps of specially invited guests, which included the seven Black members of Parliament, the head of Bermuda's General Theatres Chain, headmasters of the schools, and the press. Edwards wrote, "Reviews were favorable."³ There were some who stood adamant and did not want *Home of the Brave* to be shown to the general population but Edwards was undeterred:

> I went directly to the mayor of Hamilton. He asked that a special screening be given for the city's board members. This was speedily arranged; the board members approved the film unanimously and *Home of the Brave* got the green light. General Theatres promptly booked the film into its five movie houses. All told, my Bermuda holiday was gratifying.⁴

Home from vacation, Edwards had new film offers. He had survived his setbacks and was aware of and grateful for his good fortune. He wrote in 1952:

> Once in a while someone in the movie industry tells me, "Jimmy, it's too bad you're not white. With your talent and the acting jobs you've done, you could go further and surely be a great star." Now this may be true, but I say SO WHAT! Consider the talented, hard-working actors who for years have tried unsuccessfully to crack the films. I'm different. I was lucky.... I made it where many, many others have failed.⁵

Edwards was indeed lucky. Over the next few years he worked television, radio, and the stage. He earned respectable parts in successful motion pictures. By 1955, triple-threat Edwards would once again manage the feat of appearing in three motion pictures playing at the same time. And by the end of that year, he would vie with Dorothy Dandridge for the lead in the *Pittsburgh Courier* reader's theatrical poll of favorite entertainers.

The Member of the Wedding

In 1952 Edwards was cast as Honey Camden Brown in the Stanley Kramer production of the award-winning Carson McCullers novel cum theatrical play cum motion picture, *The Member of the Wedding*. Directed by Harold Clurman, the Broadway production starring Ethel Waters and Julie Harris won the New York Drama Critics Circle award for best play of 1950. Depending on the source, Kramer paid either $75,000 or 100,000 for the screen rights. The film version debuted in December 1952 and was distributed by Columbia Pictures. Veteran Fred Zinnemann, whose credits include the Stanley Kramer productions *The Men* 1950 and *High Noon* 1952 served as director.[6]

Edwards (with Brandon DeWilde, Ethel Waters, and Harry Bolden) as the tragic Honey Camden Brown in *The Member of the Wedding* (1952), his second Stanley Kramer film.

The Member of the Wedding is the story of a twelve-year-old girl named Frankie, played with proficiency by adult actress Julie Harris. Harris, born in Grosse Point, Michigan, attended the Yale School of Drama. Her stellar performance as Frankie in the stage version of *Wedding* afforded her critical acclaim.

Somehow, Frankie has gotten it into her head that after the wedding, she will join her brother and his new wife on their honeymoon and subsequently their new lives. In sum, she plans to be more than a spectator but a member of the wedding. Frankie is motherless, not quite a woman, but no longer a child, and is rejected by the other girls in the neighborhood for various reasons. Ethel Waters plays Berenice Sadie Brown, the family housekeeper and sister of Honey Brown. Once known as the singer, dancer, and performer "Sweet Mama Stringbean," Waters had, by now, metamorphosed into a large, asexual Mammy type. The motion picture cast also includes young Brandon DeWilde playing John Henry, who began his acting career as a child. DeWilde was also a member of the stage version of the play.

The tribulations of Honey Brown serve as a secondary theme to Frankie's story. Set in the postwar Deep South, Honey's travails provide a gloomy portrayal of racism, dejection, disappointment, and, as noted by Nolleti in his discussion of Zinnemann's work, "the imprisonment of the Black characters within a white society." Another Black character, Berenice's friend Harry, deals with the rigors of racism and bigotry by becoming a bit of a Tom. But Honey will assume no such role.[7]

Honey is a trumpet player who drinks too much, smokes reefer, and can't hold his temper. Like the character Moss in *Home of the Brave*, he is overly sensitized and reacts angrily to every real or perceived racist slight; he is ready to assail any White man who looks at him the wrong way. The playscript describes Honey as "high strung and volatile"; he is "brusque and there is about him an odd mixture of hostility and playfulness." It is interesting to note that this character description in some ways mirrors Edwards himself, that is, as described by his contemporaries (a fiery but charming, talented but tormented soul with a penchant for alcoholic beverages). Though the playscript describes Honey as a young man of twenty, Edwards was thirty-two years old at the time of the picture's release. But his boyish good looks, slender build, and high energy made for a perfect screen interpretation of Honey Camden Brown.[8]

In one scene, Honey lets loose his pent-up frustrations. In the playscript, the dialogue reads:

I'm so tensed up. My nerves been scraped with a razor.... I'm so tensed up and miserable. The nigger hole. I'm sick of smothering in the nigger hole. I can't stand it no more.

In the film version, the lines are altered:

Times like this I feel like I got to bust loose or die!⁹

Later in the story, the world crashes in on Honey. He has been involved in a hit-and-run accident and has possibly killed a White man. (In the play he pulled a razor on a White man who wouldn't serve him.) In both cases, Honey doesn't stick around long enough to see if the man has died. He is now a fugitive on the run. His sister rebukes him: "You fool, Honey Brown, you fool."

The rather melancholy story ends with a shot of Berenice, who mourns the death of John Henry (DeWilde), the loss of her job as family housekeeper, and the loss of her brother to a ten-year prison sentence. Frankie has gotten over her disappointments and has discovered boys. As the story closes, Berenice hums the song "His Eye Is on the Sparrow," which became Waters' own theme song.

Zinnemann considered *The Member of the Wedding* among his best work. Unfortunately, the film was probably a bit too talky and introspective for the average movie fan who ignored it in droves. To some it was an art house film and at the time there were very few art houses. As one critic noted, such an analytical play makes for "difficult screen material." Bosley Crowther (*The New York Times*) wrote that *Member of the Wedding* was "considerably less arresting or persuasive in the picture medium." Other reviews, when one can find them, are often unkind. "Poor Frankie!" chided Hartung of *The Commonweal*. Today, many consider the film to be a significant film work.¹⁰

Even after his triumph in Hollywood, Edwards never abandoned his stage roots but maintained strong ties to the theatre, appearing in shows coast to coast, including his former adopted hometown of Chicago and his new hometown of Los Angeles. Further, he explored his options as a writer, director, and producer.

After moving to Los Angeles in the late 1940s, Edwards began his long association with Nick Stewart, a talented actor and performer of vaudeville, radio, motion pictures, and television; Stewart would appear with Edwards in films and on the television show *Ramar of the Jungle*. Stewart made his film debut in the early 1930s and appeared in the cast of two World War II-era Black-cast musicals, *Cabin in the Sky* and *Stormy Weather*.

With his wife Edna, Stewart financed and founded the Ebony Showcase Theatre in 1950.

The Ebony Showcase was a place where Black performers could write, produce, act, and appear in the kinds of productions that they would most likely never be cast in mainstream theatre. Edwards once called it "tops and a proving ground for new talent." The season bill and the casting were configured without regard to race, actor Juanita Moore said in a recent interview. "Stewart would do what he thought would be entertaining."[11]

For many years Edwards would maintain a presence at the Showcase, where he acted, directed, and built sets. "He realized the importance of legitimate Black Theatre in his art," Stewart said. "He was the only one who was big enough and great enough to come back to the black community and work in black theatre."[12]

For the Ebony Showcase in 1953, Edwards appeared in a mounting of French writer Jean Paul Sartre's one-act play *Huis Clos* (*No Exit*). The production consisted of one setting and four characters (the others were played by Maidie Norman, Juanita Moore, and Charles Crawford). He later directed the same play. In 1955 Edwards played the lead with Camille Cannady in a production of the Sidney Kingsley play *Detective Story*.[13]

It was at the Showcase that Edwards earned the distinction of appearing in one of the earliest, if not the first, Black-cast production of Tennessee Williams' *A Streetcar Named Desire*. "This is a vital, realistic interpretation," wrote the *Hollywood Reporter*. "Nick and Edna Stewart have gathered a fine all-Negro cast[.]" Directed by John Blankenship, it starred Edwards as the uncouth, ill-mannered, and violent-tempered Stanley Kowalski, made famous by Marlon Brando. The *Reporter* noted that Edwards lacked the roughness required for the part, but made up for it in "acting prowess."[14]

But Edwards did not limit himself to the confines of the Showcase nor did he limit himself to acting: "The first big time stage production ever done entirely by Negroes in California is scheduled to open soon at the Lincoln Theatre in Hollywood," reported the *New York Amsterdam News* in 1952. The play was *The Voice of the Turtle*. Written by John Van Druten, this romantic comedy ran on Broadway for more than 1500 performances between 1943 and 1948. *Voice of the Turtle*, the paper noted, was Edwards' first attempt at producing and directing.[15]

Three years later in August 1955, Edwards directed *Detective Story* at the Geller Theatre Workshop in Los Angeles. Leon Lord, president of the theatre, told the *Los Angeles Sentinel*:

It is with extreme pleasure that I have James Edwards associated with me as director of *Detective Story*. I have never met a man more devoted to the theatre, nor one more capable than he of infusing his actors with that same inspired devotion.[16]

"Edwards has been the guiding hand in half a dozen playhouse productions ... all big hits," declared *Hue* magazine in 1955. The magazine made a point of emphasizing that the casts of his productions were "all White," but offered no commentary about whether this was a good thing or a bad thing. In addition, *Hue* quoted Edwards as having announced his wish to be the first of his race to direct a feature film for a major studio. Acting no longer held a challenge for him, he declared; "I only act now because I have to eat."[17]

Even with his ever-increasing stature, Edwards did not earn a part in one of the more celebrated Black-cast films of the period, the 1955 20th Century–Fox production of the musical, *Carmen Jones*. Still, he managed a good deal of press by appearing in a five-page, 21-photograph feature article highlighting Dorothy Dandridge's screen test for director Otto Preminger. Preminger chose some of the more sexy sequences to test actresses for the part of the tramp, Carmen. Sitting in for Harry Belafonte, who was already cast in the part of Joe, Edwards kisses the ankles, caresses the toes and helps undress Carmen, all scenes that would eventually appear in the film.[18]

Why didn't Edwards the play of Joe, instead of Belafonte? In his memoir, Preminger seems to have decided all along to go with Belafonte, who had just won a Tony Award for his appearance in the 1953 J. M. Anderson musical *John Murray Anderson's Almanac*. Belafonte had recently done a picture with Dandridge, the 1953 production *Bright Road*; though that movie was unremarkable, the two actors were both singers, were fashionable and "easy on the eyes," and made for an appealing movie couple. Moreover, who but Belafonte could have played, convincingly, the role of the good colored boy, the naïve Army private who ignores Carmen's sultry sexiness and her alluring charms for those of his plain-looking and child-like sweetheart Cindy Lou, and who reluctantly and after much cajoling gives in to the charms of the bad girl, Carmen? Edwards, worldly, dark-skinned, older, and sexual, would have made for a much different kind of Joe.

Particularly intriguing is the lack of chemistry that seemed to exist between Edwards and Dandridge, as least as communicated through the non-verbal clues in the *Ebony* photographs. They were professional actors doing a job, the shoot was reportedly quite grueling, and earning the role of Carmen was important to Dandridge, who was told by Preminger that she didn't look the part. Still, the shots reveal little merriment. In one, the two stand facing each other: Edwards stares one way and Dandridge the other and both have dour looks pasted onto their faces.

Edwards coached newcomer Diahann Carroll, who also appeared before the intimidating Preminger to audition for the part of Carmen. Carroll said, "[Edwards] was very helpful, urging me to go over my lines with him." Edwards reportedly told Carroll that he was offered an unknown part in the picture but turned it down for "something better."[19]

Seven Angry Men

In 1955 Edwards appeared as Ned Green, a former slave who joins John Brown in his effort to force the end of slavery, in the Allied Artists production *Seven Angry Men,* an interesting adaptation of the life of 19th century abolitionist John Brown. Charles Marquis Warren, a writer-director-producer of low-budget B-pictures and later television, took on the tricky job of depicting the life of this much-debated historical figure. Sam Peckinpah, who would go on to direct such memorable offerings as *The Wild Bunch* (1969) and the ultra-violent *Straw Dogs* (1971), is credited as a dialogue coach. The script was written by Daniel B. Ullman, who was careful not to portray Brown as either villain or hero, but perhaps misguided, idealistic, uninformed—or mentally ill. The cast featured veteran actor Raymond Massey as Brown. Massey, still remembered for his portrayal of Abraham Lincoln in the 1940 RKO production *Abe Lincoln in Illinois,* had earlier played John Brown in Warner Brothers' *Santa Fe Trail* (1940). Cast as Brown's sons are: Jeffrey Hunter, James Best, Tom Irish, Larry Pennell, John Smith, Dennis Weaver, and Guy Williams.

Who was John Brown? Brown was born in Connecticut in 1800 to a deeply religious family vehemently opposed to slavery. To support his family of twenty children, he took on, mostly unsuccessfully, the life of a merchant, land speculator, tanner, and farmer. He met Frederick Douglass in 1847 and over the ensuing years, with the help of his sons, he waged an all-out anti-slavery guerilla war, before being wounded, captured, and hanged in 1859. He remains a topical figure in history with his motives, methods, and degree of sanity still debated by scholars.

One of the sequences in *Seven Angry Men* depicts Brown's standoff at Harper's Ferry, Virginia, where Brown and most of his band met their end. In one scene, we see Edwards, driving a horse-drawn cart full of guns and ammunition. With a son named Owen, they set up in a schoolhouse near the arsenal that Brown eventually takes over. Brown believes that once news of the stakeout and hostage-taking gets out, the Black population will rally to the cause. They do not. After a shootout with local lawmakers, Brown has lost two sons and is now surrounded by Union troops.

"The Lord has forsaken me," he cries aloud.

Back in the schoolhouse, it is clear that all is lost, that Brown's crusade has failed. In a poignant moment, Green convinces Owen that that he should save himself: "You can't help him now, nobody can. Right now it's finished ... your father's finished, and so's his dream of freedom."

Gently, he touches the shoulder of Owen, reassuring him that he is doing the right thing by not being a martyr. Together, they leave the schoolhouse and slowly take the road to return home. Edwards' part is meaningful in this film and he delivered a thoughtful interpretation *sans* obvious typing.

The cast of *Seven Angry Men* also includes other Black actors in bit parts, such as Jordan "Smoki" Whitfield, who, like Edwards, were not compelled to play types or speak in so-called Negro dialect. *Seven Angry Men* premiered on March 30, 1955, in Osawatomie, Kansas. Reviews were kind, with the *New York Times* noting, "The misguided, bloody saga of John Brown unfolded yesterday ... in a competent if inspired Allied Artists presentation[.]"[20]

The Killing

With its dark lighting, rapid-fire dialogue, *Dragnet*-style voiceover narration, and cast of shady characters, *The Killing* resembles more of a film noir classic than an offering from Stanley Kubrick, the director who would produce such cinema landmarks as *2001: A Space Odyssey* (1968) and *Full Metal Jacket* (1990). A Casper Milquetoast of a husband, a philanderer, a scheming wife, ex-cons, and bad cops: All have one thing in common in this taut story-greed. They conspire to hold up a racetrack and make *a killing* that will render all of them rich. Edwards' part in this 83-minute tale is so small it is surprising that he received an "also starring" credit. In retrospect, however, the scene in which he appears is noteworthy as it is but one of the many essential turns in this riveting tale.

One of the pieces of the complicated scheme involves a hood named Nikki (Tim Carey), who is hired to cause a ruckus by shooting one of the racehorses. His plan is to position himself at a nearby parking lot and kill the horse from long distance using a high-powered rifle. Upon his arrival, the unnamed Edwards character, the lot attendant, brusquely informs him that the lot is full and therefore closed. After a bit of cajoling, a lie about being a wounded war veteran, and a bribe, the Edwards character allows him into the lot to watch the race from his car.

Edwards appears again to give Nikki a program. He is dressed in an immaculate service uniform, his tie tucked into his shirt, and his belt adorned with a change counter. He engages Nikki in conversation before returning to his post. Just as Nikki settles in and reaches for his weapon, Edwards returns, again, this time holding a horseshoe.

> ATTENDANT: I brought you this, mister. I figured you might need it. [For Nikki, timing is all-important, and he puts off the attendant as rudely as possible.] Is there anything wrong?
> NIKKI: Yeah. You're wrong, nigger. Now be a nice guy and go on about your business.

Dejected, the attendant throws the horseshoe to the ground and takes off. Ironically, the horseshoe is the cause of Nikki's blown tire, which allows him to be captured by police.

Kubrick's budget for the film was a measly $320,000; he wrote the screenplay himself, based on the Lionel White novel *Clean Break* (1955). The shooting took place on studios sets and Kubrick sought out lesser-known actors he could hire on the cheap. Edwards' co-stars include Sterling Hayden, remembered for his role as Johnny Guitar in the 1954 Republic film which starred Joan Crawford.* Other cast members include Jay C. Flippen, Marie Windsor, Vince Edwards, Ted de Corsia, and Tim Carey.

United Artists allotted only a tiny budget for the promotion of *The Killing* and the film was not widely reviewed. However, when it premiered in New York in May 1956, the *New York Times* described it as "an engrossing little adventure."[21]

As the decade hit its midpoint, the fortunes of James Edwards seemed to be have righted. As an actor, he had not again found another role like that of Moss in *Home of the* Brave. Whether this achievement was important to him is unknown. What were his priorities? Screenwriting? Direct-

---

Hayden also had a role in John Huston's The Asphalt Jungle *(1950), another story about a gang of crooks who plan a sophisticated theft.*

ing a motion picture? Producing plays? Perhaps all of the above. Still, he had called himself lucky and appeared content. In July 1956, he was featured in a photograph in *Ebony* magazine smiling broadly and holding a skewer of shish-kebob in each hand. The article notes that Edwards loved to prepare beef dishes, and that "next to just plain stew," shish-kebob was his "command performance."[22]

17. A Khaki-Clad Stereotype?

James Edwards became such a veteran of the war and combat film that one publication dubbed him "a khaki-clad stereotype." In *Home of the Brave* he portrayed an Army private; he was later cast in films as a Navy mess man, Seabee, Army lieutenant, Air Force pilot, Army engineer, Army sergeant, medic, and combat trooper. He may have played a soldier numerous times, but a glance at the film credits of his contemporaries proves that he was no more typecast than any other actor during a period when feature films about war and combat were a popular genre. Still, Edwards offered fans his assurances, saying, "Playing a GI is all right so long as the part is realistic and has a purpose."[1]

Like many Black performers of the period, Edwards knew well that as a Hollywood actor, he served as a symbol of his race. He was also aware that his appearance as a soldier in a combat film served as more than entertainment, but signified for Negro citizens the death of the Jim Crow Army.

The exigencies of the Cold War helped to bring to the forefront the debate about race and the United States military. By 1947, the United States Air Force would establish itself based on a policy of nondiscrimination; African Americans could now enlist in the Marine Corps and be promoted to higher rank, and the hierarchy of the U.S. Army finally agreed that racial segregation was contrary to combat effectiveness. By 1950, the USO would employ integrated entertainment units. On July 26, 1948, President Harry Truman created a fair employment system for Federal employment and established a committee to end race bias in the military. He also issued Executive Order 9981, a directive requiring "equality of treatment and opportunity for all persons in the Armed Forces without regard to race, color, religion, or national origin." Truman wrote: "Integration is the best way to create an effective combat organization in which men will stand together and fight."[2]

While Truman's directive would be the catalyst for change, it did not mandate an end to racial segregation in the military. It did not affirm when the equal treatment or equality would begin, or how it would be enforced by the advising committee that would make recommendations to the president and military hierarchy. For some time to come, the features of a racially biased American military force would remain a grim and often confusing symbol of American life.

"Ambivalence" best describes the attitude toward Blacks by the military hierarchy during the immediate postwar period, wrote one author. In addition, the perception of Blacks as cowardly, ignorant, and lacking the mental capacity for combat-based largely on the mythologies about the Black race in general can be found in the writings and policies of the Army and other military organizations years after Truman's order. Of particular concern was the suitability of Black men as combat soldiers.[3]

Popular magazines such as *Saturday Review* and *Life* featured full-length investigative articles detailing the progress and pitfalls of recently integrated units, and behaviorists compiled data, statistics, and theories regarding the Black man's ability to perform in combat. The African American press, most notably the *Pittsburgh Courier* and *Afro-American*, offered a decidedly different look, with emphasis on the hardships of tan Yanks, many of whom were stationed in unfriendly Jim Crow communities in the Deep South.

As African American citizens slowly and painfully negotiated the military color line, the postwar Hollywood war film came to include the Negro soldier. Filmmakers integrated glimpses of Black soldiers in crowd scenes as a part of the normal scheme of things while some films such *Red Ball Express* (Universal, 1952) and *All the Young Men* (Columbia, 1960), both starring Sidney Poitier, include racial issues as part of the story.

The Caine Mutiny

The appearance of Humphrey Bogart, the inclusion of actual combat footage, and Technicolor did little to help this adaptation of the best-selling Herman Wouk novel *The Caine Mutiny*. Edwards, in his first color picture, worked once again with producer Stanley Kramer in this 1954 Columbia feature. Steve Brodie, who appeared as T.J. in *Home of the Brave*, earned a small role as an officer, representing the third time the two actors appeared together on screen. The picture also starred Fred MacMurray, who long before he became the TV father of *My Three Sons* signed with Paramount in the early 1930s. He is well-remembered for his portrayal of a murderous insurance salesman in the 1944 noir classic, *Double Indemnity*. Puerto Rico native Jose Ferrer plays the role of the officer assigned to defend the men accused of treason on the high seas. Most notably a stage actor, Ferrer earned an Academy Award nomination for his film debut in Victor Fleming's 1948 production of *Joan of Arc*, but is perhaps better remembered for his Academy Award–winning portrayal of Cyrano de Bergerac in the 1950 Stanley Kramer–produced film. Van Johnson plays Maryk, one of the officers. The object of desire of 1940s-era bobby-soxers, Johnson earned a respectable living at MGM where he was often cast in combat and wartime pictures such as *Thirty Seconds Over Tokyo* (1945) and *No Leave, No Love* (1946). For Robert Francis, who plays the role of a young ensign, *Caine Mutiny* was his fourth picture. He died a year later in an accident. May Wynn, who serves as Francis' love interest, adapted her stage name from her *Caine Mutiny* character. Her real name was Donna Lee Hickey. The cast of *Caine Mutiny* also includes a young newcomer named Lee Marvin, who plays the part of Meatball.

Kramer had to negotiate many hurdles to get his film done. First, under contract to Columbia, he had to contend with the notoriously cantankerous studio boss Harry Cohn. Cohn's budget for *Caine Mutiny* was about half of what Kramer believed he needed to attract a starring cast. Further, Cohn imposed a tight 54-day shooting schedule and mandated that the film could not be more than two hours long. Then, Kramer had to alleviate the anxieties of the Navy hierarchy who were fearful that the film would put the organization in a poor light. After a contentious round of negotiations, the U.S. Navy gave Kramer the use of its facilities in Pearl Harbor, Hawaii, along with a destroyer, aircraft carrier, landing crafts, and 2,000 Marines. Interior scenes were shot in Los Angeles on the Columbia lot.[4]

According to the Sperber-Lax bio of Humphrey Bogart, the cast of *Caine* was far from chummy. MacMurray's wife had died recently and he was depressed and withdrawn; when not shooting, Bogart apparently preferred the company of his family to that of his fellow actors and made himself scarce. And then there was the director, Edward Dmytryk, a refugee of the infamous Hollywood Ten, who had given in to the pressure and prison sentence imposed upon him by the House Un-American Activities Committee and had named names. Still, "[W]hen the cameras rolled, it was a textbook operation by an ensemble of thorough professionals," noted

17. A Khaki-Clad Stereotype   115

Edwards as Whittaker, a Navy mess man (standing, second from right), joins (clockwise from lower left) James Best, Herbert Anderson, Jerry Paris, Arthur Franze, Joe Haworth, Fred MacMurray, Robert Francis, Van Johnson and Humphrey Bogart in the famous "strawberries scene" from *The Caine Mutiny,* (1954), Edward's third Stanley Kramer film.

Bogart's biographers. A photograph that appeared in *Our World* magazine featured Edwards, Dmytryk, MacMurray, and producer Kramer, all in smiles as they relax between scene changes. In one shot, Johnson shares the contents of his thermos with Edwards.[5]

The fictional story of the *Caine* takes place on a Navy minesweeper on duty in the Pacific. The vessel is commanded by Captain Queeg, played by Bogart, whose neurotic behavior threatens the morale of the entire crew. Queeg's quirks, lies, cowardice, and incompetence eventually become too much for the ship's officers to bear. At a pivotal moment, when the survival of the men and the vessel are at stake, the senior officer, Lt. Maryk, with the support of the other officers, decides to take over the ship. The result: The officers are deemed mutineers and must appear before a court martial board to explain their actions.

Edwards plays the part of Whittaker, a mess man who gets caught up in the controversy. We first glimpse him in a scene with the other men who are enjoying a Western film, only to have their fun, and the movie, curtailed by an irate Capt. Queeg, who is angry that he wasn't informed. Later, Whittaker is a featured player in the famous strawberries scene, one of the most darkly humorous and telling sequences in the story.

At one o'clock in the morning, Whittaker arrives on deck to summon the two officers on watch. He alerts Maryk:

> WHITTAKER: The captain wants a meeting of all officers, immediately.
> MARYK: Do you know what it's about?
> WHITTAKER: Yes, sir ... strawberries.[6]

Queeg's wish is to determine what has happened to the remainder of a quart of strawberries that, according to his calculations, should have been left over from the night's dinner. Dressed in his mess man's uniform of white undershirt, white trousers and white web belt, Whittaker is ordered to dole out portions of sand (used in lieu of the missing canned strawberries) in an attempt to determine how much should have been left over after everyone had been served.

"*The Caine Mutiny* ... won't be released until August," wrote Richard Coe, critic for the *Washington Post*, "but all year everyone will say it's 'the picture of the year.'" Coe's prophecy proved wrong. *The Caine Mutiny* suffered cinematically from a host of reasons including a tight budget, the equally tight shooting schedule, and screenwriter Stanley Roberts' need to condense a dense 800-page novel into a two-hour presentation. Many pages were stricken from the script at the last minute to make Cohn's limit. Moreover, Kramer was obliged to make more than a few concessions to the Navy who wished to ensure the institution's good face. "[T]he structure of the story presented in Mr. Wouk's book," wrote Bosley Crowther in a tepid review for the *New York Times*, "was not entirely felicitous for the playing of a drama on the screen."[7]

Still, *The Caine Mutiny* would do reasonably well at the box office and garnered eleven Academy Award nominations, including one, ironically, for Best Screenplay. Bogart, whose face graced the cover of *Time* magazine in June 1954, was widely praised for his performance. He died three years later of cancer.

Battle Hymn

Directed by Douglas Sirk (*Magnificent Obsession*, 1954; *Imitation of Life*, 1959), the Universal film *Battle Hymn* was based largely on the true story of a fighter pilot and minister, Colonel Dean Hess of the U.S. Air Force, who dedicated himself to saving hundreds of children during and after the Korean conflict. Under an initiative that came to be called "Operation Kiddy Car," abandoned and starving South Korean children were shuttled to Cheju Island off the southern coast of Korea where an orphanage was established. By the time Hess was transferred, notes an essay on the Air Force Museum website, "his orphanage had taken in more than 1,054 Korean children who most likely would otherwise have died."[8]

Hess' autobiography *Battle Hymn*, published in 1956, was made into a feature film in 1957, produced by Ross Hunter with a screenplay written by Vincent B. Evans and Charles Grayson. The Technicolor film features Rock Hudson in the top role, along with Dan Duryea, Jock Mahoney, Richard Loo, Alan Hale, Philip Ahn (Edwards' co-star from "Mr. Pak") and Anna Kashfi. Edwards appears as Lt. Maples. *Battle Hymn* is a film that Edwards fans should see if for no reason other than the fact that his character appears liberally throughout and in one scene, Edwards provides a brief but tantalizing soundbite of his singing ability.

Even though the screenwriting credit for *Battle Hymn* indicate Grayson and Evans, Edwards, who had in April 1956 signed a contract as a screenwriter for Universal-International, seems to have made some contribution, at least in the development of the character he portrayed. His character is fully fleshed out, integral to the story, and appears as one of the heroes throughout the entire film.

The story begins in 1950, about a month after the invasion of South Korea by the Communist North. Col. Hess, a veteran of the Second World War and now a civilian and minister, suffers from the lingering depression brought on from an experience he suffered in Germany, when he accidentally bombed an orphanage, killing 39 children. With the outbreak of war in Korea, he decides to leave behind his wife, give up his ministry, and return to active duty. He is stationed with an air group whose mission is to train South Korean pilots in tactics and flying. He is warned by his commander not to lose any precious planes to "needless heroics."

We first see Edwards when Hess arrives at the base and addresses his troops. Maples is one of perhaps twelve Air Force flight instructors. Hess scolds them for the poor condition of the runways, airfield, and buildings and warns them to get the base, and themselves, in shape.

On Thanksgiving, the men are overjoyed to have a change from their usual rations. In their mess hut they are served Thanksgiving dinner. Maples, cigarette in hand, mills among the men, who are singing songs

Col. Dean Hess (Rock Hudson) consoles a saddened Lt. Maples (Edwards) in *Battle Hymn* (1957).

and celebrating the holiday with tin cups of beverage. Col. Hess leaves the tent only to discover a dozen Korean children in search of scraps to eat. Hess orders they be fed, and over the next few weeks the group grows substantially to the point that the pilots complain about base security.

In a later scene, when a training mission attracts enemy fighters, Maples reveals his concerns to Col. Hess about being unable to defend themselves.

> HESS: You made contact with enemy aircraft?
> MAPLES: We had to tuck our tails and run. You know, colonel, it feels kinda naked up there with no experienced wing men.
> HESS: From now on, you'll have hot guns ... only for protection.

In one harrowing scene, another training mission turns into battle and Maples is ordered by flight commander Skidmore to take out a column of enemy who line a road. Maples reminds him that they are not supposed to engage the enemy but he relents, and follows the order to take

17. A Khaki-Clad Stereotype

out an escaping truck. We see a helmeted Maples in the cockpit of his P51 fighter which soars through a clear blue sky. He chases after the escaping vehicle and lets fly a barrage of bullets. He circles his prey only to find the vehicle did not contain North Korean soldiers but civilian refuges, mostly children.

Back on the ground, Maples is shattered. He pounds the side of his aircraft in heartfelt anguish: "Those kids. Those poor little kids!" Later, Hess visits Maples in his quarters to find him reading a Bible. Maples apologizes, "I'm sorry I lost control out there. I'm better now."

Hess reveals to Maples his similar experience in Germany. Maples, who has turned to his faith for solace, offers his commander his take:

> Sir, it's the way of things, I guess ... God's will.... No sparrow shall fall to the earth unless He first gives His nod.... It's all we have to trust in, sir.... You see, colonel, God and all His reasons are invisible to the eyes of man....

Maples' words seem to invigorate Hess; he knows what he has to do.

The film is rife with religious references: The men pray before Thanksgiving dinner, and the song "Glory, Glory Halleluiah" is an integral part of the musical score.

The remainder of the film is devoted to Hess' efforts to rescue the children. Maples generously offers his free time to assist with the project. In a Buddhist temple, a woman, (Anna Kashfi) has taken a number of orphans into her care. Hess cajoles her into taking on more. His men, including Maples, bring in supplies, and Maples repairs the bombed-out roof with some tarpaulin that a sergeant has "borrowed" from the Navy.

But the enemy is on the offensive and the children must be evacuated. Maples joins the others, who move the children and supplies to a makeshift camp while Hess begs higher-ups for an airlift. The children are tired and frightened and Maples, with a child asleep in his lap, softly croons "Sweet Low, Sweet Chariot" in a melodious baritone.

The next day, enemy fighters strafe the base. Some of the men manage to get their aircraft off the ground and into the sky where they may defend themselves. At one point, Maples finds an enemy fighter on his tail. He radios Hess for assistance. Hess seems hesitant; the old "Killer Hess" died long ago, replaced by the Reverend Hess. Maples is desperate: "Cut him off, colonel.... Help me!" Hess makes short work of the enemy fighter.

Battle Hymn is replete with postwar proselytizing, war movie character types, corny coincidences, and too-cute Korean children who sing "America the Beautiful" in perfect English. Bosley Crowther of the *New*

York Times wrote, "[T]his picture ... doesn't miss a single cliché as it makes a calculated circuit of the old militant sky pilot."[9] Still, some reviews were wholly positive. The *Fitchburg (MA) Sentinel* said, "The authenticity of this picture rings like a huge clear bell."

As for Edwards, in depth and scope, the part of Maples should be counted as Edwards' best film performance since *Home of the Brave*. He is positioned as an everyday human being, not a racial issue; he is a savvy fighter pilot and a humanitarian united with his comrades in a single, important cause.

Sirk revealed that he wanted a Black pilot included in the cast. His experiences in Nazi Germany had made him very interested in "race issues." Hess himself wrote about his disgust at the segregation he encountered while stationed at Napier Field, Alabama, where church services were conducted in the chapel for Whites and in the gym for Blacks. He writes about a Black colleague, Lt. Ernest Craigwell, whom he "came to love like a brother."[10]

Regardless of the character's origin, Maples comes across as authentic and is a valuable element of the film. Edwards provided a strong and admirable positive filmic image of an African American officer, gentleman, and hero.

Director Sirk reflected upon interference from the real Col. Hess, who demanded that he always "stick to the truth" and eschew any filmic embellishments that might have strengthened the Hess character and bettered the film. "[H]e was always on set, hanging around, supervising every scene.... I even suggested [the character] take a drink, but he kept saying 'I never drink.' He was definitely a split character." In addition, Sirk broke his leg and was forced to finish the picture from a wheelchair. "It removed me from my actors and camera.... I couldn't demonstrate a scene. I guess I let things go that I ordinarily wouldn't."[11]

Battle Hymn, shot in Arizona and on movie sets, premiered on February 20, 1957, in Los Angeles. Because of the presence of Korean actor Philip Ahn, the film enjoyed great popularity in South Korea, where for many years it was screened on television in commemoration of the Korean Conflict.

Men in War

After the shooting for *Battle Hymn* was finished, Edwards immediately began work on *Men in War* (1957), a story based on the novel *Com-

bat! by Van Van Praag. The screenplay was penned by HUAC casualty Philip Yordan, who worked under an assumed name at the time, and was directed by Anthony Mann. Robert Ryan, Edwards' co-star from *The Set-Up*, portrays the gruff, exhausted, but decent Lt. Benson. The cast also includes Aldo Ray, Robert Keith, Nehemiah Persoff, and a young Vic Morrow. Edwards plays the role of Killian, a sergeant described in an early scene as "the best mechanic this side of the Hudson."

The film is a compilation of long and bloody battle sequences that only incidentally lead in the end to an American victory, one that costs far too many lives. The men of 2nd Platoon, Dog Company, are nearly surrounded by enemy; they suffer from sleep deprivation and jagged nerves. Breakfast for some consists of a cigarette and a swig of lukewarm water from a canteen. They are dirty, bearded and perspiration-soaked.

Edwards receives mention in reviews for his contribution. However, Killian is killed in the first half-hour of the film. He is an intelligent, likable fellow. In one scene, he tenderly replaces the helmet on the head of an obviously scared and shivering young soldier. In a very tense moment, when the same soldier is obviously sick and having trouble keeping up with the group, Killian gets him permission to sit in the only available seat in a Jeep intended only for the hauling of supplies. Eventually, Killian meets his death, not from an enemy bullet but because of his own recklessness. He is assigned to patrol a road, to protect his company from being picked off by snipers. He stops to admire some wildflowers. He picks one, then two, then removes his helmet to insert his small floral arrangement. He sits down and puts down his gun. He unlaces, then removes a boot and rubs his tired foot. The silent enemy, recognizable through nearby bushes, comes upon him and he is stabbed to death. He is never even able to cry out.

In his review of the film, Bosley Crowther of the *New York Times* describes the Killian character as a "careless Negro." Though the American military had been working towards integration for nearly a decade by the time of the film's release, Crowther's words reflect the still persistent general feeling amongst many associated with the military that African Americans were not only undependable under fire, but lacked courage, mechanical aptitude, and the capacity for leadership. In this case Killian not only endangered himself, but his entire company as well.[12]

Moreover, Killian is the only discernable Black soldier in *Men in War*. Tokenism, the inclusion of a lone Black face, was another element all too typical in postwar-produced combat motion pictures. In *Men in War*,

Black faces are all but absent from the gruesome scenes of fighting and dying. Except for Edwards' brief appearance behind the trigger, Black soldiers are not shown contributing to the effort in a significant way, presenting a decidedly false picture of the Korean Conflict.

Fraulein

In 1958, Edwards was cast once again as a soldier in this intriguing depiction of postwar West Germany. The screenplay, written by Leo Townsend, was based on the 1956 novel *Fräulein* written by James McGovern. *Fraulein*, produced by 20th Century–Fox, was shot in DeLuxe Color on location in the cities of Cologne and Berlin, Germany and at film studios in Los Angeles. The 90-minute film was directed by Henry Koster, later famous for his 1966 production *The Singing Nun*.

The story follows a young woman named Erika, played by Dana Wynter. Wynter, born in Germany but raised in England, left her medical studies to pursue an acting career and appeared, mostly uncredited, in British-produced pictures. Before her appearance in *Fraulein,* Wynter was cast opposite Rock Hudson in the 1957 MGM production *Something of Value.*

In the story, Erika struggles to survive after her father loses his life to Nazi brutality. She falls into the clutches of her father's former tenants, a man and his wife who, unbeknownst to her, now make their living operating a bawdy house. They offer her a place to stay. She signs a form, not realizing that she has just registered herself as a prostitute. When she realizes her predicament, she flees, with her handler close at heels. Edwards, as the character Cpl. Hanks, appears in a Jeep, attired in a smartly pressed Army uniform, his trousers bloused and his feet adorned with gleaming black jump boots. Upon his head a helmet is emblazoned with the letters "MP." Hanks rescues Erika from the man, who returns the favor by insulting him with a veiled racial epithet. Erika apologizes for him. He asks her, "Have you any place to go?" She thanks him but refuses further assistance. He smiles at her. "Good night, Fräulein. Fräulein, that's a nice word."

Erika goes on her way. Grateful for her kind words, Hanks gazes upon her until she disappears from sight. It is impossible to tell whether he is simply concerned for her safety or is perhaps smitten.

By the end of the film, Erika has fallen in love with an American officer played by Mel Ferrer. He wants to marry her and take her to live

17. A Khaki-Clad Stereotype

Edwards as the gallant Cpl. Hanks who comes to the aid of war refugee Erika (Dana Wynter) in *Fraulein* (1958).

in America. But first, she must pass muster. By now, she realizes that she is registered as a prostitute but is afraid to tell her fiancé. She finds her way to the American security administration office, hoping to convince someone of the truth. Fortunately for her, Cpl. Hanks is on duty. He remembers her and volunteers to take care of her request. He pulls her records, but warns: "I'll make copies ... it'll take a little time."

Hanks types up the paperwork that will allow her to marry an American. By the time he is finished, they are the only two people in the office. He hands her the papers, she reads them and is startled. She and thanks him, and he replies, "No trouble at all. That's what we're here for. Something wrong? I told you I was a lousy typist."

The papers make no mention of her registration as a prostitute. She is now clear to marry her American and leave Germany for a life in the United States. Once again, Hanks has come to her rescue. In a bittersweet moment, he gazes upon her from a window as she runs out to meet her husband-to-be. Clearly, his interest in her went beyond his duties as a soldier. She was young and pretty and many Black GIs stationed overseas formed alliances with German women in the aftermath of the war.

The *Syracuse (NY) Post-Standard* described the picture as a "sentimental yarn ... about a pretty Fraulein," but noted that the script "suffers from too many neatly contrived situations." In *Variety*, Edwards is mentioned as being part of the strong support, but the *New York Times* review of the picture chides: "[S]hots of bomb-torn Berlin and Cologne and the picturesque Rhine wine country contribute more color to *Fraulein* than its plot."[13]

Critics apparently did not care to comment on the implications of Hanks' romantic interest in Erika. The film features a number of good performances and some intriguing characterizations. Edwards' part, though small, is charming as he manages to make substantive use of his relatively brief time on screen.

Pork Chop Hill

In 1959, Edwards landed a respectable part in the United Artists production *Pork Chop Hill*. The film was directed by Lewis Milestone, whose deft hand can be appreciated in such film mainstays as *Rain* (1932), *A Walk in the Sun* (1945), *The Strange Love of Martha Ivers* (1946), and the Academy Award–winning World War I epic *All Quiet on the Western Front* (1930). The screenplay was written by James Webb.

The story is based on a true and tragic saga compiled by Brig. Gen. S. L. A. Marshall, USAR, retired. In 1953, a brave but beleaguered company of soldiers attempts to hold onto a piece of real estate that for all practical purposes holds little in the way of a gained advantage for either side. There are no intriguing parallel stories, no clever plot devices. There is little time in this fast-moving story to identify with any particular character; men who spoke a few lines in one scene are casualties in the next as American soldiers fight and die trying to fend off swarms of well-armored Chinese troops. The men are tired and dirty. Most are bearded. Dozens of grenades are detonated from both sides. There is much gunfire and death. Helmets and personal effects fly high into the air with every earth-shattering explosion. One sequence features an instance of the classic Milestone touch: In documentary-like fashion, a row of young men is gunned down in a long panoramic shot that makes clear the horror and waste of war. As white-haired generals continue talks in a Quonset hut in Panmunjom, Korea, some seventy miles away, this nearly stranded and seemingly forgotten company of men continues their relentless barrage up the hill to the sound of enemy propaganda spewing from a loudspeaker. Pork Chop Hill is dusty and rock strewn; it is a place of violence.

Gregory Peck portrays Lt. Clemons, the troop commander. Peck, born in California in 1916, reportedly left a career in medicine after being bitten by the acting bug. He was a good actor and during the war, with the scarcity of men, he found plenty of work. He made his film debut in the 1944 RKO production *Days of Glory*, a war film. Of course, he will always be remembered for his performance as Captain Ahab in John Huston's 1956 production of the classic *Moby Dick*. With *Pork Chop Hill*, Peck took on another role, that of a film producer.

George Shibata, acting in his first feature film, plays Clemons' executive officer Lt. Ohashi, a Japanese-American. Edwards portrays Cpl. Jurgens. Former professional football player turned actor Woody Strode portrays Franklin. By the time Strode earned the part in *Pork Chop Hill*, he had played bit parts in nearly twenty films, playing characters with names like Walu, Malaka, and Eseu in stories often set in the mythical jungles of Africa. In 1956 he achieved a measure of notoriety for his role as the King of Ethiopia in Paramount's classic *The Ten Commandments*.

Pork Chop Hill, which depicts an incident that occurred during the Korean Conflict, offers an illuminating depiction of the changing social order of the postwar American military. In the film's opening sequence, a multi-racial group of soldiers emerges from a bunker that has been converted to a chow hall. A Black corporal serves as a runner for the company commander; there are Black artillerymen.

Franklin does not want to fight; he is a malingerer with a chip on his shoulder honed by his resentments and anger and his perceptions of how he has been mistreated. In one scene, he announces, "I'll be damned if I die for Korea." Feigning a sprained ankle, he volunteers to stay behind and assist a truly injured comrade. He attempts to conceal his huge frame behind a piece of debris as his comrades dodge bullets hurrying through an opening in the barbed wire. Lt. Clemons is never fooled by Franklin's attempts to get out of duty. He reprimands him and orders him, "Stick close to me!" With his finger on the trigger of his weapon, Franklin makes a threatening motion toward Clemons, who exhibits little fear of this angry Black soldier with murder in his eyes. He warns Franklin not to do "anything stupid."

As Jurgens, Edwards provides contrast as an intelligent and self-assured Black trooper. In one scene, he barks out orders to a multi-racial group of soldiers.

With an expansive cast comprised of nearly 100 speaking parts (the cast also featured Harry Guardino, Rip Torn, George Peppard, Norman Fell, and Robert Blake), it would have been easy for Edwards to disappear into the maze of supporting players. But he managed to garner a tiny bit of press for his performance, with the *Oakland* (CA) *Tribune*, for example, citing him along with Woody Strode for providing compelling performances. The *Paris* (TX) *News*, singling him out (along with a handful of other actors) as one of the "top featured players." The *California Eagle* remarked upon the appearance of Edwards and Strode, calling them "a credit to the race."[14]

It was Edwards who was instrumental in getting Strode the part. Edwards worked with Strode, teaching how to deliver certain lines. Strode wrote in his biography, "[W]hat Jimmy did was teach me to underplay.... He would play the scene for me, then I would step in and copy him.... Well, every black actor in Hollywood showed up for that job, and I got it."[15]

Later, in another scene, Franklin has a confrontation with Clemons. "I was over my head," Strode revealed, "but Jimmy walked me through it." Edwards coached Strode from the sidelines. When the scene was printed, he thanked Edwards, noting, "Because you're the one who taught me to do this stuff!"[16]

Pork Chop Hill, which might well have made the list of the top war pictures of all time, suffered from the interference of some of the individuals involved in the production, including Peck, who was also one of the film's producers (and perhaps Joseph P. Clemons, whose exploits are highlighted in the film). At times the film seems disjointed and incoherent, and nearly comes to a halt. Joseph R. Millichap, a Milestone biographer, notes that Peck "exercised a great deal of control over the production.... Peck more than anyone else interfered with Milestone's artistic vision of *Pork Chop Hill*." Milestone apparently wanted a different ending, one that would add to the irony of Panmunjom and the hill as opposed to focusing on the heroic bravery of the men. The version of the film that was released was the version that Peck preferred. The result, "Gregory Peck and a gun," was all that is left, complained Milestone.[17]

Still, the film was received warmly by many critics. "The realism of combat is an impossible thing to convey dramatically, but *Pork Chop Hill* ... comes as close to it as I have ever seen," wrote the critic for the *Berk-*

shire (MA) Eagle. The *California Eagle* described *Pork Chop Hill* as "one of the greatest war pictures ever made by any studio" while the drama editor for the *Oakland (CA) Tribune* said, "Lewis Milestone ... has directed the picture with no false moves.... A more heartbreaking combat story could hardly be imagined than this[.]"[18]

Blood and Steel

That same year, Edwards appeared in the stinker *Blood and Steel,* which premiered in Los Angeles on New Year's Eve. The story very much resembles the plot of *Home of the Brave* and involves a squad of Seabees who come to an enemy-infested Pacific island to scout a place to build an airfield. They are assisted by a native girl played by Ziva Rodann. The cast includes John Lupton as Lt. Dave, Brett Halsey as Jim, Edwards as George and John Brinkley as Cip. Released by 20th Century–Fox, *Blood and* Steel was directed by Bernard Kowalski.

"James Edwards is fine as one of the GI's," wrote the *Oakland Tribune*, which added, "This might have been a gripping movie, if so much of it didn't look like one of those repetitious TV dramas made on a small budget."[19]

As he himself alluded, from the heroism of the character Lt. Maples in *Battle Hymn*, to his appearance as a Seabee in the awful *Blood and Steel,* Edwards' film roles in war and combat pictures served a purpose in that they offered an illuminating and significant image of the times: that of a Black soldier in integrated American armed services treated as an equal by his White comrades.

18. Tarzan, Eartha Kitt, and the Strip Scene

"There has always been a Tarzan," wrote Barbara Berch in an article on Lex Barker's installment as the newest Tarzan, "and as long as men are men ... there'll always be one."[1]

James Edwards was a popular and established actor who openly rallied against Black caricatures in film and television, and who prided himself on accepting only dignified roles. Why did he, then, consent to appear in not one but two Tarzan pictures? Even in the still innocent 1950s the African adventure genre was considered by some as little more than crass, idiotic, escapist pap, often awash in racist imagery. It was once one of filmdom's most popular genres; by the postwar period, the African adventure film was slowly losing its drawing power. However, for a brief time just before Tarzan and Jane's eventual (but temporary) banishment, the African adventure film experienced a brief resurgence. Films such as *King Solomon's Mines* (MGM, 1950), *The African Queen* (United Artists, 1951), *Mogambo* (MGM, 1953), and *Congo Crossing* (Universal, 1956), featuring well-established stars such as Rock Hudson, Katharine Hepburn, Humphrey Bogart, and Clark Gable, led the field, followed closely by cheaply made thrillers and B-movies sometimes assembled from leftover footage from other films. Twenty-three Tarzan pictures had been released in the past 15-year period, Berch claimed in 1949; "[T]hey have turned out to be the biggest consistent money-making bonanza in the business."[2]

Moreover, the employment outlook for serious Black actors in Hollywood had improved only slightly since *Home of the Brave* had opened some doors.

In 1959, William Walker, African actor and member of the board of the Screen Actors Guild, told *Variety* that there were only an estimated 25

Black actors who were members of the Screen Actors Guild (half a result of the 1959 film *Porgy and Bess*), and that only a small percentage of members of the Screen Extras Guild were Black. Walker revealed, "[T]he Negro in [feature] pictures is a case of feast or famine." Combined with Hollywood's financial difficulties, job-hunting in Hollywood for serious Black actors was difficult at best. And any actor who wanted to continue to work and pay the bills could not afford to be too choosy.[3]

In 1957 Edwards signed a contract to appear in the low-budget film *African Manhunt*. The picture was directed by Seymour Friedman, from a story written by Arthur Hoerl. Friedman's directing credits include perhaps six episodes of the 1950s television show *The Lone Wolf* and such forgettable Hollywood flicks as *Boston Blackie's Chinese Venture* (1949) and *Counterspy Meets Scotland Yard* (1950).

Edwards plays Native Guide, an unnamed character who leads a group of investigators — a woman and two men, accompanied by a criminal — through the mythical jungles of Africa. The cast consists of Myron Healey, Karin Booth, John Kellogg, Ross Elliott, and Ray Bennett. This black-and-white feature film (replete with stock footage of wild animals and costumed natives) was released by Republic Pictures, a studio that by the 1950s was surviving on its production of serials and low-budget B-movies, many set in the mythical old American West and the equally mythical African jungle.

African Manhunt opened at the 46th Street Embassy in New York in April 1957. The *New York Times* suggested:

> The only thing to do with a film like *African Manhunt* ... is to wave it on its way as quickly as possible.... It is another African safari without credential, but let it pass.[4]

In the 1958 MGM film *Tarzan's Fight for Life,* Edwards plays the part of Futa the witch doctor of the Ngasu tribe, who tries to wipe out the evil White people and wrest power for himself. The picture was produced by Sol Lesser, who had made a successful living on Tarzan films since the 1930s.

Tarzan's Fight for Life was filmed in Metrocolor. Indeed, this was no cheapie; production values are above average. *Variety* described the picture's "handsome color, wide screens, capable acting and able direction;" But bettered values did little to improve the rather juvenile story and script, which was sprinkled with preposterous dialogue. "You can get away with almost anything in a Tarzan picture," wrote the *New York Times*, "but Sol Lesser is pushing his luck with...*Tarzan's Fight for Life*."[5]

Edwards, attired in the requisite feathers and face paint, shouts his way through most of his lines. He is usually having someone beaten or doing the job himself, chasing or being chased through the jungle. But his character played an important part in the story and his role was ample.

The cast of *Tarzan's Fight for Life* also includes Gordon Scott in his second picture as Tarzan, Eve Brent as Jane, Ricky Sorenson, Jill Jarmyn, Nick Stewart, and Woody Strode, who plays the part of Ramo. Edwards has many scenes with Strode, and it is interesting to note that Edwards, 6'2" and athletically built, looks delicate in comparison to the massive physique of Strode, whose hair was trimmed into a Mohawk for the part. Strode wrote about the experience in his biography, and explained how he was glad to shave his head for a salary of $500 per week. "They took all kinds of license," he commented about the out-of-place hairstyle. Strode held no pretense about his skills as an actor. "I was strictly a mechanic," he said, "They told me what to do; I did it, and took the money and got out of there."[6]

After a few months shooting that spring, *Tarzan's Fight for Life* was released in July 1958. Publicity for the film included display ads, some of which featured Edwards' face surrounded by lines reading:

> STRANGE VOODOO RITES OF THE MAD WITCH DOCTOR;
> FILMED WHERE IT HAPPENED IN SAVAGE SEETHING AFRICA.

Edwards and Strode were also featured in a multi-photograph piece printed in *Ebony*, one that submerged all discussion of the film and its shortcomings for a story about the young Cub Scout who earned a part in the film.[7]

Anna Lucasta

The backstory coinciding with the release of this 1959 film is long, complicated, and well beyond the scope of this book. Briefly, however, the 1936 Philip Yordan play, originally written about a Polish family living in a Pennsylvania mill town, went unproduced until it was adapted by the American Negro Theatre (ANT), a tiny, struggling troupe organized by seminal African American actor Frederick O'Neal. The goal of the ANT was to create a place where Negro players could hone their craft.[8]

With a cast that included Hilda Simms, Canada Lee, Rosetta LeNoire, and O'Neal, the play *Anna Lucasta* opened in the basement of the Harlem

Public Library on June 16, 1944. The production received such acclaim from the community that the seats in the tiny room filled, and five weeks later, the production was mounted at the Mansfield Theatre on Broadway where it ran for 600 performances and spawned a number of touring companies. Edwards, too, would appear in productions of the play as it toured Chicago. In 1949, a Columbia Pictures version of *Anna Lucasta*, featuring a White cast and starring Paulette Goddard as Anna, came and went with little fanfare.

O'Neal and Simms (who appeared with Edwards as Joe Louis' wife in the 1953 film) became stars. Others were not so lucky. "[T]hose who began the first stage of the play with an all-colored cast has [*sic*] long since been forgotten..." wrote the Baltimore (MD) *Afro-American* in 1959. The onstage success of *Anna Lucasta* ended with lawsuits and acrimony about profits and rights.[9]

Directed by Arnold Laven, the second film version of *Anna Lucasta* was released in February 1959. The cast featured Eartha Kitt as Anna; Frederick O'Neal as Frank; Henry Scott as Rudolph Slocum; Sammy Davis, Jr., in his first film role, as Joe; and Rex Ingram was cast as Joe Lucasta, Anna's father. Kitt had recently made her film debut in the 1957 Film Productions International picture *Mark of the Hawk*, which starred Sidney Poitier. Veteran actor Ingram, whose film career began during the era of silent pictures, earned prominence by appearing in the all–Black World War II MGM musical *Cabin the Sky* (1943) and the same-year Columbia Pictures combat feature *Sahara*, which starred Humphrey Bogart.

Edwards had a brief but memorable part as Eddie, the proprietor of a local club who sees himself as a big-shot deserving of respect. Anna, who doesn't like him, brushes off his overtures in a wonderful sequence at the beginning of the film, where several of the players are grouped in one of the main sets, Noah's Bar, a waterfront dive. Eddie wants to lure Anna to work for him at his establishment; he also, incidentally, wants to lure her into his bed. He loses his patience with her smart-alecky tone, grabs her and pulls her toward him trying to kiss her. She retaliates.

> EDDIE: Why you little...She burnt me with her cigarette — right on the neck.... I ain't wasting my time with waterfront tramps.... You'd better change your mind and quit being so particular. Some day you'll need a pal.
> ANNA: I'd sooner pal with rats.
> EDDIE : Keep it up and you soon will.[10]

Kitt was well identified as an actor who liked to dominate and overpower her fellow cast members in a given scene but Edwards did not capitulate to her presence and instead holds his own.

Anna Lucasta had great music, including songs sung by Davis, who also danced and played the drums. A debate ensued over advertisements for the picture, with the censors objecting to the image of Kitt walking away in a tight dress which they felt over-emphasized Anna's shapely posterior.

The film was not particularly well-received; some critics were downright unkind. *The Monthly Film Bulletin* remarked:

> [T]he play does not wear particularly well — some of the character motivation, especially that of the father, is irritatingly obscure and the heroine has now become a well worn theatrical symbol.... Arnold Laven contributes little to the author's original conception.[11]

Time magazine wrote:

> [Kitt's] extraordinary animal glitter makes her histrionic limitations irrelevant. Sammy Davis, Jr., is Danny, the oversexed sailor, and there are at least three major scenes in which Sammy, with superhuman energy, takes over the screen like a blackface Bugs Bunny.[12]

A critic for the *Algona (IA) Advance* described the empty seats in the theatre and declared:

> The enjoyment of a picture of this sort depends almost entirely on your reaction to colored folk. The acting was violent and dramatic and the plot was sordid and unappetizing.... [T]here is little interest in movies of this type.[13]

Albert Johnson, writing for the influential journal *Sight and Sound* suggested:

> It would be well for Hollywood producers to hire an observant and perceptive member of the Negro race (James Baldwin, the novelist, would be my choice) as "technical adviser" on any future films of this kind.[14]

Indeed, it seems that some critics preferred the poor, stereotyped, semi-literate Negro inhabitants of Catfish Row to the machinations of a middle-class African American family that tries to exploit their wayward kin for money (the film *Porgy and Bess* was released in August but the story performed as opera since the 1930s). "Oh, Where's Porgy's Bess?" was the headline for Richard Coe's review for the *Washington Post*. He called it a "poor, tasteless film" and stated, "I think *Porgy and Bess* is a valid Negro drama and *Anna Lucasta* a phony drama." Bosley Crowther of the *New*

18. Tarzan, Eartha Kitt, and the Strip Scene

Eddie woos an intractable Anna Lucasta, played by Eartha Kitt, in the Black-cast film version of *Anna Lucasta* (1959).

York Times* wrote, "If someone dug down into the play-bin and brought up 'Bertha and the Sewing Machine Girl,' they could probably turn it into a better movie than has been made by Philip Yordan of *Anna Lucasta*." He described the production as "an incredibly artless film ... played with surprising amateurism by a big-name Negro cast."[15] In response to the *New York Times* review, one man wrote:

> You describe the entire film as being amateurish.... In fact you had sour comments for every single performer. I would wonder if it isn't your racial unconscious that is prejudicing your acrid opinion [of the film and its performances].[16]

To add insult to injury, referring to theatres in the Southern market, Eartha Kitt claims in her biography that 2,500 cinemas across America had declined to screen the film. Kitt asserted that she looked "too white" for Southerners who thought the film included an interracial romance.[17]

Anna Lucasta did not click with critics or the movie-going public. The offbeat and taboo nature of the story didn't help matters.

In spite of it all, Edwards' brief appearance as Eddie did not go unnoticed. In his otherwise unflattering review, Johnson of *Sight and Sound* singles out Edwards' performance, noting:

> [He] sketches a keenly detailed characterization of a sinister pander and brings to the memorable bar-room sequence the sense of style that is so wanting in the rest of the film.[18]

Edwards also appeared a two-page, nine-photograph article on the film published in the December edition of *Ebony* magazine. Publicity for the picture sometimes capitalized on Edwards' name recognition by featuring him prominently in publicity stills.[19]

Night of the Quarter Moon

Edwards next provided a sincere portrayal of a trial attorney in the B-grade MGM potboiler *Night of the Quarter Moon*. This 1959 production was directed by Hugo Haas (*Pickup*, 1951, *Thy Neighbor's Wife*, 1953, *Bait*, 1954), a specialist in lurid B-thrillers, and was produced by Albert Zugsmith, known for his penchant for taboo and odd subject matter in his exploitation films. Some of his productions, including *The Tattered Dress* (1957), *Touch of Evil* (1958) and *High School Confidential!* (1958) were condemned by religious and community censors.[20]

18. Tarzan, Eartha Kitt, and the Strip Scene

The publicity campaign for *Quarter Moon*, which was to be exploited differently in various markets, included such teaser promos as:

"THE SHAMELESS STORY OF GINNY—A GIRL WHO PASSED FOR WHITE!"
"I DON'T CARE WHAT SHE IS.... SHE'S MINE!"
"EXPOSED!"

Ginny is played by actress-singer Julie London. London, whose credits include numerous low-budget features and television shows before she was cast in *Quarter Moon*, is perhaps best known for her 1955 hit song "Cry Me a River." As the story opens, we see Ginny standing wordless as four young toughs throw rocks through the window of the front room of her home. They then proceed to clip the branches of her rose bushes (using pruning shears they apparently just happened to have handy). As they yank her landscape bushes from the ground, while her neighbors stand and watch, Ginny is compelled to run from the house. She doesn't utter a word; she clearly can't fight off four healthy young men, so her motivation is unclear. Finally, her husband Chuck, whom she has telephoned, arrives on the scene. He picks a fight with one of the men, but when the police arrive, but only he and Ginny are hauled off to the police station.

In separate rooms they are interrogated. The police accuse Ginny of enticing the boys into a vandalizing frenzy by flirting with them and exposing herself. For unknown reasons, a group of photographers and reporters are permitted to stream into the room where Ginny is being held and they interrupt the proceedings. In between peppering her with questions, one reporter yells, "Why don't you go back to Mexico?" It is then that we learn, in flashback, the story of Ginny, the "girl who passed for White!"

Edwards received third-billing in this film, with singer Nat "King" Cole billed as the star. Cole has perhaps three scenes and a respectable number of lines of dialogue. Clearly, the main reason he was cast was to capitalize on his surging celebrity. Seated at his rightful place at the piano, he performs a full number, "To Whom It May Concern." Other cast members include Dean Jones, Jackie Coogan, Charles Chaplin, Jr., as one of the young thugs. Billy Daniels, a popular singer, was cast as a waiter. Anna Kashfi, who appeared with Edwards in *Battle Hymn*, plays Cole's wife. Chuck, Ginny's husband, was played by John Drew Barrymore. He had recently appeared in another Zugsmith film, the truly horrible exploitation film *High School Confidential!* Barrymore also appeared as the character Little Horse in the Westinghouse-Desilu production "Silent Thunder." The screenplay was based on a story written by Edwards.

Edwards as attorney Asa Tully in the notorious strip scene from *Night of the Quarter Moon* (1959), with John Drew Barrymore and Julie London.

In a long flashback we see Ginny, who likes to swim naked in the moonlight, explain to her husband-to-be that she is one-quarter Portuguese Angolan. Her mother, she explains, "was much darker than she."

At first, her new mother-in-law, played by veteran actor Agnes Moorehead, is overjoyed to meet Ginny. Ginny has married Charles Nelson of an important, wealthy family. When his mother finds out about the girl's background, she turns into a snake, asking Ginny, "Where did my son propose to you, on the beach or in a cotton field?"

Indeed, as soon as Ginny's parentage is revealed, the entire town turns against them. They are tossed out of their honeymoon suite and buy a house only to find that the neighborhood has a restrictive covenant: no Negroes allowed. The local newspaper devotes the whole of their front page to the fact that Ginny is a quadroon, complete with a huge bannerhead.

We return from the flashback to learn that during the police interrogation (where his mother, brother, lawyer, and doctor all squeeze into the tiny room), Chuck, Ginny's husband, a former Korean War POW, has lost his grip on reality. We see him as he hallucinates about his experi-

18. Tarzan, Eartha Kitt, and the Strip Scene

ences with his Korean captors. His mother takes this opportunity to whisk him away to a sanitarium and, using power of attorney, she sues Ginny for an annulment of the marriage.

Enter Asa Tully, played by James Edwards. We first see him as the guitarist in a jazz trio featuring a lounge singer (played by Cathy Crosby of the famous Crosby family). Tully puts his guitar down in the middle of the number to talk to Ginny. They move to a table in the sparsely populated club as Crosby howls through a rendition of the song "Blue Moon." Tully lights a cigarette and explains to Ginny that he only works there to make money because as a Black man, the only work he can find is preparing brief for others. Ginny pleads with Tully: "I've gotta know now. Are you going to help me?" Tully answers affirmatively: "Sure. Sure, I'll help you. First, I gotta knock out a few beats."

The ensuing trial scenes are perhaps the most compelling and best done of the entire film, with Edwards doing a superior job in his role as a trial attorney. He appears throughout the sequence attired in a well-tailored dark suit and striped tie. His courtroom demeanor feels authentic. He doesn't simply take on the persona of a lawyer, he *is* a lawyer. As Tully, he exudes confidence and clarity. At one point, Mrs. Nelson remarks, "Her lawyer is one of the shrewdest I've ever seen."

Tully questions Chuck's brother John in defense of Ginny, who is accused of setting her sights on Chuck only because she knew that he was a Nelson and therefore rich.

> Mr. Nelson, did you ever meet a woman who did not use her feminine wiles to entice a man?... Did you ever witness the defendant making love to your brother?... Did you ever see her go into his room?... Did you ever find them in a compromising position?... Did you ever witness them kiss?

John cannot recall witnessing any of the above acts and therefore, the argument that Ginny was little more than a gold-digger is neutralized.

The next matter is to prove that Ginny, indeed, informed Chuck of her Negro blood. Ginny is ordered to disrobe, to show that Chuck had to know that her color was not due to a heavy tan but was truly the color of her skin. In a mildly titillating scene, Ginny slowly undoes the buttons to her jacket. She is clearly embarrassed and hesitates. Tully tears open her jacket, revealing her bared back. Chuck, full of remorse, removes his wife from the courtroom. The case is over and there will be no annulment. We see Ginny and Chuck as the couple fight through a barrage of reporters. Once again the audience is subjected to Crosby's vile singing; this time she delivers a rendition of the film's title song, "Night of the Quarter

Moon." In a wide shot, we see Tully alone, carrying his valise, as he strolls through the front door of the courtroom and onto the busy street.

Though the limitations of this film are clear (the *Monthly Film Bulletin* called it "vulgar, sensational and humanely false"), some viewers were so empathetic toward the story about the problems befalling two sincere young lovers of different races that they overlooked the contrived story, inane dialogue, flubbed lines, and implausible circumstances. The *Los Angeles Sentinel* claimed that the film had established attendance records at "fifteen important theatres throughout Los Angeles County."[21]

Critiques of Edwards' performance were positive. The *California Eagle* gushed:

> James "Jimmy" Edwards, unquestionably one of Hollywood's most versatile thespians, has the memorable ability to elevate any mediocre role into a portrayal of brilliance.[22]

The Commonweal, which called the film "a hopped-up melodrama," noted, "[I]ts best role is played by James Edwards as Julie's Negro lawyer[.]"[23] A similar plaudit came from the film critic for the *Oakland Tribune*, who said:

> Actually, the film's best performer is James Edwards as the Negro attorney fighting the annulment suit ... his portrayal has dignity, depth and sincerity, nonetheless.[24]

The *California Eagle* proclaimed, "James Edwards gives one of the greatest performances these eyes have beheld in a long time." *Variety* wrote of Edwards' performance, "Smoothest portrayal in cast is offered by James Edwards as the Negro lawyer defending the young wife."[25]

19. "The Role Was a Cheat"

In 1955, Edwards played a small but consequential part in the film adaptation of one the most newsworthy items of the year: the story of Phenix City, Alabama.

There was a time when Phenix City was known as the wickedest town in America. Located only a few miles from Fort Benning Army Post in Georgia, the city served as a destination for soldiers, tourists, and anyone else with a taste for gambling and vice. Referred to by some as the Hellhole of the South, Phenix City provided a haven for all manner of criminal activities. Liquor and narcotics flowed freely at gambling joints, nightclubs, and whorehouses. Corruption ran rampant: A small band of gangsters and thugs reigned over all local businesses. Criminals controlled the courts, police, Chamber of Commerce, school and hospital boards, elections, and even some churches. One prosecuting attorney wrote in 1956, "Phenix City was not merely a community where crime was rampant and violence shrugged off ... it was a state of mind — the philosophy of 'get it while you can and the methods will not be questioned.'"[1]

The beginning of the end came in June 1954. Albert Patterson, one of the founders of the Russell County Betterment Association, ran for attorney general on the promise that he would clean up the city. Despite the efforts of racketeers to steal the election, he won. And as he himself predicted, before he could be sworn in, he was murdered by in cold blood while sitting in his car on a city street. The subsequent investigation, which saw hundreds of individuals indicted, made headline news as newspapers across the country covered the proceedings taking place in Phenix City.

The Phenix City Story purports to dramatize the true story of the town which was eventually cleansed of its evil reputation with the help of its citizens, the government, and two brave men. The film was directed by Phil Karlson, a veteran of such pictures as *Kansas City Confidential* (1952),

99 River Street (1953), and *Tight Spot* (1955). He is regarded by some as the master of the film noir crime film. The producers were Samuel Bischoff and David Diamond; the screenplay was written by Crane Wilbur and Dan Mainwaring, who interviewed the people of Phenix City for their scenario. The story is based largely on fact, but like all cinematic interpretations of historical events, the script contains its fair share of stylistic embellishments.

The film opens with a rather droll prologue consisting of interviews with real citizens, conducted by journalist Clete Roberts, whose purpose it is to find out "what happened here, in Phenix City." This preamble continues for more than ten minutes and goes so far as to act as a spoiler. Today this sequence seems painfully tedious, but to viewers at the time of the film's release, with no access to RSS newsfeeds, blogs, Internet or cable news networks, the story of Phenix City had only just begun to appear in the pages of newspapers; therefore, the film's long introduction was most likely well-received and appreciated.

At the conclusion of the preamble, the fictional dramatization of the story of Phenix City begins at the Poppy Club. A vocalist slinks her way through a number, enticing an appreciative all-male audience. Moments later, a man realizes that he was cheated at a card game; indeed, he discovers he has been playing with marked cards. (The club also featured loaded dice and rigged slot machines.) He demands his money back. Two ruffians appear, beat him to a pulp, and dump his limp body into the gutter in broad daylight. A young woman named Ellie (played by Kathryn Grant), employed as a card dealer, is horrified.

Edwards is cast as Zeke Ward, who works at the Poppy Club as a porter. After the beating incident, we see Zeke outside the club, broom in hand. A young, rather innocent-looking man lingers at the door of the club. He asks Zeke for a match, who lights his cigarette. Zeke then issues the man a warning: "You ought to keep away from here."[2]

In the next scene we see Zeke clearing tables; a look of chagrin creases his face as he takes in the raucous atmosphere and tawdry shenanigans.

We meet Rhett Tanner, Poppy Club proprietor, local businessman and hoodlum. He meets any attempt to usurp his power with unabated viciousness. One by one, the members of the town's Betterment Association (a small group of citizens determined to challenge the hoodlums head-on) are brutally beaten or murdered, all without interference from the police who are in the hip pockets of Tanner and his cronies. In sum, the story is about the bad guys who prefer Phenix City to remain a cesspool

19. "The Role Was a Cheat"   141

of corruption and flagitiousness vs. the good guys who want to clean up their hometown.

Zeke is compelled to leave his job with Tanner and join the good guys. He is a married man with a child, a young girl of six or seven. We see her in ribbons and pigtails, playing and riding her bike like any child. But Zeke must pay for his disloyalty. In a brutal scene, his daughter is snatched from the street, murdered, and thrown from the window of a moving car onto the lawn of the home of John Patterson, Tanner's opponent. A note is pinned to the child's clothing, warning, "THIS WILL HAPPEN TO YOUR KIDS, TOO." Chilling is the medium shot of the murdered child with her eyes wide open and blood streaming from her head.

At the police station, an officer hangs up the telephone and blithely announces that he has received report of "a dead nigger kid." We never see Zeke or his wife's reaction to their daughter's cruel murder. We don't know if they demanded justice. Their part of the story, their grief and anger, is never explored or even mentioned.

John Patterson's father, Albert, decides takes on Tanner by running for attorney general. The film depicts how mobsters attempted to ruin the election through rape, arson, drug peddling, assault, and murder. After Patterson is elected we witness his brutal murder. Now John is left to take on his father's burden. A recently discharged veteran, he likens the fight against Tanner to the war against Hitler.

Ellie leaves Tanner's employ and decides to join the crusade to clean up Phenix City. She, too, must pay and is in fear of her life. She hides at Zeke Ward's cabin. John tries to rescue her but he is too late: He arrives at Zeke's outbuilding to find her lifeless body. Tanner and his henchman are still on the property and now John and Zeke are pitted man to man against them. Two horrific fights break out, one between Zeke and Tanner's hired muscle, and another between John and Tanner, who roll down an embankment and into a pond.

In his cabin, Zeke, who has gotten the better of Tanner's brute, can now take revenge for his daughter's cruel murder. He stands over the man, ready to pummel the life out of him with the butt of a shotgun. We return to John, who is prepared to avenge the murder of this father by holding Tanner underwater and drowning him.

"The role was a cheat," Sidney Poitier said of the part of Zeke Ward. He had seen the script but refused the part.

> It was a lie, an absolute out-and-out lie, and they used it in an uncourageous manner.... This father ... his daughter was killed and thrown on the

lawn ... he's got him in a shed and he's going to kill him. And then they put in this mouth the most ugly compromise ... crappy words like, "I suddenly realize the Lord doesn't want me to do this."[3]

In a scene that is both compelling and gripping, Zeke joins John and Tanner in the pond. He wrestles with John in the dim waist-deep water and screams at him in a voice strident and pleading:

> No, Mr. Patterson ... please, don't do it ... you can't take the Lord's revenge into your own hands ... the Lord said not to kill, thou shalt not kill, the Lord said ... Mr. Patterson, please! Back there a few minutes ago I was gonna beat a man's brains out ... and my wife took my arm, and she was crying and all bloody ... where they'd beat her, and I was going to do it anyway ... but she said, "No, Zeke, no" ...so I handed her the gun, and I come out here....

After some moments of heartfelt cajoling, John relents and Zeke pulls a shaken, shivering Tanner from the pond. With so much murder and mayhem, this scene, affecting and forceful, is certainly one of the high points of a rather gloomy story, signaling that the corner has been turned and eventually, things will be set right. Poitier was not completely wrong in his assessment of the scene's truth and Zeke's motivation, but little did he suspect that, within context, the scene would be especially resonant and one of the best of the film.

The role of Rhett Tanner was played by Edward Andrews, a Georgia native and stage actor usually seen as characters much more amiable than his one he plays in *Phenix City*, which was his motion picture debut. Before his role as Albert Patterson, veteran actor John McIntire achieved a measure of fame for his appearance as a police officer in the hit 1950 film, *The Asphalt Jungle*. Richard Kiley, who played the role of John Patterson, was a Chicagoan who began his acting career as a child. Mostly a stage actor, Kiley was excellent in support of Richard Widmark in the chilling 1953 Samuel Fuller production *Pickup on South Street*.

The Phenix City Story was filmed on location in Phenix City, Alabama. Charles Crawford, theatrical columnist for the *California Eagle*, reported that Edwards said he was "feeling no pain" while working on the picture on location in the Deep South. This statement stands in direct contrast to other reports, including one appearing in the *Pittsburgh Courier*, which reported how Edwards, along with other members of the crew, feared for their own safety. The lives of cast and crew were threatened, which limited their movements around town. Edwards, the paper reported, was supplied with an armed driver who drove him to and from the set each day.

The film crew claimed that their work was "sabotaged in many small ways." *Variety* reported how mobsters intimidated booksellers who tried to sell copies of the book *Phenix City*, written by Gene Worstman, state political writer for the Scripps-Howard *Post-Herald*, and Edwin Strickland, a political writer. For their efforts, the two authors suffered nuisance arrests, intimidation, threatening phone calls, and public recriminations. Diamond, one of the producers, told *Variety*, "I'm in here and I'm shooting this movie if I have to hire guards." The premiere was moved from Columbus, Georgia, to Edwards' former hometown of Chicago out of safety concerns.[4]

Not surprisingly, *Phenix City* received more than its share of complaints from the Production Code Association about the amount of violence and brutality, its depiction of prostitution, and in particular, the murder of Zeke Ward's child. Some concessions were made to appease the censors, but the prostitutes and the murder of the child remained a part of the film, which debuted on August 15, 1955.

The *Los Angeles Sentinel* described the film as "a blood and thunder tale as full of dead bodies as any Shakespearean tragedy." *Time* magazine was less than complimentary, calling the treatment of the story of Phenix City "overexcited."[5]

"Allied Artists has come up with one of the grimmest and darkest documentaries ever to be attempted by a motion picture studio," wrote the *Syracuse (NY) Herald-Journal*. "There is nothing entertaining in this picture[.]" A critic for the *Cedar Rapids (IA) Gazette* wrote, "*The Phenix City Story* is a shocker…. The picture deals with unpleasant facts and there is nothing pleasant about it."[6]

Most surprising was the complimentary opinion of the film tendered by Bosley Crowther of the *New York Times,* who went as far as to call it one of the best films of 1955. He wrote,

> Despite some efforts to dismiss this picture as a cheap, low-budget job, it is a surprisingly candid, comprehending and crisply cinematic account…. It had the sharp documentary quality of some of our best journalistic films.[7]

A review tendered by Richard Coe of the *Washington Post & Times Herald* was equally complimentary, noting how the story was "far more than the fairly familiar crime yarn," and how the events were "excitingly, compellingly, pictured."[8]

Except for his final scene, Edwards' appearances in the film are relatively brief, but as usual he makes the best of his time onscreen. Coe wrote,

"In the fully adequate supporting cast, James Edwards, as the young Negro, is outstanding." The *Oakland Tribune* called Edwards' performance in his big scene "powerful," and the *Syracuse (NY) Herald-Journal* wrote that Edwards (along with other supporting actors) "stood out" in supporting roles. *The Cedar Rapids (IA) Gazette* declared, "James Edwards is the colored man who is excellent in a telling part."[9]

It is interesting to note that Edwards' popularity was well exploited in promotions for the picture. Advertisements in newspapers in some markets, for example, featured his face in silhouette accompanied by the words:

"You'll never forget the sensational performance of James Edwards!"[10]

Today's viewers, accustomed to clever, more graphic, sophisticated, and less preachy and predictable storylines, may find *The Phenix City Story* a bit artificial; the script is doddering at times, and the dialogue occasionally teeters on the banal. At the time of its release, however, the film was hailed for its courageousness, its realistic treatment of a current news story, its politics, and its message. Warts and all, *The Phenix City Story* was, Crowther wrote, "an uncommonly good little film[.]"[11]

20. Black Cowboys on a *Mission*

As television's dramatic anthologies quietly faded from primetime, the Western emerged as one of America's most popular television genres. Programs such as *Gunsmoke* (1955–1975), *Wells Fargo* (1957–1962), *Have Gun Will Travel* (1957–1963), *Maverick* (1957–1962), *Colt .45* (1957–1960), and *Wagon Train* (1957–1965) captured large audiences of devoted viewers who eagerly followed the lives of the characters. In 1956 alone, nearly one dozen new Western series premiered.

The average American knew little of the role that African American men and women played in the settling of the American West, nor had most ever heard of Black cowboy William Pickett, or the Buffalo Soldiers, whose history dated back to the Civil War. Notes one writer on the history of the Black cowboy:

> Almost totally missing from the traditional history of the American West is the role of the Black cowboy.... The exclusion was extended into the twentieth century by the Hollywood producers (documentary and movies) who not only excluded them, but slanted and twisted the facts regarding the overall western scene.[1]

While the TV western featured women, Hispanic, and Native American characters, more often than not, life in TV's dusty Western towns were devoid of Black citizens except for the occasional guest star appearance by a name performer like Lou Rawls. Black faces were not only absent as main characters and minor characters but missing in street and crowd scenes. George Norford, an NBC writer-producer, claimed that producers told him, "We produce shows set in 1870, 1880; it would be unrealistic to put Negroes in those scenes." Norford disputed this claim and informed producers that newly freed Black slaves came West in droves and worked in all manner of occupations.²

William Walker, actor and member of the board of directors for the Screen Actors Guild, told *Variety*, "A particular sore spot is the TV western.... [T]he people who make westerns seem to absolutely exclude the Negro." This truth was not lost on Black television viewers who were often vocal in their complaints to television networks.³

In 1959, Edwards joined a mostly Black cast in an unusual Western tale that highlighted the exploits of Black cavalrymen of the old west.

Dick Powell's Zane Grey Theatre

Dick Powell's Zane Grey Theatre, which ran from 1956 to 1962, was hosted by the actor himself. Though Powell is perhaps better known for his roles as a boy singer in Busby Berkeley musicals of the 1930s, by the 1950s he was the head of Four Star Productions, one of the biggest producers of television programming.⁴

Zane Grey Theatre featured adaptations of the stories by Zane Grey, author of *Wyoming* (1952) and *The Fugitive Trail* (1957). His novels were too long for a 30-minute show and when the supply of suitable short stories ran out, original teleplays were commissioned. The program attracted name stars such as Jack Lemmon, Edward G. Robinson, Joan Crawford, Danny Thomas, Hedy Lamarr, and Lloyd Bridges.

In 1958, Edwards appeared as Sgt. Morgan in an episode called "Mission." As the story opens, we see Morgan in command of a squad of men on horseback. Black men, members of the 10th Army U.S. Cavalry stationed at Fort Warren, they are also known as the Buffalo Soldiers.

Morgan leads them to a secret location where they meet a Native American whose dress indicates his high stature. Morgan describes him as "a guest of the government." The men head back to the fort only to be ambushed by a group of Apaches. Only then does Morgan reveal what their mission was truly about: They must deliver the mystery man, who happens to be the chief of the Cheyenne nation, to a nearby Army post where he will sign a treaty that may be the catalyst for peace in the region between the Indian nations and the U.S. The Apaches are suspicious of the treaty, believing that it will weaken their position. They consider the Cheyenne chief a traitor and consequently, the men are attacked repeatedly. Morgan suffers an arrow to his chest.

Cpl. Harper, played by Sammy Davis, Jr., dislikes and distrusts all Indians. He is derisive and mean-spirited and treats the Cheyenne chief with contempt. He is summoned by the dying Morgan:

> MORGAN: I messed it ... the first real job we get, and I messed it.
> HARPER: Anything we can do for you Sarge?
> MORGAN: Get back, keep your eyes open! They're not through! Harp, you've got to get him back to the fort!
> HARPER: Why us?
> MORGAN: Who'd figure us? Never thought they'd figure us! Too important![5]

Sgt. Morgan dies of his wound. Now Harper must lead his men, outgunned and short on supplies, to their ill-fated mission. Edwards does an admirable work of his death scene, which has him lying upon the ground covered in perspiration and stiffened in pain. Too, unlike some of his fellow actors, he looked the experienced horseman, and reportedly kept his own horse at the Muse-A-While ranch of actor Clarence Muse. Sammy Davis, Jr., received top billing in the episode. Though he, too, provides a fine acting job, he appears a bit out of place with his mop of processed hair and hep-cat air. "Mission" would be the earliest if not the first television American Western featuring a Black cast. But the episode has a noteworthy albeit disquieting backstory.

Davis, who appeared with Edwards in the 1959 film *Anna Lucasta*, was reportedly a big fan of the western and sought a dramatic role on a television show. Aaron Spelling's original script cast him as a deputy with Dick Powell as sheriff. In the story, the deputy would save the life of his sheriff by killing the villain. However, the idea of a Black man carrying a gun and killing a White man, even if the White man was the villain, was too controversial for 1959 television, particularly for the program's sponsors, Lorillard Cigarettes.[6]

At the time of his death in 2006, Spelling, a former actor who became a writer and independent producer, was one of television's household names. He is the creator of such popular programs as *The Mod Squad*, *Charlie's Angels*, *The Love Boat*, and *Dynasty*. In 1959, however, he was still trying to break into the television business. He recalled the issues surrounding the "Mission" episode in an interview in *American Film*:

> I wrote a show for *Zane Grey Theatre* and cast Sammy Davis, Jr., in it. One cigarette sponsor — I'll never forget it — said, "No, we cannot have Sammy Davis do one of our shows ... we don't want a black sheriff, because he has a gun." They didn't mind that I had the Indians going over the

Buffalo Soldiers and saying, "But you're colored like us, why do you care about the white man?" They thought that was OK but I couldn't have the blacks carry guns. Oh God, I hated those days.⁷

In the end, if Black men were going to carry guns, Spelling had to rewrite the script (which he called "Buffalo Soldiers") containing no White people at all. "The sponsors' racist attitude really stunk, but here I was using their forum to point out bigotry and that was okay with them.... Didn't make any sense."⁸

Not everyone was convinced of television's good intentions. The *California Eagle* noted ruefully:

> The fact that Sammy Davis and Company on the TV show ... gave an eye-opener to the nation on the part Negroes played in the Old West doesn't encourage the powers to be to feature Negro actors in horse operas!⁹

Some members of the Black community hoped that the *Zane Grey Theatre* airing of "Mission," with a nearly all-Black cast that included Abraham Sofear, Felix Nelson, Roy Glenn, Ernie Anderson, Hari Rhodes, and Bobby Johnson, would be the first of many Westerns featuring African American characters.

Texas John Slaughter

Two years later, in 1960, Edwards made another, even more intriguing appearance as a Black cowboy on the television show *Texas John Slaughter*.

Walt Disney Studio's early alliance with the ABC network is considered a major turning point in the Hollywood-television partnership as the Disney programs *Disneyland*, *Davy Crockett*, and *The Mickey Mouse Club* became three of *the* most popular shows. The concept for one Disney television program, *Texas John Slaughter*, was based on the real-life story of John Slaughter, a Confederate Civil War veteran. Set in 1880s Texas, this miniseries presented feature-length programs geared toward a younger audience. Slaughter, played by actor Tom Tryon, "made 'em do what they oughta, 'cause iffen they didn't they die...."¹⁰

Edwards was cast as John Raymond Beaumont, otherwise known as Batt, in at least three of the seventeen episodes. In the story "Apache Friendship," Edwards stars with Jay Silverheels, known for his portrayal of Tonto on *The Lone Ranger*. The episode presents Slaughter as a widower with two young children. The woman he wishes to marry, Vi (played by Betty Lynn), won't accept him unless he stops wearing guns and changes his combative ways. Batt shows up at the Slaughter ranch and thrills the children with his carving. He makes toys for them and they beg their father to hire him. The two men talk. Batt reveals that he is from the South and that his profession was a tracker:

> Well, sir, I became just about the best tracker in Florida, then Georgia, Alabama, and Mississippi.... Naturally, I just had to expand west.

Slaughter asks Batt if he can do any other work, such as cooking or looking after horses, and Batt responses affirmatively but adds:

> Well, Mr. Slaughter, I'd rather be put in the books as a tracker, that being my proper profession.

In 1955, Edwards vowed, "I'd rather dig mines than say one 'yassah' on the screen." In this episode, he nearly does just that. Too, the Batt character is positioned as somewhat comical in that he believes himself to be good at everything, from wrestling alligators to growing hair on bald people. Indeed, Edwards appears uncomfortable in this role and occasionally lapses from a Southern drawl back into his natural, plain way of speaking, as if he had trouble making peace with the type of character he was contracted to portray.[11]

In "Geronimo's Revenge," Batt appears as one of Slaughter's ranch hands. He is treated casually, as an equal. In one scene, he mounts his horse to join the others as they chase after the so-called bad Indians. He had a number of short lines of dialogue. Curiously, in the VHS version of the show obtained for this study, Edwards' voice has been replaced with the voice of another *sans* any hint of a Southern drawl. Why? A technical glitch or a purposeful move on the part of Disney?

In his study of Disney Television, David Brode describes a more nuanced Batt in the episode "Kentucky Gunslick." Batt has become a hero of sorts to Slaughter's boy Willie, and confidant to the new Mrs. Slaughter. It would have been interesting to see the further development of Batt, had Edwards appeared in subsequent episodes.[12]

Gary Yoggy, who wrote a detailed history of the television western, credits Edwards' appearance in *Texas John Slaughter* as the first Black cowboy character to appear on a recurring television program. For Edwards, his role represented a part in three full-length features and a paycheck during a lean time in Hollywood. Still, with the ever-so-slightly stereotypical role he portrayed, and the possibility that his voice was dubbed over, one wonders what Edwards would have thought about this achievement.[13]

Death Valley Days

Edwards also made an appearance in the television western *Death Valley Days,* a syndicated program with 558 episodes produced from 1952 to 1975. The program had its beginnings on radio during the 1930s. It aired on television for more than twenty years, making it one of the longest running television series. The setting was the 19th century American West and each story, which began with a brief narrated introduction, was supposedly based on real facts and events.

In 1963, Edwards appeared as Scipio Gates in a half-hour color episode called "The Other White Man." In this rather thin yarn, a government man from Washington, D.C. (played by Michael Hinn), arrives at an Army post in South Dakota. He sets out to convene with the nearby Dakota Indians, hoping to negotiate a new treaty before the arrival of new White settlers to their lands. Treaty or no treaty, one of the Dakota warriors is set upon killing any White man who dares to set foot on Dakota land. He kills two White men and injures the agent.

Scipio Gates has been living among the Dakotas since he escaped slavery as a young man. The Dakotas call him "the other White man." A Dakota woman asks Gates to help get the dying agent to the Army post but he is reluctant because he does not want to be captured and returned to bondage. After some cajoling, he relents, referring to the man as "slave catcher" and telling him, "You might as well start calling me 'boy' so I can get used to it again."

The agent explains that he is not a slave catcher; moreover, slavery ended twelve years earlier. He informs a stunned Gates, who was prepared to give up his freedom to save the man's life, that he is now a free man.

As the 1960s evolved, Black characters would appear only intermittently in the primetime television Western. By the time producers of such shows could be convinced that Black people indeed made contributions to the settling of the American West, and sponsors were no longer afraid of the reaction they might receive from the South if a Negro face appeared in a given program, the Western genre itself was on the decline.

21. Comeback in a Big Picture

There was a time when the face of Dorothy Dandridge appeared regularly in the entertainment sections of Black and mainstream newspapers as columnists eagerly documented her every move and reported upon her personal and professional activities. By 1960, the fanfare about Dandridge had ebbed to a trickle and it is difficult to find her mentioned at all by the correspondents who once covered her career so carefully. What happened to the film career of Dorothy Dandridge? In 1961 a columnist for the *Los Angeles Sentinel* questioned her "dwindling presence." After her appearance in the much-hyped Otto Preminger production *Porgy and Bess* (1959) and the atrocious British-produced film *Malanga,* Dandridge's film career seemed be in a freefall.[1]

The same question could have applied to the film career of James Edwards, who seemed to all but disappear from the picture. His appearance in *Home of the Brave* and the impact that this film made on American society was, by now, nearly ancient history. In 1959, he had appeared in three pictures but none in 1960 or 1961. Sidney Poitier took command as the reigning Black screen god and soon became the first Black man to win an Oscar for Best Actor for his performance in the film *Lilies of the Field* (1963). There was barely enough work in Hollywood for Poitier, let alone the other talented and serious Black male screen actors. Was Edwards' film career over?

Edwards' groundbreaking performance had opened doors as it highlighted the ability of a serious Black actor to play the lead in a dramatic film. Still, eleven years later, Hollywood opportunities for Black actors remained few and far between.

In truth, times were tough for many of the people who made a living in Hollywood. With the launch of the new decade, unemployment in the film industry became an equal-opportunity condition. Even well-established stars from Hollywood's so-called golden years, some of them attempting to "seem relevant in the new times," wrote one scholar, would find decent film parts hard to come by. Hollywood legend and Academy Award winner Bette Davis made no pictures in 1960 and survived the sixties via parts in campy horror films like *What Ever Happened to Baby Jane?* Edwards' *Home of the Brave* co-star Lloyd Bridges hadn't appeared in a feature film since 1958 and made a living from television, as did Douglas Dick and Frank Lovejoy.[2]

The Hollywood film industry, which survived the upheaval of the 1950s, suffered near-collapse in the 1960s when many of the dream factories that once churned out dozens of pictures per month closed and bolted their doors. A number of the Hollywood old guard died, including Harry Cohn, Walt Disney, William Fox, Louis B. Mayer, David O. Selznick, B.P. Schulberg, Joseph Schenck, Albert Warner and his brother, Harry Warner. Along with them, for better or for worse, went the vestiges of the Hollywood studio system.

Film studios changed hands, merged, suffered hostile takeovers, or were purchased by conglomerates with little or no connection to the art of filmmaking. Some studios sold their lots to developers. In December 1962, a real estate firm bought Hal Roach Studios in Culver City. The studio, established during the silent era, was responsible for the production of thousands of one-reelers and full-length comedies featuring early stars such as Stan Laurel and Oliver Hardy. Some companies stayed alive by selling their film libraries to television or by producing television shows. In 1964, the once-mighty Paramount Pictures sold television rights to 200 of its films produced before 1948. Even the once-mighty MGM, in desperate need of cash, auctioned off costumes to the highest bidder. The Hollywood of 1949, which watched bright young actor James Edwards burst onto the scene, all but ceased to exist as the motion picture business struggled to get patrons away from their television sets and into the theatres.

In addition to impending financial ruin, Hollywood was compelled to acknowledge the effects that rapid social change inflicted on the tastes and sensibilities of 1960s moviegoers. America had evolved tremendously since the year that people flocked to the theatre to see *Home of the Brave*. The Cold War, Vietnam, television, student activists and the new American left, gay rights, women's rights, and an increasingly militant civil rights movement — all served to transform the cultural fabric of American society.

Hollywood filmmakers could no longer rely solely on the tried and true formulas of the past. Heroes became anti-heroes, the leading lady was not always appealing, the good guy did not always come out on top, and stories no longer routinely ended on a positive note. Public tastes changed. International film moved from the art houses to the screens of American neighborhood theatres as European and Asian filmmakers used film to comment on the realities of life after World War II. Swedish director Ingmar Bergman offered appreciative cinemaphiles *The Virgin Spring* (1960) and *Persona* (1966), while the bizarre fantasy sequences contained in the works of Italian film director Federico Fellini would coin a new word, *Felliniesque*. As usual, Hollywood would adjust to its rapidly altered circumstances. "The old cinema had not vanished," one scholar observed. "It proposed to coexist with *Psycho, Manchurian Candidate*, and *Little Shop of Horrors*."³

Hollywood, like television, would also be obliged to react to the demands of Black leadership and their allies for more opportunities in front of and behind the camera, as well as for the inclusion of positive depictions of Black life and culture in feature films. Throughout the decade, African Americans appeared in minor roles, cast as everyday citizens; in other movies, most notably those produced by independent producers, scenarios explored graphic racial violence and bigotry. Pictures such as *A Taste of Honey* (1961), *A Raisin in the Sun* (1961), *The Cool World* (1964), *A Patch of Blue* (1965), *For the Love of Ivy* (1968) and *The Learning Tree* (1969) provided fresh and uncommon portraits of Black life as filmmakers explored the pressing issues of the day. Poverty, crime, interracial relationships, Southern-style bigotry, and racial discrimination were depicted in surprisingly frank and occasionally controversial productions released by Hollywood during the decade. Stanley Kramer thrived during the 1960s with his deft production of edgy films that explored timely subject matter, such as *Guess Who's Coming to Dinner* (1968). Opportunities behind the camera for African Americans still remained scarce but were no longer nearly unattainable; and Black filmmakers began to take matters into their own hands and formed their own production companies.

Was James Edwards' film career over? Would he be able to negotiate the Hollywood that would emerge from the ashes of corporate takeovers?

Edwards turned 42 in 1960. His marriage to Leola Mosley was ended and in January 1961 he married Everdinne Wilson, a comely 36-year-old actor-singer who had earned a small part in the 1959 Otto Preminger production *Porgy and Bess*. Eventually, the couple would be comfortably ensconced in Wilson's hometown of San Diego, California. In 1963, they had a baby girl whom they named Eugenia Anne. Edwards' desire to raise a family no doubt had some effect on his career, perhaps a positive one. Though he was no longer employed as a writer with Universal-International, he was still developing screenplays for independent production companies and appeared in theatre.

In 1962 he was cast in a Gene Frankel production of the Jean Genet play *The Blacks*, which explored Black–White relationships. Robert C. Wylder, writing for *The Long Beach Independent Press Telegram (CA)*, described the play as "rebellious," "unorthodox," "nonconformist" and "thoroughly fascinating," noting, "Gene Frankel has worked with what must be one of the best all–Negro casts every assembled on the West Coast, and together they make the play a colorful, gripping experience."[4] The cast included Juanita Moore, with whom Edwards had worked on radio and television.

Edwards' film acting career was not over. In 1961 he hinted to the *California Eagle* that he would come back in a big picture. And in 1962, he appeared, once again as a soldier, in one of the more extraordinary feature films of early 1960s Hollywood.

The Manchurian Candidate

The Manchurian Candidate is considered by some to be the most eerily peculiar Cold War–era political suspense films released by Hollywood during the twentieth century. Edwards appears as the character Corporal Melvin.

The screenplay was written by George Axelrod, drawn from the Richard Condon novel. The film was directed by veteran John Frankenheimer, who learned to shoot pictures as a member of the Air Force Motion Picture Squadron during the Korean Conflict. Before *Manchurian*, he honed his craft by directing dozens of anthology productions on early live television.

Manchurian Candidate featured an extensive cast: Laurence Harvey as the programmed assassin Raymond Shaw, Frank Sinatra as Major Marco, Janet Leigh as Marco's love interest, James Gregory as the reprehensively oily politician Senator Iselin, and Angela Lansbury, who received an Oscar nomination as the intimidating, control-freak traitor, mother to Shaw and wife to Iselin. Harvey, born in 1928 in Lithuania, worked as an actor in England and came to the forefront as the womanizing charmer in the 1960 production *BUtterfield 8* starring Elizabeth Taylor. Janet Leigh, handsome as well as capable as an actor, became a household name with her performance in the shocking Hitchcock thriller *Psycho*. Angela Lansbury, born in London in 1925, was already one of the most respected actors of the period before *Manchurian Candidate*. She earned an Academy Award for her debut Hollywood performance in the 1944 MGM production *Gaslight*, which starred Ingrid Bergman and Charles Boyer. James Gregory was a well-known character actor of both film and television. Sinatra, of course, requires no introduction. Indeed, Edwards was in the company of some of the best performers in Hollywood.

The film opens with a shot of Corporal Melvin (Edwards), a soldier on duty in Korea, who is holed-up in a sleazy dive of a nightspot, surrounded by his squad mates and the comfort women who keep them entertained. The drinks are plentiful and cigarette smoke fills the room. One woman is draped across Melvin's lap and they trade kisses. Sgt. Raymond Shaw, their platoon leader, enters in a huff and calls off the fun, much to the men's dismay. Clearly no one likes him; they mockingly refer to him as St. Raymond. Moments later, while on patrol, the men creep around in murky darkness. Suddenly they are captured, not by the Korean enemy but by Soviet and Chinese operatives.

In a flashback-linked, bizarre and creepy unraveling of the story, we learn that the men were brainwashed during their captivity. Sgt. Shaw, in particular, has been programmed as an assassin. He is triggered to act when he sees the red queen of diamonds in a deck of cards.

In one memorable scene, we see Melvin's squad displayed in front of an audience of Soviet and Chinese operatives described by one critic as "Moscow Frankensteins." The group of perhaps one dozen soldiers in uniform has been programmed to believe that they are sitting at a garden lecture for ladies and in their eyes the audience in front of them consists of women dressed in fancy hats who sip tea and eat cake from saucers. As a female lecturer drones on about the characteristics of the hydrangea, the men yawn and shift in their seats. They cannot see or hear the villains who refer to them as though they were zoo specimens.[5]

To prove that a hypnotized subject can be compelled to commit an act against his moral nature, Raymond is ordered to strangle to death one of his comrades. He submissively complies. Then, as his comrades sit impassively, Raymond uses a pistol to assassinate Bobby, a young, baby-faced squad member.

Eventually the plot begins to unravel. It is Melvin, now a civilian and married man, who suffers from terrible dreams in which he relives the murder of Bobby. We see him awaken with a jolt in the middle of the night to emit a spine-tingling scream. Wide-eyed with horror, he sobs and turns to his wife for comfort.

> What's so awful is to keep dreaming a thing like that about Sgt. Shaw.... I must be going crazy! Raymond Shaw is the most bravest, kindest, warmest, most wonderful human being I've ever met in my life.[6]

Indeed, the man he disliked intensely is now framed in Melvin's mind as a friend, and he recites the same mantra about Shaw that others, too, recite by rote. He sends a letter to Shaw, and we hear Edwards' voiceover as he describes his nightmares. He inquires whether anyone else in their squad has experienced the same problem. With the help of Marco, a Soviet plot is discovered just in the nick of time.

In an interview, writer Axelrod revealed:

> The main trick of *Manchurian* was to make the brainwashing believable. What I did was dramatize the way the prisoners were brainwashed into believing they were attending a meeting of a lady's garden society. I had the further idea of making Corporal Melvin [Edwards] black and doing the whole second half of the dream with black ladies.[7]

The Manchurian Candidate premiered in New York in January 1962. The two-hour black-and-white film opened to mixed reviews. *Time* wrote, "[T]he story is notable chiefly for a systematic error it makes. It tries so hard to be different that it fails to be itself." In his *New York Times* review, Bosley Crowther makes light of the film's implausible, almost ridiculous premise, but concedes, "[I]t must be added that the film is so artfully contrived, the plot so interestingly started, the dialogue so racy and sharp and Frankenheimer's direction is so exciting ... that the fascination of it is strong."[8] Reviewing the film for *Variety*, Vincent Canby presumed that the picture would earn Oscar kudos and wrote,

> Like all the best films, there probably has never been anything quite like *Manchurian Candidate*.... [The film] restores a topical excitement to American films which has been almost totally lacking since Hollywoodites starting taking up residence abroad.[9]

In a chilling quirk of fate, *Manchurian*'s plot centered on the assassination of a presidential candidate. Thirteen months after the film was released President John F. Kennedy was killed by Lee Harvey Oswald, who is believed to have been influenced by Communist ideology, just like the villain of the film. Bad press notwithstanding, in the end the picture was withdrawn because of a dispute over profits between Frank Sinatra, one of the producers, and United Artists head Arthur Krim. The picture was rereleased in the 1980s and has enjoyed an enthusiastic following ever since, and it is now considered an authentic American film classic.

The Sandpiper

In 1965, Edwards appeared in the MGM melodrama, *The Sandpiper*. With a screenplay written by the Hollywood Ten's survivor Dalton Trumbo, the inspired direction of Vincente Minnelli, and the breathtaking photography of Milton Krasner, the operative word for this film is *beauty*. Elizabeth Taylor, young, lithe, and at her best, is simple beautiful as Laura, a free-spirited artist. Taylor's costumes, as well as the main set, an art-filled oceanfront bungalow, are also immensely beautiful. Richard Burton, playing the standoffish Episcopal minister who falls in love with her, is as yet untarnished by the drinking problem that would contribute to his early death. In this film, he is handsome and trim, his blue eyes bright; he too is strikingly beautiful. The photography, particularly the panoramic Panavision and Metrocolor shots of the rugged wave-tossed ocean and the immaculate sands of Northern California's Big Sur region of Monterey provide, as described in *Variety*, "some of the most startlingly beautiful coastline effects ever filmed." All this against the beautiful strains of the Johnny Mandel standard "The Shadow of Your Smile."

Minnelli revealed in his memoirs:

> Though I found the premise of the story ludicrous and dated, I let the Burtons' enthusiasm color my judgment.... [T]he more Dalton Trumbo worked on the story, the more we realized it was too ponderous and pretentious.[10]

The story involves Laura, an artist who wants to raise her son to be liberated. The boy, however, gets himself into trouble with the law and she is ordered to send him to a nearby Episcopal boarding school where Dr. Hewitt, played by Burton, is the headmaster. As soon as Laura enters his office, Hewitt is immediately attracted to her. He fights gamely to hold back his feelings but he soon gives in and they engage in a full-fledged affair.

Hewitt's wife (Eva Marie Saint) seems oddly unaware of her husband's infidelities. Saint, a native of East Orange, New Jersey, was a stage actress who broke into film with her role as Marlon Brando's girl in the 1954 production *On the Waterfront*.

Edwards' appearance in this feature is intriguing. We first see him as he leaps from an open Jeep, dressed in an ocher turtleneck sweater and his face adorned with a scruffy goatee. He is Larry Brandt, friend of sculptor Coz Erickson, played by Charles Bronson. They offer Laura a ride, Brandt assists her into the vehicle, and they speed off.

Later, we see Brandt and Laura at a local gallery where she attempts to convince the reluctant proprietor to exhibit her work. The Reverend Hewitt appears and quickly snaps up the painting. Laura is too flabbergasted to speak so Brandt speaks for her. Dressed in a burgundy jacket and pants, and white turtleneck, he serves as her surrogate manager, and informs the Reverend Hewitt that the painting goes for $100. He assures Laura: "Look baby, with the parson as your patron, you got it made. Think of all those Renaissance cats."

Indeed, the Brandt character is presented as a hipster, replete with colorful clothes, facial hair, and dialogue full of modish slang. In one scene Coz, who also has feelings for Laura, engages Hewitt in a philosophical discussion about the meaning of Nirvana; he attempts to make the reverend look foolish. But it is he who ends up as the butt of the joke. Brandt exclaims, laughing, "Coz, you just been dropped!"

Indeed, the character Larry Brandt is very different from the rather staid and upstanding citizens that Edwards generally portrayed.

Even though Taylor's appearance in the disastrous 1963 Twentieth Century–Fox production *Cleopatra* was still fresh in the minds of Hollywood, for approximately five weeks' work she and Burton would receive $1 million and a percentage of the gross, which totaled more than $14 million. Burton apparently took some offense at Minnelli's direction and challenged him about some of his scenes. At the end he conceded, "For the money, we will dance." *The Sandpiper* was produced by Martin Ransohoff, based on his own story. The cast also featured Robert Webber, Tom Drake, and Morgan Mason, who plays Taylor's eight-year-old son. Minnelli revealed that Taylor wanted Sammy Davis, Jr., for the part of Coz but no one particularly cared for the idea. Minnelli wrote in his memoir, "This would add the suggestion of an interracial romance to the already overburdened story."[11]

In the final sequence, Laura realizes that she is madly in love with

Hewitt. At a raucous, bacchanalian beach party, she has a long scene with Brandt, seeking him out as her confidant as she ponders the ramifications of her affair. They move away from the crowd and the noise. He asks her: "What's so special about this preacher? "All right, come on, let's get it out."

To Brandt, her Negro friend, she bares her soul, revealing how she never knew that any man could be so tender.

For all its beauty, *The Sandpiper* was panned by most critics, some of whom seemed preoccupied with Taylor's brief semi-nude scene where she poses for Coz' sculpture. Hewitt arrives unexpectedly and she covers her bare breasts with her hands.

Edwards as Larry Brandt, Laura's (Elizabeth Taylor) ultra-hip confidant in *The Sandpiper* (1965).

"Charles Bronson and James Edwards represent the more forthright of the character's freethinking friends," wrote Bosley Crowther for the *New York Times*. Edwards "scored," *Variety* noted. Edwards' appearance was casual, not in any way stereotyped, and not part of a racial issue. He was accepted as simply part of the group, a fact that was probably not lost on Black viewers of the period. Moreover, the film was improved with Edwards' appearance, which helped to lend credence to the group's uninhibited lifestyle.[12]

It is interesting to note that even though his stardom had somewhat waned, in 1965 Edwards' name still had enough draw that in some markets he received star billing alongside Taylor and Burton in *Sandpiper* newspaper advertisements. Just as interesting is the fact that just a few years earlier, Edwards appeared in another MGM film—clad in feathers and carrying a spear!

In 1966 Edwards made an appearance in a curious documentary created by self-exiled performer William Van Prince, whose credits include the 1951 Broadway production *The Green Pastures*. The film, called *The Exiles*, documents the stories of self-proclaimed "lost souls": African American performers who had exiled themselves overseas to avoid the racism and discrimination inherent in American society.

While Edwards spent time overseas shooting films, little has been written to suggest that he maintained ties to, or had a permanent home in any foreign country, or considered himself an expatriate. Unknown is what remarks Edwards made in the film about American-style racism or about his experiences as a Hollywood actor. However, Samuel A. Boyea, drama critic for the *Long Beach (CA) Independent* who reported on the film, mused, "Old Mr. Sullen Self, actor James Edwards, was in the vanguard of those who felt the monkey off their backs once they had left the U.S. for Europe. But it was hard to tell whether the monkey ... was self-created[.]"[13]

Coogan's Bluff

In 1968, Edwards played a police officer in the film *Coogan's Bluff*. In this vehicle, Clint Eastwood plays Coogan, a go-it-his-own-way Arizona sheriff who is sent to New York to extradite a dangerous prisoner. His garb, including pointy-toed cowboy boots and ten-gallon hat, cause many to taunt him and refer to him as "Tex." Truly, he looks a fish out of water in comparison to the crumpled suits and ugly neckties worn by his New York police comrades. Further, except for a pretty police psychologist played by Susan Clark, no one likes him and he doesn't particularly like any of them. Coogan accidentally allows the prisoner to escape, and though he is ordered to get out of town and leave the capture of the prisoner to the New York police (Lt. McElroy, played by Lee J. Cobb, coldly tells him he's "out of his league"), he remains, employing his own brand of tactics.

When Coogan visits the mother of the escaped prisoner in her apartment, he encounters Edwards, disguised as a drunken, disheveled bum, camped out in the stairway of the building. In his hand, he grasps a liquor bottle enclosed in a brown paper bag. Coogan rudely lifts him by the scruff of the neck to clear the way. Leaving the apartment, Coogan is swiftly arrested by New York police who haul him away. In the office of Lt. McElroy, Coogan learns that the drunken bum was actually Sgt. Jackson, an undercover police officer staking out the apartment in case the prisoner visited his mother. Jackson is still attired in his costume of a filthy coat; his face is covered with stubble. In no uncertain terms, he relays to Coogan his anger at having had to sit around a grubby, cockroach-infested building for three days, "stinking like a goat," all for naught.

> Do you know what it means when someone's got a stakeout like that established, and some rock-head comes in and blows it ... aw, damn!

The two men eye each other with malice, exchanging barbs, until Lt. McElroy hands Coogan a telegram from his superior. He has been taken off the case. *Coogan's Bluff* was produced and directed by Don Siegel *(Invasion of the Body Snatchers*, 1956, *Dirty Harry*, 1971) from a screenplay by Howard A. Godman, Dean Riesner, and Herman Miller. Though predictable, *Coogan's Bluff*, clearly an Eastwood picture, was well-received, even as it drew criticism for its sex and violence. Particularly striking is a scene where Coogan fights a band of hoods in a pool hall, using balls and cues as weapons. In his *New York Times* review, Richard Coe wrote, "The switch on Eastwood's usual Western settings is cleverly, even wittily thought out."

The Young Runaways

Also in 1968, Edwards appeared as Sgt. Joe Collyer, a police officer, in the Four Lear Productions story *The Young Runaways.* The picture starred Brooke Bundy, Kevin Coughlin, Patty McCormack, Norman Fell, Dick Sargent, and a young Richard Dreyfuss. The film, which premiered in September 1968, dramatized the travails of three rebellious teenagers who run away from home. Some scenes were shot in Edwards' former adopted hometown of Chicago, Illinois.

Doomsday Voyage

Edwards played a small but respectable part in John Vidette's production *Doomsday Voyage*, a film released after his death. Fifteen years after their work together on an episode of *Alfred Hitchcock Presents*, Edwards is once again paired with veteran actor Joseph Cotten, who plays the captain of a freighter.

This curious drama involves a murderous, ideological drifter named Wilson (John Gabriel) who has assassinated a politician. In order to reach safe haven in international waters, he takes as a hostage the young daughter (Katherine Jason) of the captain of a freighter. He threatens to kill her unless he is allowed passage. Edwards, playing the part of an unnamed investigator, boards the vessel and orders his men to conduct a thorough search for stowaways. The killer escapes detection by ordering the girl to pretend to take a shower and he hides in the stall with her.

In what was probably his final film appearance, Edwards appears fit and hail, smartly attired in a well-tailored suit complete with silk handkerchief and hat. Though his hair is flecked with strands of gray, he could easily have passed for a man much younger than his fifty years. In a pivotal scene in their one sequence together, the captain asks his daughter how long she will be in the shower. Edwards, as the officer, makes a sly attempt to peek through the slightly opened door of the bathroom, ostensibly, of course, as part of his job. The father of the girl gives Edwards the eye.

With its flashbacks, flash-forwards, cross-cutting, and purposeful pairing of veteran and no-name actors, *Doomsday Voyage* is most likely one of the more novel films in which Edwards appeared.

22. The Black Revolution

When four Black students from North Carolina A&T launched their sit-in at the segregated lunch counter of a local Woolworth's in 1960, they helped to set the stage for the most revolutionary changes in the status of African Americans since emancipation. Over the coming years, freedom riders risked their lives to integrate public accommodations; volunteers helped Black citizens to exercise their rights as voters; marchers joined arms for protest rallies; and, on a warm day in August, a Baptist preacher named the Rev. Dr. Martin Luther King, Jr., organized the March on Washington for jobs and freedom, attracting more than 200,000 people.

The 1960s was a bellwether for the American civil rights movement, the high point of which was the 1964 signing of the Civil Rights Act by President Lyndon Johnson, giving the federal government the power to prosecute discrimination in education, employment and voting. The effects of these events would transform most sectors of American society.

On American television, none of the most-watched programs of the early 1960s, including *The Andy Griffith Show* (1960–1968), *The Beverly Hillbillies* (1962–1971), and *The Dick Van Dyke Show* (1961–1966), featured a Black character in a central, recurring role. In the perennially popular television Western, the settling of the American West was generally portrayed as all–White history. Appearances on television by a Black performer were limited largely to variety shows and to infrequent parts written specifically for a Black actor.

Media critics and civil rights officials tendered their complaints: about the absence of Black faces in television commercials; about the negative typing of Black life and culture in television programming; about the dearth of Black professionals working behind the scenes as writers, directors and technicians; and the fact that stories that foreground Black issues were often deemed too controversial for primetime. "DOGS HAVE TELE-

VISION SHOWS. NEGROES DON'T" read a sign carried by one protester at the August 1963 march.[1]

In 1962, Hilda Simms, Sidney Poitier, and Ossie Davis testified before the House Committee on Education and Labor, headed by New York Representative Adam Clayton Powell, Jr. Simms voiced her dissatisfaction on a number of issues, including the scarcity of television and film parts for Black actors and the negative typing of Black life and culture in the various entertainment media. Poitier, who revealed that he had not played a suitable role on television since 1955, told the committee, "It is virtually impossible for Negro actors to earn a steady livelihood in the American theatre, movies, or broadcasting."[2]

But the complexion of American television would soon be changed. "There are still no continuing programs with Negroes as stars," notes the *Washington Post* in a 1963 article, "but one of the most easily observable features of the new television season is an increase in the number of Negro performers." *Time* magazine noted, "[T]his fall, as never before, television shows are reflecting the Negro revolution. Negro actors are finding work — and they are getting roles that could be filled by whites."[3]

With some trepidation, television programmers attempted to provide a more equitable treatment of Black life and culture in the primetime lineup. A subtle but significant shift took hold. Dramatic programs such as *Naked City* (1958–1963), *The Eleventh Hour* (1963–1964), *East Side/West Side* (1963), *The Defenders* (1961–65), and *The Fugitive* (1963–67) cast Black actors in parts not necessarily written for Black characters, and presented stories that touched upon problems such as social unrest in the Black community. Some programs experimented with interracial parity, including *NYPD* (1967–1969), *Mission: Impossible* (1966–1969), *Daktari* (1966–1969) and the mainstay *Star Trek* (1966–1969) which co-starred African American actress Nichelle Nichols as Lieutenant Uhura. Clarence Williams III appeared afroed and militant in the show *The Mod Squad* (1968–1973), while the articulate and sensible multi-racial educators of *Room 222* (1969–1974) addressed the concerns of a diverse student population. In the espionage program *I Spy* (1965–1968), Robert Culp and Bill Cosby shared equal status. And no discussion of the period would be complete without a mention of *Julia* (1968–1970), featuring Edwards' companion Diahann Carroll in the leading role of Julia, facetiously referred to as the most assimilated Black character to appear in the American mass media.

In November 1967, the Public Broadcast Library ran a broadcast of the Douglas Turner Ward play *A Day of Absence*. The plot is a fictional day when all Black folks in America disappeared. Suddenly there were no butlers to answer the door, no nursemaids, cooks, cleaners, bootblacks, porters, street-sweepers, or others to do the taken-for-granted menial work of the community. The thinly veiled, anti–White message ruffled more than a few feathers. Yet in some ways, the fantasy depicted was mirrored in primetime American television, as the image of Black citizens as the happy, ever-faithful Black maids and servants so common on early programs gave way to Black characters with intelligence and assertiveness.

The shift would not go unnoticed. Networks suffered backlash from advertisers, media critics, and local officials who railed against programs that contained glimpses of race mixing, fearing that such would promote familiarity between Black men and White women. In October 1963, the Knights of the Ku Klux Klan staged a well-attended rally in Rayville, Louisiana, to protest television shows that "exaggerate the use of Negroes in their casts and advertising."[4]

Edwards was a principal player in postwar social problem theatre and motion pictures that explored controversial issues such as American style racism; it is interesting that he found himself a frequent player in social problem television of the 1960s. Storylines dealing with sensitive issues such as race relations would have been considered subversive during the dark years of Communist witch-hunts. But as Buhle and Wagner note in their discussion of the Hollywood blacklist, by 1963 such subject matter would be explored in a number of series starring "well-known progressives such as Ossie Davis and Ruby Dee, but also Diahann Carroll, James Edwards, Cicely Tyson and Diana Sands."[5]

Edwards appeared comfortable with the medium's limitations and some of his early '60s performances are striking. But his portrayals are unusual for other reasons, as he was one of a handful of Black actors who was cast in roles, not as the token *Negro character* but as an everyday American facing life's problems, challenges, and triumphs. He played a cowboy, a professional, a family man, and a police officer, offering television viewers of the period a rare glimpse of an authentic Black American citizen.

East Side/West Side

In 1963, Edwards appeared on the television drama *East Side/West Side*; one of the most challenging, controversial, debated and discussed, overtly political primetime shows to air during the decade. It was developed by seminal writer, producer, and talk-show host David Susskind. Talented, driven, sometimes abrasive, and outspoken, he is reported to have declared that 95 percent of what was shown on television was trash. Still, he claims that the development of *East Side/West Side* was his response to FCC Chair Newton Minow's complaints about the poor quality of television programming.[6]

East Side/West Side, ran at 10 P.M. on CBS. The episodes were filmed mostly in New York. The cast featured George C. Scott as Neil Brook, a social worker assigned to a blighted urban neighborhood (in '60s terms, a slum). Cecily Tyson, who would later earn applause by appearing in the seminal film *The Autobiography of Miss Jane Pittman*, was also featured as a regular on the show, as the secretary Jane.

Taking on such contentious subject matter as prostitution, rape, mental handicaps, and the plight of Puerto Rican immigrants, *East Side/West Side* was largely well-received by critics. The *Washington Post* noted, "As the weeks go by, appreciation grows for the extraordinary quality that continues to turn up on *East Side/West Side*."[7]

In one of the more storied episodes, "Who Do You Kill?" Diana Sands and James Earl Jones play a lower-class couple living in a Harlem slum. They answer the cries of their infant child only to find, to their horror, that a rat attracted by the smell of milk is attacking the baby. Not surprisingly, many Southern television stations refused to air the episode.

East Side/West Side often presented episodes that dealt with the ramifications of life in the slums. By 1960, 95 years after the end of slavery, Black citizens had made immense progress. Many had even achieved the American Dream of owning property, receiving a college education, and/or finding success in government, politics, business, and the military. Still, a large segment of the Black population was left behind, awash in a world of poverty and despair. Hundreds of thousands were segregated in ghettos: neighborhoods replete with vermin, vice and violence, located on filthy avenues strewn with the homeless, vagrants, criminals, junkies, uncollected trash, feral cats, and packs of stray dogs. Poor people were warehoused in "the projects": dilapidated and ill-kept government-sanctioned, high-rise housing. In some cases, even the local police were afraid to venture into the dimly lit, urine-streaked hallways of the projects to assist someone in need. Indeed, for some American citizens, attempting to negotiate life in the slums was a cruel fact of life. Surviving, rising above, or escaping slum life was a topic popularly addressed in plays, films, popular music, jokes, and dramatic television shows created during the period.

In addition, America in many ways remained a nation where systematic discrimination and overt or covert racism remained a fact of life for people of color. Innocent Black citizens too often found themselves victims of police brutality, residential segregation, disfranchisement, lynching, and injustices in the court system.

This delicate subject matter also made its way into teleplays of programs such as *East Side/West Side*.

In 1963, Edwards, billed as "special guest star," appeared as Mr. Jackson in the episode "Where's Harry?" It is the story of Herschel "Harry" Bernstein, played by Simon Oakland, who simply and inexplicably picks up and runs away from home. He is a late middle-aged man with a successful business and, as he later describes, "a big house with a built-in bar, garage, faithful wife, and handsome son." He turns up at the door of Mr. and Mrs. Jackson, a lower-middle class Black family operating a small grocers in an all–Black slum neighborhood. Bernstein wants to rent the ill-furnished room above the shop. Mrs. Jackson is immediately suspicious: Bernstein is in distress, he's obviously quite ill, and she wants no part of him. "Why is trouble always White?" she asks no one in particular. Indeed, "Where's Harry?" is two stories in one. There is Bernstein's emotional crisis and the story of a lower class Black family trying to rise above their circumstances.[8]

Mr. Jackson shows more empathy towards Bernstein; moreover, he is glad to have the $50 rent. His family is preparing to move out of the ghetto and into their first home: a huge achievement and a big occasion. In the secondary storyline we follow Mrs. Bernstein who, seven months after her husband's disappearance, is falling apart emotionally. Fate brings her to the office of Neil Brook, who sets about to help her.

Bernstein rented the meager space because it just happens to be the room where his immigrant Jewish family lived when he was a child. The space hasn't changed much in 25 years: It is sparsely furnished with a sink and an icebox. A single light bulb hangs from the ceiling. Bernstein is a man in despair because although he has achieved much in terms of money and status, as an individual he feels empty. When Jackson asks him how things changed for him, Bernstein ruefully reflects upon his success: "The houses got bigger, but the people got smaller."

In a later scene, dressed in an open-collared plaid shirt and trousers covered by a white butcher's apron, Jackson checks on his tenant.

> A man who takes a room like this is at the end of the line. But you're not. Look, you've got money, your clothes are fancy tailored, and you're wearing a wedding ring on your finger. Now, what are you doing here?

Bernstein wants Jackson to appreciate what he has; they debate the pros and cons of being poor. He asks Jackson if he's been happy here, where his family has lived for many years. Jackson reveals:

> Sometimes at night when the store is closed ... the boy is doing his homework ... the baby's sleepy and soft in my lap ... my wife's brushing her hair ... yes, yes, I guess it's good then.

With the help of a physician, who happens to have known Bernstein for years, and with the help of Brock, Bernstein is reunited and reconciled with his wife. The Jacksons enjoy their moving day. No fancy explanation or clever plot devices tie up loose ends; indeed, "Where's Harry?" is a think piece.

Edwards provides a consummate and well-reasoned interpretation of the character Mr. Jackson. He commands the space of the small screen, revealing his character's makeup with sensitivity, efficiency and realism, and without obvious overplaying. Indeed, Edwards seems much more at ease than George C. Scott, who, at times, looks stiff and uncomfortable. Further, as the character Jackson, he is no one-dimensional set piece. He has a wife (who is a bit of a shrew) and two children, one a precocious boy of about ten. Jackson is not bloodless but real; he is allowed his humanity.

For various reasons, *East Side/West Side* (called by one scholar a "pragmatic program with little action but deep thought") would last only one season. Scott revealed that he was uninspired by the television medium. Some Southern stations chose not to air programs with Black themes and characters. In November 1963, Arnold Perl, executive producer of the show, decided not to continue but to "go on to other things." Additionally, the assassination of President John F. Kennedy in November 1963 darkened the mood of the nation; gloomy themes became a bit less appreciated. Indeed, most scholars agree that the program's authentic depiction of life was well done but the program was perhaps ahead of its time.[9]

The Fugitive

In 1963, Edwards appeared as Joe Smith in a splendid episode of ABC's hit program *The Fugitive* (1963–1967). "The Decision in the Ring" is notable in that it presents issues of race although the story is not about race but the desire of one man to overcome his circumstances.

The Fugitive presented the story of Dr. Richard Kimble, who is falsely accused of the murder of his wife. He adamantly maintains his innocence and claims that he saw a one-armed man running from his home on the night of his wife's slaying but he is convicted anyway. He manages to escape from the police and the program follows him, on the run, as he takes on various personas and odd jobs to remain hidden, support himself, and continue his search for the one-armed man. *The Fugitive* featured David Janssen in the title role.

In "Decision in the Ring," Ruby Dee plays Joe's wife Laura Smith and Hari Rhodes plays Dan, his sparring partner and up-and-coming middleweight hopeful. The fact of Edwards' appearance on the show was widely covered in the press, with papers reporting how the television industry and Hollywood responded to pressure from the civil rights movement to produce storylines about race, and to use Black actors in roles.

In the opening teaser, we see Smith stripped to the waist and attired in silk boxing trunks as he takes on an opponent in a boxing ring. The crowd noise is deafening, nearly drowning out the sound of the bell ending the round. It is exciting to watch Edwards, a former Golden Gloves alternate, utilizing the skills he acquired some thirty years earlier when he briefly made a living as a prizefighter. By this time, Edwards was nearly 45 years old but easily plays the part of someone who could be half his age. Trim and athletic, he dances around the ring, feinting and showing a bit of fancy footwork; Edwards' acting is spot-on. While this is not the first or only time he was cast as a prizefighter, it is the only time he is actually seen boxing.

Smith suffers a bad cut above his left eye and is bleeding heavily but early in the next round he knocks out his opponent, winning the bout. Back in the locker room, when his corner man is unable to stop the bleeding, Kimble, working incognito as an orderly for the coliseum, comes up with a solution of adrenaline crystals to ebb the flow of blood. Joe's manager, a shyster named Lou (played by veteran actor James Dunn), hires Kimble, much to the consternation of sparring partner Dan, who doesn't trust Kimble.

Later, Joe and Dan go running and Joe outruns the car that follows them. We see Joe in the ring during a sparring match with Dan, who tries to best him but who himself is bested. Joe teases, "What you trying to prove, Dan?"

At a racially integrated party, Lou excitedly extols the virtues of "his boy," the soon-to-be champion, Joe Smith. Smith appears with his wife Laura. They are very affectionate: He places his hand around her waist and hers around his. Alone with Kimble, Laura reveals that Joe was a boxing champ in college but that his real ambition was to become a doctor. After two years of medical school he turned to prizefighting, not only because he didn't want her to be the family's breadwinner but, as she explains, "It's complicated ... Joe's complicated."

Later we learn that there are other matters that trouble Laura Smith. Joe's cognitive skills show signs of compromise. He forgets things. We later find that Joe realizes the truth about his health but remains in denial.

Not until Act III do we learn Joe's reasons for choosing the fight game over a medical career. As he sees it, he not only earns a good living as a boxer but, as a popular figure, he commands the respect denied the average Black man in America. He tries to persuade an unconvinced Laura:

> People pay $5 to see me fight ... would they pay it for treatment if I were a doctor? No, Laura, I couldn't take it after feeling how nice and warm it is here.... Oh, Laura, Laura, can't you understand? I can hold up my head! I can't go back!

It is Kimble who suggests a strategy for Laura to use to save her husband from possible permanent injury: "I only know that before a person gives up one thing for another, he has to want that one thing more."

Just hours before the big fight, Laura, in a calm but unambiguous way, tells Joe to give up fighting or she will leave him. She moves her luggage from their hotel room and returns home.

Now Kimble works on Joe. They are alone in his room in the arena. Lou, Dan and his other handlers are upstairs watching the other fights in progress. Kimble and Joe have it out; there are no raised fists or voices, just debate. He tries to explain his motives to Kimble:

> We'd be choking to death for the rest of our lives. A Negro doctor in some slum, a ghetto? Who are you to stand there so high and mighty and tell me to go back when now they say, "There goes Joe Smith the fighter?"

At the end, a detective sent to investigate Lou figures out Kimble's real identity. Joe relents and reveals to Lou that he is sick and can no longer fight. He returns home to Laura and in a tender scene they embrace. He takes her face in his hands and plants a kiss upon her lips. "Decision in the Ring" addresses a daring theme for the time: one Black man's determination to overcome the limitations imposed upon him. Too, the episode provided another audacious depiction: a rare glimpse of an affectionate, married Black couple.

By 1963, Edwards had been married to the former Everdinne Wilson for nearly two years. His daughter Euginia was born that year. Perhaps family life appealed to him: He not only appeared in great physical condition but seemed comfortable and confident. The part of Joe Smith is one of Edwards' best early '60s television roles. He appears in many scenes (action-filled and dramatic), the fight scenes are realistic and well choreographed, the dialogue was first-rate and the good story compelling.

The Eleventh Hour

CBS's pseudo-medical drama *The Eleventh Hour* (1962–1963) distinguished itself with good writing and acting. The program portrayed the life of a forensic psychiatrist, Theodore Bassett, played by Ralph Bellamy. The episodes tackled themes then considered taboo: illegitimate children, teenage pregnancy, abortion, rape, and homosexuality.

Some sources note that Edwards appeared as Ettinger in a November 1963 episode called "Who Chopped Down the Cherry Tree?" The episode featured Robert Ryan, Edwards' co-star from the 1949 film *The Set-Up*, and Peggy Ann Garner, Richard Anderson, Harvey Korman, Walter King, and Buzz Martin.

The story concerned big-time small-town politics. Considered a shoo-in, politician Franklin Hopp chooses to do the right thing by rallying against a pork-barrel project. His actions raise the ire of local businessmen who stand to line their pockets and who conspire, with the help of Hopp's own brother, to have him committed as a psychiatric case. With the help of Bassett, Hopp is discharged but his political career is over. Still, he has succeeded in canceling the project and retaining his dignity. Edwards was perhaps cast as one of the three businessmen who attempt to bully Hopp into reconsidering his position; his lines of dialogue are few.

The Joey Bishop Show

In 1963, Edwards made one of his seemingly rare forays into comedy, appearing in an episode of *The Joey Bishop Show* (1962–1964, NBC; 1964–1965, CBS) called "Double Exposure." Bishop's program would undergo a number of changes over its three-year history, but in 1963 Bishop played the character Joey Barnes, a comedian. This sitcom was more comic than situation, with a focus on shtick and humorous repartee, heightened by Bishop's deadpan delivery. In "Double Exposure," comedian Barnes performs a set at a men's prison. One of the prisoners, Lightfingers Leon (also played by Bishop), looks remarkably like Barnes, save his thick glasses. When he catches Barnes alone, he whaps him over the head and changes clothes with him. Before he can manage his escape, he encounters two prison guards dressed in dark uniforms and carrying billy clubs (Frank Lewis and Edwards). The guards chat with the man they think is Barnes, ask for his autograph, and are pleasantly surprised that he knew their names without being told. Though the part is small and his lines are few, Edwards, not a complete stranger to comedy, seems to enjoy himself in the Bishop vehicle.

Going My Way

In 1963, Edwards was cast as Sgt. Wilson in an episode of the short-lived "dramady" *Going My Way* (1962–63, ABC). The show starred actor-dancer Gene Kelly and veteran performer Leo Carroll as parish priests who apparently have so much time on their hands that they can spend most of it embroiled in the problems of their parishioners. In the episode "Run, Robin, Run," Juanita Moore plays the mother of a troubled young man, portrayed by Ivan Dixon. When the man is accused of a crime, it is Wilson, a gruff, no-nonsense precinct sergeant, who gives the priests one day to find the boy before he is picked up.

DuPont Show of the Week

In 1955, Edwards appeared in the *DuPont Cavalcade of America*'s biographical presentation of the life of African American educator, civil rights leader, and Nobel Peace Prize winner Ralph Bunche. The episode was titled "Toward Tomorrow." In June 1964, Edwards appeared on the *DuPont Show of the Week*, one of the few anthology programs still airing in primetime. The episode, "Ambassador at Large," was a story about the State Department's involvement with the dictatorial leader of a fictitious Latin American country. Cast members include Larry Hagman, Peter Falk,

Oscar Homolka, Andrew Duggan, and Arthur Kennedy, who co-starred with Edwards in the 1951 film *Bright Victory*. The episode was directed by Franklin Schaffner, with whom Edwards would work on *Patton* in 1970.

The Nurses

The storylines of the program *The Nurses* (1962–1965, CBS) exploited such socially conscious themes as euthanasia and capital punishment, while depicting the workings of a large urban hospital. Hilda Simms, former star of the stage version of *Anna Lucasta*, who appeared with Edwards in *The Joe Louis Story*, was a regular during the second season of the program. In one noted episode, Ruby Dee portrays a nurse determined to divest herself — physically and emotionally — from her ghetto upbringing. In the February 1964 episode "The Roamer," Edwards appeared as Hudson, a strong-willed social worker trying to rehabilitate a young delinquent boy. He clashes with a nurse who prefers to mother the wayward lad. "Edwards offered an excellent example of a social worker attacking the core of this job," noted a critic for the *Bridgeport (CT) Post*.[10]

Dr. Kildare

Today, the popular 1960s television hospital drama *Dr. Kildare* (1961–1966, NBC) looks like the period piece it is: Patients smoke in their rooms; nurses are bedecked in starchy white cotton dresses and high hats; telephones are black analogue sets with noisy rotary dials.

In 1965, Edwards appeared as Dr. Lench in a compelling three-part story about a group of people who must choose who will live and who will die. In the teaser of the first episode, "The Life Machine," a group of physicians gather around a new piece of medical equipment, a room-sized contraption of aluminum and plastic. Dr. Lench explains, "For the first time in medical history, patients whose kidneys have ceased to function can go on living."

They are referring to an artificial kidney, commonly referred to today as dialysis. In part two of the story, "Hour of Decision," Edwards joins a group made up of physicians, community leaders, and a member of the clergy to commence the unenviable task of selecting the candidates who will receive the new life-saving treatment. Lench explains, "There's only room for four more persons out of the eleven who are medically eligible. Let's make sure that we choose the most deserving."

Lench and his colleagues sit at a round conference table covered with patient charts and reports. Who will live and who will die? Cigarette in hand, Lench joins his colleagues in a brief summation of each patient's spiritual values, artistic talent, intellect, marital status, and family responsibilities; they, too, must explore their own, unconscious prejudices. One candidate is an unemployed man with few prospects beyond a recent job offer contingent upon his being healthy enough to work. A doctor callously dismisses him with "But the man never amounted to anything!"

Lench explodes: "Amounted to anything? Because he's never made the money you have? You have been more concerned about material things!"

The chaplain interjects himself into the fray and the argument is defused. The two men apologize to each other and Lench concedes that it was all his fault.

The candidates for the life machine are not revealed until episode three. Lench does not appear in the episode. Cloris Leachman, who was enrolled at Northwestern University at the same time as Edwards, appears in this episode as the wife of a patient.

23. Final Curtain

In 1969, Edwards told his hometown paper, "Now I am 51. I know my work and I am very competent."[1] Not only was Edwards competent, he was a survivor. Professionally, he had survived the lean years when Hollywood teetered on the brink of financial collapse; the awful period of the Red Scare when blacklisting made good acting jobs increasingly more difficult to obtain; and the dearth of parts for serious Black Hollywood actors. Too, he was a survivor on a personal level, having battled back his own demons and staying alive long enough to witness the final memorials of some of his colleagues and associates.

James Gow, co-writer of *Deep Are the Roots,* the play which helped put Edwards' name onto the entertainment pages of the newspaper, died of a heart attack at age 44 in 1952; Humphrey Bogart, star of *The Caine Mutiny,* died of cancer a few years after the release of the 1954 film; Frank Lovejoy, Edwards' co-star in *Home of the Brave,* died of heart failure in 1962; Dick Powell, the brain behind Four Star Productions and the personable host of *Zane Grey Theatre* and *The Lloyd Bridges Show,* died in 1964. Performer Nat "King" Cole, who appeared with Edwards in *Night of the Quarter Moon,* succumbed to cancer in 1964 at age 50. How surprising it must have been for Edwards to learn of the death of Dorothy Dandridge in 1965. Though they had not appeared in a film together, in 1954, he had worked with her on her *Carmen Jones* screen test.

Edwards came back to his hometown of Anderson, Indiana, in 1969, visiting with his father, James Valley Edwards, and an aunt. He had recently returned from shooting a film in Germany and was on his way to Spain to begin work on *Patton*. He told his paper how he had managed to carve out a niche in one of the most competitive businesses: "I didn't care whether I was green, blue, purple, or white. "I knew if I was good enough, they'd have to come along and buy me someday ... and they did."[2]

Twenty years had passed since his triumphant portrayal in the history-altering *Home of the Brave*. His acting style had evolved. He was now the elder statesman, an acting veteran, and his performances took on an attention-grabbing luster. He often portrayed characters with chips on their shoulders: police officers who barked out orders and rarely smiled, or bad-tempered cowboys with personal problems. Was this persona a style that he purposefully cultivated or did his real guise spill over into his portrayals? How much of what he portrayed was clever acting vs. his actual demeanor? Edwards is sometimes described as having been angry. No doubt his final acting performances contributed to this perception of him.

Regardless, Edwards' late work displays some of his best acting, from minor roles where he appeared in only one sequence, to the parts that allowed him to display his full range of skills as an actor. As usual, whether walk-on or lead, he never disappeared into the haze of characters but managed to make his presence known. With finesse and skillfulness, and no doubt a good measure of egotism, he always stood out.

Color Me German

The NBC show *Experiment in Television* represented a unique programming concept in that the network tried in earnest, as described by *Newsweek*, to "put something different on the tube":

> Black poets read their lines on a street corner in Watts. A deaf actor plays out a Hamlet soliloquy on his hands ... now in its second season, *Experiment* is a rarity in network television.[3]

Working with a tiny budget of less than a half-million dollars per season, Tom McAvity, program manager for the series, ran both dramatic and non-dramatic programs that included pseudo-documentaries, dramatic readings, and love stories. Unfortunately, *Experiment in Television*, which aired on Sunday afternoons, attracted a tiny audience and an even tinier roster of regular sponsors. Though the recipient of a 1969 Peabody Award, the program was cancelled after three seasons.[4]

In February, 1969, Edwards appeared in a film that aired on the program: *Color Me German* was produced and directed by Victor Vicas and written by Manya Starr, creator of the short-lived soap ABC soap opera *The Clear Horizon*. *Color Me German* is the story of a middle-aged Black schoolteacher visiting Germany to see his Afro-German nephew, a boy who wants to believe that he is accepted by German society even though his German mother has been ostracized by her family for birthing an illegitimate, mixed-race* child. The idea for *Color Me German* was Edwards' own. He had a real-life Afro-German nephew named Charles whom he visited in Switzerland and brought to America to meet the Edwards family.

Color Me German was shot in Munich, Germany, and starred Ron Williams as Hans; Edwards was cast as Wesley Potter; and Rosemarie Fendel plays Helga, Hans' mother. Amongst her other problems, she must choose between her love for her 23-year-old son and the love of the German man who wishes to marry her but who doesn't want Hans around. Potter wades through his own personal challenges. He is unsure of his place in the new, more militant Black community in the United States and even considers a permanent move to Germany. At the same time he feels it is his duty to school his nephew about the way of the world, including the plain fact that he is *not*, as he believes, accepted by most of German society. Furthermore, he must deal with the attraction he has for Helga.

While the audience may have been small, the airing of *Color Me German* did not go unnoticed and attracted good reviews. On February 16, 1969, Edwards, Williams, and Fendel were featured in a large publicity shot that appeared on the television page of the *New York Times*. A week prior, NBC Television ran an advertisement citing the success of the *Experiment in Television* series, using "Color Me German" as an example. A review in *Time* magazine was complimentary of the direction of Victor Vicas but complained of the script, noting:

> The structural weakness of the play was the poorly defined visiting uncle of the boy who vacillated between wanting to find acceptance by whites and committing himself to the cause of Negro rights.[5]

However, most critiques were highly positive. The *Independent Press-Telegram (Long Beach, CA)* declared, "There was no major 'experiment' in the fine piece of work by writer Manya Starr. It was simply a first-rate contribution to television, far superior to almost anything seen in the prime time...." *Time* later called "Color Me German" one of the four most impressive shows of the *Experiment in Television* series.[6]

This was Edwards' second performance in a story dealing with issues of Afro-German identity precipitated by liaisons between African American men and German women during the Second World War: In 1955, he appeared in a General Electric Theatre *called "D.P." ("Displaced Person").*

Amos Burke, Secret Agent

The program *Burke's Law* was a spin-off of an episode of *The Dick Powell Theatre*, starring actor Powell as the first Burke. *Burke's Law* featured Gene Barry as a suave and dashing, millionaire private detective. In 1965, network executives decided to fiddle with the program's premise. "ABC threw us a curve with the 'James Bond' craze," wrote Aaron Spelling, the show's producer. "Suddenly secret agents were in ... *Burke's Law* was forcibly changed." Therefore, by the time Edwards appeared in 1966, the ABC program had been transformed into *Amos Burke, Secret Agent* (1963–1966). While Napoleon Solo and Illya Kuryakin worked for U.N.C.L.E., Burke worked for SECOR.[7]

Edwards was cast in a two-part episode called "Terror in a Tiny Town," written by Marc Blandel and Murray Golden. The premise and staging of this curious story is unusual, resembling a mixture of *Twilight Zone* and *The Manchurian Candidate*, and though far-fetched and implausible, the story nonetheless is very engaging.

The people of the small town of Sorrell are maniacal in their defense of their close-knit community. They are especially proud of their radio station, KJAH. Moreover, they are hostile and suspicious of outsiders. When questioned, like automatons they recite the same mantra. After a man is shot and killed by a police officer under strange circumstances, Burke is sent by SECOR to investigate, only to become entangled in the bizarre goings-on.

At first glance, one might be dismayed to see that Edwards, who appears as John Norton, is the proprietor of a shoeshine stand. Edwards, who refused roles as a menial and prided himself on taking only dignified parts, cast as a lowly bootblack? After finishing Burke's shoes, he receives a silver dollar as payment. But this is no ordinary silver dollar. Earlier, we watched Burke make a recording of his findings onto a tiny CD-like cylinder which he hid in a coin. Norton is no bootblack but a secret agent working with Burke. They tip each other the wink. Later, a Sorrell police officer questions Norton as to what happened to the man who used to run the stand. "He's on vacation. I'm his cousin. Can't you see the family resemblance?"

This veiled dig at the old "all Negroes look alike" jibe is one of many written into this unusual teleplay. Later, Burke meets a woman named Ruth, played by Monica Keating, who does not act as oddly as her fellow townspeople — but then, she does not listen to the town radio station. The two make plans to meet at the Kit Kat Klub. As the door of the club opens, we see the letters "KKK" emblazoned over the bar, an obvious reference to the violent American organization.

In Part 2 of "Terror in a Tiny Town," we learn from Burke that agent Norton's stand was destroyed by hooligans and Norton is in the hospital. The townspeople next conspire to get rid of Burke. They set him up: When he walks into the neighborhood laundry and discovers the lifeless body of a man stuffed in a still-running clothes dryer, he is charged with the murder.

At the trial, Norton is summoned to testify against Burke. "I know about him," Norton reveals. "I knew he wasn't up to any good ... everybody in town knows that."

Norton appears hesitant and confused; his words are halting. It appears that he, too, has been indoctrinated into the regime ... or was he?

> PROSECUTOR: Mr. Norton, you've been in Sorrell Hospital for several weeks now. Did you receive good treatment?"
> NORTON: Yes, I received good treatment.... Music? Yeah, I had plenty music. I had a radio ... it was playing all the time.

Hence, we learn that the entire town has been brainwashed through the local radio station which runs 24-hour subliminal suggestions. A right-wing subversive organization is using the town as part of a plan to take over the U.S. government and turn America into "an obedient, disciplined nation ... all tuned into the same wavelength."

It must be noted that in close-ups, Edwards does not look particularly well. His once attractive face instead appears haggard and careworn; his lips swollen and his face marked. Was his less than healthy appearance a consequence of the technological shortcomings of sixties television? Or was he perhaps not at his best?

Television viewers apparently did not care very much for *Amos Burke* and the show never attracted enough loyal fans to sustain the program. Producer Aaron Spelling said, "I hated it."[8]

The Outsider

In 1968 Edwards was cast as Lt. Wagner, an ill-tempered police detective, on the NBC crime drama *The Outsider*. Darren McGavin plays the renegade private investigator David Ross. With his appearance on this program, Edwards makes his transition from the murky black-and-white imagery of early television to the clearer, sharper technology of color television. He appeared in perhaps two episodes of the program. In "Tell It Like It Was ... and You're Dead," an aging but vivacious former burlesque dancer decides to reveal the indelicate details of her past in a tell-all book. There are people who do not wish to see the book published and she hires Ross to find out who is trying to kill her. Unfortunately, she ends up dead before he can unravel the mystery.

Wagner, who doesn't care for Ross' style, picks him up for questioning on a regular basis. In one scene, he circles the seated private investigator, glaring at him and peppering him with questions about the dancer's murder. Cigarette in hand, Edwards looks dapper in a dark suit, his face adorned with a thin mustache and short-cropped hair. Though there are other officers present, it is clear that Wagner is in charge of this investigation. Ross eventually solves the case without the help of the police. The episode also featured Ted Knight, like Edwards a former cast member of the daytime soap *The Clear Horizon*, and former child star Jackie Coogan, who worked with Edwards in *Night of the Quarter Moon*. Edwards again appears as Wagner in the episode "I Can't Hear You Scream," which paired him with Juanita Moore, with whom he worked in film, radio, and television; and Myron Healey, his co-star from *African Manhunt* (1955).

Cowboy in Africa

ABC's pseudo-western *Cowboy in Africa* (1967–1968) featured Chuck Connors as a former rodeo star hired by an Englishman to run a Kenyan ranch. The program, which was filmed in Africa and on American sets, ran for one year on ABC. In the 1968 episode "A Man of Value," Edwards plays Shendi Suakin. The leader of the fictional African country New Gali, he is kidnapped by criminals of the colonial powers who wish to silence him and his political movement. Edwards spends most of the first two sequences prostrate, with his face completely bandaged in gauze and his acting limited to a few groans of pain. The third sequence shows Suakin, who has escaped his captors, being led through the forest by an orphaned boy named Sampson. Edwards, now in his late forties, exhibits a receding hairline but was apparently in good enough condition to play the rather physical part which had him climbing through a window. Only in the very last scene, when Suakin's kidnappers have been rounded up, could Edwards put his acting skill to any good use. He lies prone and bleeding from his injuries, with his eyes focused wistfully at the sky as he offers an emotive speech about how the experience changed his thinking and reinvigorated his commitment as he declares, "I am involved in all mankind."

The Outcasts

In 1969, Edwards appeared in an episode of ABC's short-lived, hour-long Western, *The Outcasts* (1968–1969). The premise of this program seems a bit out of place for the hip and socially conscious year 1969: Don Murray plays a former Virginia aristocrat and Otis Young is Jemal, a recently freed slave. A quirk of fate forces them together and though neither trusts the other, they work together to eke out a living as gunman and bounty hunter in the post–Civil War West. In the episode "My Name Is Jemal," Jemal is mistaken for another man, played by Edwards, who is wanted by the authorities.

"A few fine Negro performers are given a showcase in this complicated western tale," wrote the *Kokomo (IN) Tribune*. "James Edwards gives an interesting performance as the wanted man with an unusual history."[9]

The Virginian

Based loosely on the 1902 Owen Wister classic *The Virginian: A Horseman of the Plains,* this Western aired on NBC from 1962 to 1970. The program is notable as being the only 90-minute show of the genre.

Many episodes featured well-known stars with whom Edwards had worked with previously, such as George C. Scott, Charles Bronson, and Lee Marvin, as well as up-and-coming young talent like Kurt Russell and Robert Redford. The regular cast, which changed over the years, featured Lee J. Cobb as Judge Henry Garth (1962–1966); Gary Clarke as Steve Hill (1962–1964); Pippa Scott as Molly Wood (1962–1963); Roberta Shore as Betsy Garth (1962–1965); Randy Boone as Randy Benton (1963–1966); Clu Gulager as Deputy Emmett Ryker (1964–1968) and David Hartman as David Sutton (1968–1969). The setting for *The Virginian* was the 1880s Wyoming territory.

In 1968, Edwards appeared in a superb episode called "The Mustangers," which aired in December. In the first scene, we see Edwards as Ben Harper confronting a stranger who has appeared at the Williams Ranch where he lives and is employed as a mustanger (a horse buster). Turns out the stranger is his son, Dewey. Ben's joy turns to disappointment when he learns that Dewey has left school.

Ben questions his son with his voice tinged with ire. "You just up and left?"

Dewey tries to explain just how fast the money he (Ben) sent ran out, and how he could take on a job busting broncos, just like his father. But Ben is unconvinced.[10] Ben says, "You don't know nothing about no mustangs ... these ain't horses, they're mustangs, and it takes a man to work 'em."

Ben's reluctance to allow his son a chance to make a living is puzzling. The boy is keen and obviously needs money; why is his father so adamantly opposed?

Chuck Daniel, in only his second appearance on television, was well cast as Dewey. The two greatly resembled each other except for the fact that Edwards stood more than a few inches taller. Edwards sports long sideburns tinged with grey and his hair is streaked with white, as is his mustache. Even with makeup rendering him an older man, Edwards seems youthful and fit.

Dave (David Hartman) and Dan (James Drury) arrive, seeking horses. But that evening Dave and Ben, who are on watch, are beaten by horse rustlers who make off with the mustangs. Everyone knows who committed the crime: Cal Hobson, a local hood.

Before this, however, we learn of Ben's fame as a mustanger. Indeed, some locals jokingly believe that he is part mustang. Bit by bit we learn other things about Ben, for example, his lack of schooling:

> Never got pass the third grade myself ... the closest I got to college was looking at one. I looked at it a long time ... imagine being able to learn all you need to know in a few years.

We then learn that Ben, formerly seen as the very best horse-buster that ever lived, is now past his prime. But he remains in denial.

The men set out to find another herd. Dewey comes along, much to Ben's chagrin. Dewey asks if he can participate in the round-up of wild horses. Ben warns him:

> You left Fort Worth without my permission. You come here against my will. Now you're here but you're a cook's helper and that's all.

Unfortunately, the roundup of fresh horses causes Ben to take stock of himself. Twice he makes a mess of things and then injures himself trying to force his will on an angry horse. It is Dewey who tames the recalcitrant creature. Ben sadly concedes, "I just ain't fast enough for 'em any more."

Ben realizes that he's finished as a mustanger and, in desperation, he turns to the crook Hobson, who earlier had offered to pay him a large sum of money for inside help in stealing more horses. Ben agrees. The money would pay for Dewey's schooling. Later, in a poignant scene, Ben, holding back tears, finally reveals his true feelings to his son:

> Just like watching myself up there ... long time ago. I remember the praise and the backslapping. With one ride I could really become somebody. The first time anybody knew what my name was. Yeah, son, it's a nice, warm, cozy feeling knowing you're the best there is. Kind of feeling I never wanted you to know, Dewey. Not here, not busting broncs! It's not enough ... when there's a whole big country out there, that's bigger than this and you got to get yourself ready for it. You spend enough time with 'em, you start to hate it, yeah, I hate 'em.... Now you look at me and see yourself twenty years from now.

The script for "The Mustangers" was written by Norman Jolley. The part of Ben Harper offered Edwards full range, and he took advantage of the opportunity to display his gifts. The splendid story touches upon a variety of issues, including the relationship between a father and son, a man coming to grips with his own mortality, and a father's fervent wish that his son does not follow in his footsteps, but instead gets an education and takes advantage of new opportunities. In sum, the episode features one of Edwards' best television performances.

Mannix

In 1969, Edwards appeared on the highly popular 60-minute crime drama *Mannix* (1967–1975, CBS) starring Mike Conners. African American actor Gail Fisher, co-starred as a regular as assistant Peggy Fair, and Robert Reed, best known as Mr. Brady of *The Brady Bunch*, appeared as Mannix's friend and police contact, Lt. Adam Tobias.

In this episode, Mannix is blinded by the effects of wounds he received in a shootout with a mysterious gunman. Naturally, he is angry and resentful. He announces to Peggy and Tobias that it's time to "close up shop." Peggy berates him for feeling sorry for himself and asks what happened to his courage. She offers to introduce him to a friend of hers who works with the blind.

Edwards, playing Jerry, is an ex–Marine and Medal of Honor recipient who was blinded for ten years and now works as a therapist. Edwards has finally begun to take on the features of an older man. His once stunningly handsome features have given way to the slightly puffy face of maturity; his hair has been refashioned into a somewhat misshapen Afro haircut. Still, in this program, he is an imposing presence. In his first scene, he is nattily attired in dark gray trousers, blue button-down oxford shirt, navy blue sport coat, and striped tie. He exudes confidence and an almost haughty air.

Mannix throws him a curve: He doesn't want to be taught to be blind, but how to survive if his stalker comes after him. Indeed, he has pieced together the rather complicated mystery that includes murder and the mob. He believes himself to be in danger.

Jerry gets to work with Mannix immediately, warning him, "It could get tough." He challenges Mannix to think differently about his surroundings in words that are firm but shaded with kindness. He shows Mannix how to move around his apartment: I'm going to condition you so that you know there's a chair there even if somebody moves it. You've got four senses left! Use them! Sharpen them!

Edwards gives a radiant performance in this memorable episode. Gail Fisher declared, "It was a gas to work with him.... [F]or the first time, I had trouble as an actress controlling my emotions because he moved me so deeply with his work."[11]

24. "James Edwards Was a Pioneer"

James Edwards was born eight months before Armistice Day, a frightful period of world war, deadly influenza, and an American society terrified of home-grown anarchy and political unrest. He lived long enough to see the start of the 1970s decade.

Twenty years had passed since he had burst onto the entertainment news pages with his performance as the lead in *Home of the Brave*—still being rerun on television. He was still a working actor. Recently, he had played a small but interesting a part in a picture called *Questions* (released in 1970 and retitled *Doomsday Voyage*); and guest starred in an episode of the TV show *Mannix*. He was still involved in local theatre. As a writer he was working on a novel and a script for Metromedia Productions.

On a personal level, Edwards had been married to Everdinne Edwards since 1963 and would have celebrated a wedding anniversary in January 1970. His daughter, Eugenia, would that year turn seven. He maintained his Indiana family ties and from time to time had returned to Hammond and visited with family.

In February 1970, Twentieth Century–Fox released the highly anticipated film on the life of U.S. Army General George S. Patton. *Patton*, directed by Franklin Schaffrer, was nearly three hours long and featured a massive cast, with George C. Scott (whom Edwards worked with on the television program *East Side/West Side*) in what would become his signature role. Edwards had a small but solid role as Sgt. William George Meeks, a member of the general's large staff of personal advisors and consultants.

Edwards appears fit, trim, and young-looking enough to assume the role of someone who would no doubt in real life have been about twenty years younger. By now, however, he had lost his boyish looks.

Edwards, as Sgt. William George Meeks, helps Gen. George Patton (George C. Scott) prepare for a pivotal battle in *Patton* (1970).

Some have described Edwards' appearance in *Patton* as little more than a servant role—a description patently unfair. As anyone with military experience can attest, it is a plain fact that everyone in the armed services is a servant of some higher-up. Even Gen. Dwight D. Eisenhower, mastermind behind the invasion of Europe during World War II, served

President Franklin Roosevelt. Too, in one *Patton* scene Lt. Col. Codman, another of Patton's aides, assumes the role of waiter and serves wine to the cadre of military brass that Patton has assembled to test out his plan for the invasion of Sicily. Patton, too, was reminded of his servitude when he lost his command because of bad behavior; he had to all but grovel and swear to behave in order to get his job back. Sgt. Meeks is an integral member of Patton's staff. He appears very early in the film, when Patton arrives at his post in Tunisia. After Meeks and Capt. Jenson set up his office, they pin the general's three-star rank onto his lapels.

Patton and Meeks treat each other with respect. In one of their more poignant scenes together, Meeks informs Patton that he has not been assigned commander of all ground forces. The reason: Patton has ruffled too many feathers, particularly after he slapped a frightened young soldier suffering from battle fatigue. Meeks quietly, respectfully reminds him,

> MEEKS: One little slap. That's what done it.
> PATTON: Oh, George.... I wish I had kissed the bastard.[1]

In one of the most evocative scenes in the picture, Meeks helps the general prepare for a challenging battle. In silence, he hands the general his ivory-handled pistols and then, almost ceremoniously, places the steel helmet onto the head of Patton. The character Meeks serves as his confidant, and scenes where they discuss wives and other subjects are sometimes poignant. Indeed, it might be argued that Edwards had one of the best parts in the film. Notes one review:

> There is a truly beautiful interior in a long corridor of windows where Patton exits from Eisenhower's office after having been rebuked for the so-called Knutsford incident. His loyal and faithful orderly (played by James Edwards) patiently waits for him and a very moving and touching scene is played between them.[2]

In a year (1970) that brought us *Love Story, Ryan's Daughter, The Great White Hope, Airport* and *MASH, Patton* was one of *the* most talked about and debated pictures, garnering Academy Awards for Acting, Art Direction, Cinematography, Directing, Film Editing, Music, Sound, Visual Effects, Writing, and Best Picture. Edwards, however, would never bask in the glory. On Sunday, January 4, 1970, he died of a heart attack.

Over the following days, reports of Edwards' death appeared in major publications such as *Variety, Time,* and *Newsweek,* and in local and community papers across the country. *Newsweek*'s obituary was brief, as was the one in *Time,* which mentioned Edwards' career highlights. The *New*

York Times claimed that on Sunday he had been working on a script in the San Diego apartment he used for writing when he complained of chest pains. He went to bed at 10 o'clock in the morning and arose at 7 P.M. and died almost immediately. He was transported to Sharp Memorial Hospital in San Diego where he was pronounced dead.[3]

In another account, Edwards' wife said he was at home working on a script which was scheduled to be delivered to Metromedia Producers Corporation that week. He often kept irregular hours that saw him occasionally work through the night. He arose in the early evening and even watched some television before complaining of chest pains. Regardless of the true sequence of events, Edwards never lived out the day. He had been working on a screenplay with the working title of *Bright Star Falling*.[4]

"Jimmy," Everdinne Edwards claimed, "had no history of heart disease." He was, she said, "in perfect health," and had just pasted "an exhaustive physical examination." Edwards died at the relatively young age of 51, approximately eight years earlier than the average life span for a U.S. Black man in 1970. Smoking, drinking, stress, overwork—all these factors no doubt served as contributors to his premature demise.[5]

Edwards was survived by his mother Anne Edwards Riley (his parents had divorced and his mother remarried), his father James Valley Edwards, his brothers Charles, Claude, Chase, and Freddy, and his sisters Jeannette, Mildred, Margaret and Barbara. In an obituary that appeared in the *Hammond (IN) Times*, no mention is made of Edwards' marriage to Everdinne; in error, his wife is identified as "Leola Mosley of New York City." Mosley was his first wife.[6]

A brief article in the *New York Times* detailed the issues that coincided with what would be Edwards' final public appearance, his funeral, the details of which apparently sparked some dissension among his survivors. As his Indiana family and former wife prepared for a hometown funeral, Everdinne was left with organizing a memorial service in Los Angeles. On January 9, 1970, at the Ebony Showcase Theatre, a place where Edwards had performed and directed shows, his acquaintances and colleagues gathered to pay their final respects. Back in Indiana, after a January 10 funeral at Mount Zion Baptist Church, Edwards was buried in his hometown of Hammond.[7]

In the weeks that followed, many who knew Edwards expressed their shock and disbelief. "Several of the people I talked to," wrote a *Chicago Defender* scribe, "were so grief-stricken that they could not speak as fully as they wanted to."[8] Columnist Gertrude Gipson, now writing for the *Los*

Angeles Sentinel, had covered Edwards' career since 1949 when she wrote for the now-defunct *California Eagle*. She noted in her column her sadness over Edwards' demise and how everyone had applauded his recent appearance on a television show:

> It was more than a shock when a call to our home related the shocking death of James Edwards.... Even just a few weeks ago ... TV reviewers were discussing the great role he portrayed as a psychiatrist in *Mannix*.[9]

Actress Gail Fisher, who appeared with in him the episode, told the *Chicago Defender*, "Looking 35 with the scars of life of 150 ... Jimmy died a winner making inroads in his lifetime." Stanley Kramer revealed in the same article, "I remember Jimmy with personal affection and with the highest professional regard. We worked together at a most critical time in both of our lives, and shared the experience of seeing the effort succeed. That is the kind of intimacy one can never forget."[10] Sidney Poitier pointed out that the opportunities he eventually received as an actor were a direct result of Edwards' efforts in *Home of the Brave*:

> Jimmy Edwards was an excellent actor. All young Negro actors today owe him a debt of gratitude because it was Jimmy Edwards who started the employment situation outside the old stereotypes.... I'll miss him.[11]

James Edwards career as a professional actor lasted a brief twenty years but in that time he made good on stage, film, radio, and television. His legacy, for better or for worse, will forever be married to his daring performance as the character Moss in *Home of the Brave*. However, through providence, a bit of good fortune, grit, and struggle, he made inroads throughout the entertainment world.

Edwards contributed to the history of American theatre with his appearance on Broadway in one of most successful and daring plays of the postwar period, *Deep Are the Roots* by James Gow and Arnaud d'Usseau. When the play reached the West Coast with Edwards in the lead, it broke local attendance records. Edwards was one the earliest members of the landmark Ebony Showcase Theatre, one of Black Los Angeles' most successful cultural venues. At the Ebony, Edwards hosted events, acted, directed, built sets, and appeared in what was most probably the first production of Tennessee Williams' *A Streetcar Named Desire* done with Black cast. He also directed and produced at other small theater venues, and for a time ran his own acting school.

Though many directories of radio credits do not mention his name,

Edwards played substantive roles on network radio despite the fact that commercial radio provided few opportunities for serious Black actors.

Edwards conquered the new medium of television both as an actor and as a writer. He developed concepts and scripts and saw at least one of his television concepts produced and aired. It was also on television that Edwards became a man of firsts, albeit small ones. He was one of a small contingent of Black Hollywood performers to play parts on programs where he was not cast as the comic servant of a White household, but was cast in serious roles on early television's dramatic anthology programs. He appeared in the first *Alfred Hitchcock Presents*, an episode directed by Hitchcock himself, and he was played the first Black cowboy in a television Western in a recurring role.

Edwards, too, earned his place in American film history. With his performance in the box-office smash *Home of the Brave*, he contributed to the success of a struggling independent producer named Stanley Kramer, who would go on to become of Hollywood's most respected filmmakers. Edwards was featured prominently in the cast of *The Steel Helmet*, the first film produced about the Korean Conflict, and he appears in two motion pictures that are now considered film landmarks, *The Manchurian Candidate* and *Patton*. He was possibly the first African American to sign as a screenwriter for a major Hollywood studio.

How properly, then, to assess the career of James Edwards? He never won or was nominated for an Emmy, Academy Award, or Tony Award; some of the motion pictures he appeared in were B-quality; and his career was cut short by an early death. It would be wide of the mark to place undue importance on Edwards' appearance in a handful of movies and television shows, some so undistinguished that they have yet to appear on DVD. Indeed, it is interesting to note how Edwards' story has sometimes been cast in a negative light. He has been labeled as a man whose career was ruined by a racist Hollywood industry unwilling to cast him in big or important roles, or as an actor undone by own drinking problems and his anger. These issues, no doubt, factor into Edwards' journey, but deemphasize his accomplishments. In spite of the exigencies associated with the highly competitive and unpredictable business of acting (the decline of the film industry; America's legacy of racial prejudice and discrimination; Edwards' own demons), he made a successful living as a Hollywood actor. Perhaps Kramer said it best: "James Edwards was a pioneer."[12]

His roles as one of the guys in war and combat films like *Men at War*, *Blood and Steel*, and *The Steel Helmet* provided a foretaste of the integrated armed forces. Furthermore, to Black citizens of the period, who often made a point of attending any film that included a Black character, Edwards' presence in a combat-war picture was far from routine, but at times an event. His roles as a fighter pilot, a sergeant in command of other troops that may have included Whites, his parts as a medic, or just another gun-toting trooper, represented inclusiveness, and showed African Americans not on the outside looking in, not as anomalies, but as part of the mainstream.

African American actor Paul Winfield, who died in 2004, said that the groundwork for his success in motion pictures was laid when, at age eight, he saw *Home of the Brave*:

> I remember everyone coming to my parent's kitchen and talking about this movie coming to town and they weren't going to sit up in the balcony. [Edwards] was not the porter, the servant. It was a soldier, somebody they could look up to. It was a real revelation.[13]

One columnist noted that Edwards made "the first step in Hollywood in the film industry where Negroes were recognized for their ability rather than the color of their skin."[14]

The appearance of a Black on early television was also hailed with approval and applause. (Indeed, even as late at 1974, when the CBS program *Good Times* hit the air, many Black families set aside time to be sure not to miss this sitcom with the all–Black cast.) Edwards appeared, not as the street-sweeper or the yardman, but as a detective, business owner, physician and astronaut. Such depictions instilled a sense of pride during a period when African Americans fought and died for respect and status. Edwards considered himself part of the struggle for civil rights, and made this clear in his interviews. As a performer, his television appearances, while perhaps not legendary, were a fitting contribution to the struggle.

Edwards seemed to have appeared at just the right time. He rose to prominence in a tentative period in the history of the Black struggle for rights in the United States. *Home of the Brave* was not just a successful picture at the box office but was the first picture to offer a candid and frank rendering of the "Negro problem" in America. Its script incorporated the hateful words and odious circumstances that many Black Americans were compelled to negotiate each day.

Moreover, Edwards stood for something. He meant something to Black people. Even though he would never be cast in the lead of another big picture after *Brave*, years later he still had star power.

Black actors of the period not only had to fight to survive in one of the most competitive fields, but they also served as a symbol of the race. Edwards seems to have kept his promise, as stated in 1951 in the *New York Age*, that he would never stoop to take a stereotyped role. Whether he could truly "afford to be picky" was his secret. Unknown is the number of offers he turned down because he deemed them unworthy

When asked why he succeeded as a Hollywood film actor when many of his contemporaries did not, Sidney Poitier told *American Film* in 1976,

> First of all, there was a great deal of luck.... Actors have a certain kind of energy, and that energy has to do with the way people receive you on the screen. There are some actors who are destined to be character actors; there are others who are destined to be supporting actors. But there are some actors, whose skills are not necessarily gargantuan, who have what some people call "force," others call "presence," or whatever.[15]

In many ways, Edwards can be considered lucky; he apparently possessed an overabundance of energy. He also seemed to emanate the "force" and "presence" that Poitier spoke of. Still, he barely made it beyond the status of character actor. Perhaps he did not live long enough for Hollywood to produce the kind of pictures that would display his immense talents. Or perhaps his pursuit of too many other activities slowed his progress. Still, this child of plain old Midwestern folks who also happened to be Black, with the odds stacked highly against him, decided to become a Hollywood actor. He became a good one and thrived, doing quite well for himself for nearly two decades. He achieved what Black men of his time could only dream about achieving, he became a movie star, a serious actor and icon. It is fitting to conclude with the words of Nick Stewart, Edwards' acting co-star and Ebony Showcase director, who said, "There was only one Jimmy Edwards."[16]

Appendix 1:
Morse v. Morse

James Edwards spent much of his life in search of recognition. In an unfortunate and bizarre twist of fate, his daughter would earn a great deal of notoriety for herself— notoriety of the negative kind.

In December 1998, twenty-eight years after his death, James Edwards' name once again appeared in the pages of San Diego area newspapers when his only child, 35-year-old Euginia Edwards Morse, now known as Eugia, was charged with kidnapping her own three children.

In 1994 Eugia divorced her husband, Robert Morse, after a turbulent and violence-tinged ten-year marriage. He remarried and the two battled over custody until Robert Morse was granted full custody in 1996. He was afraid that his wife might try to take the children so he brought a picture of Eugia to school.

In December 1996, Eugia sent a singing telegram performer to the school and while everyone was distracted, she took the children. Some sources allege that her mother, Everdinne, Edwards' widow, accompanied her daughter in the getaway car.

Eugia was described as an aspiring actress by the *Los Angeles Times*, which also noted that the case of Morse v. Morse was "a tale of accusations, counter-accusations, altercations, police interventions, and a continual tug-of-war."

Two and a half years later, the children, unharmed, were found with their mother in Texas after someone recognized pictures of the children on a website. Some sources described the family as having lived in deplorable conditions and claim that Eugia had been diagnosed as borderline schizophrenic. By the time of the 1998 trial, she was living, some said, more or less as a transient.

The case received a great deal of press coverage. Ten years later, the abduction is cited in fact sheets and publications distributed by the Polly Klaas Foundation, which include the words of Aja, one of the children, who claimed, "My brother and sister and I never went to the doctor, dentist, or to school."

Eugia Morse spent an undetermined amount of time in prison and was released. Her mother, Everdinne Wilson Edwards, died in 1999.

See Tony Perry, "Custody battles intensify at holiday time: Abductions increase as Christmas nears," *Los Angeles Times*, 23 December 1996, D8; Anne Krueger, "Suite in kidnap of 3 kids goes to trial," *San Diego Union Tribune*, 25 September 1998; "America's Hidden Crime: When the Kidnapper Is Kin: A Polly Klaas Report on Family Abduction, Public Opinion Insights and Best Practices," March 2004. As noted on their website, "the Polly Klaas® Foundation is a national nonprofit that helps find missing children, prevents children from going missing in the first place, and works with policymakers to pass laws like Amber Alert that help protect kids." See pollyklaas.org.

Appendix 2: Film, Television, and Radio Performances

1948

Ellery Queen (ABC Radio)   *Airdate:* February 12, 1948; *Episode:* "A Question of Color"; *Director:* Dick Woollen; *Writers:* Anthony Boucher and Manfred B. Lee
   Cast: Edith Gwynn, Roy Candy, Herb Butterfield, Lawrence Dobkin, Kaye Brinker, Alan Reed, James Edwards, Bill Bouchey, Roy Glenn, Frankie Lynn, Edith Wilson, and Earl Smith

The Lux Radio Theatre (CBS Radio) *Airdate:* November 15, 1948; *Episode:* "Body and Soul"; *Director:* Fred MacKaye; *Writers:* Abraham Polansky and Sanford Barnett (adaptor)
   Cast: John Garfield, Jane Wyman, William Keighley, Marie Windsor, William Conrad, William Johnstone, Wilms Herbert, Janet Scott, Douglas Evans, and James Edwards

1949

Manhandled (Paramount)   *Director:* Lewis R. Foster; *Producers:* William H. Pine and William C. Thomas; *Writers:* Louis R. Foster and Whitman Chambers
   Cast: Dan Duryea, Sterling Hayden, Dorothy Lamour, Maidie Norman, and James Edwards in his first film role

The Set-Up (RKO)   *Director:* Robert Wise; *Producer:* Robert Goldstone; *Writer:* Art Cohn, from a long poem by Joseph Moncure March
   Cast: Robert Ryan, Audrey Totter, George Tobias, Alan Baxter, Wallace Ford, Percy Helton, Philip Pine, James Edwards, and David Clarke

Home of the Brave (Screen Plays)   *Director:* Mark Robson; *Producers:* Stanley Kramer and Robert Stillman; *Writer:* Carl Foreman, from a stage play by Arthur Laurent
   Cast: Douglas Dick, Steve Brodie, Jeff Corey, Lloyd Bridges, Frank Lovejoy, James Edwards, and Cliff Clark

1950

The Halls of Ivy (NBC Radio)   *Episode:* "The Leslie Hoff Story"; *Director-Producer:* Nat Wolff; *Writers:* Nat Wolff and Don Quinn
   Cast: Ronald Colman, Benita Hume Colman, Herb Butterfield, Lois Corbett, and James Edwards

Toast of the Town (Ed Sullivan) (CBS Television)   *Airdate:* January 14, 1950
   Guests: James Edwards, Sugar Ray Robinson, Anna Maria Alberghetti, James Melon, and Sam Sneed

1951

Bright Victory (Universal)   *Director:* Mark Robson; *Producer-Writer:* Robert Buckner
   Cast: Arthur Kennedy, Peggy Dow, James Edwards, Will Geer, Nana Bryant, Jim Backus, Richard Egan, Rock Hudson, and Bernie Hamilton

The Steel Helmet (Lippert Pictures) *Writer-Director:* Samuel Fuller; *Producers:* Robert Lippert and Samuel Fuller
   Cast: Gene Evans, Robert Hutton, Steve Brodie, James Edwards, Richard Loo, Sid Melton, Richard Monahan, William Chun, Harold Fong, Neyle Morrow, and Lynn Stalmaster

1952

The Member of the Wedding (Columbia)   *Director:* Fred Zinnemann; *Producer:* Stanley Kramer; *Writers:* Screenplay developed by Edward and Edna Anhalt from a stageplay and novel by Carson Carruthers
   Cast: Julie Harris, Ethel Waters, Brandon DeWilde, James Edwards, Arthur Franz and Harry Bolden

1953

Confession (NBC Radio)   *Episode:* "The Case of Roger S. Chapman"; *Airdate:* September 17, 1953; *Director:* Homer Canfield; *Writer:* Don Brinkley
   Cast: James Edwards, Maidie Norman, Jester Hairston, and Jay Loft Lynn

The Joe Louis Story (United Artists) *Director:* Robert Gordon; *Producers:* Walter Chrysler, Jr., Stirling Silliphant, and William F. Joyce; *Writers:* Robert Sylvester and Stirling Silliphant
   Cast: Coley Wallace, Paul Stewart, Hilda Simms, James Edwards, John Marley, Dotts Johnson, P. Jay Sidey, Buddy Thorpe, and Ossie Davis

Ramar of the Jungle (Syndicated) *Episode:* "Savage Challenge"; *Director:* Sam Newfield; *Producers:* Rudolph Flothow, Harry S. Rothchild, Leon Fromkess; *Writers:* Howard J. Green, William Lively, Maurice Tombragel
   Cast: Jon Hall, Nick Stewart, Rex Ingram, James Edwards, Bernard Hamilton, Juanita Moore, Isaac Jones, and Ray Montgomery

1954

The Fireside Theatre (NBC Television)   *Episode:* "The Reign of Amelika Jo"; *Airdate:* October 12, 1954; *Director:* by Frank Wisbar; *Writer:* John Vandercook
   Cast: James Edwards, Keye Luke, Johnny Lee, and Nick Stewart

The Caine Mutiny (Columbia)   *Director:* Edward Dmytryk; *Producer:* Stanley Kramer; *Writer:* Stanley Roberts
   Cast: Humphrey Bogart, Van Johnson, Fred MacMurray, Jose Ferrer, May Wynn, Robert Francis, James Edwards, Tom Tully, E.G. Marshall, Lee Marvin, and Steve Brodie

1955

DuPont Cavalcade Theatre (ABC Television)   *Episode:* "Toward Tomorrow"; *Airdate:* October 4, 1955; *Director:* John Meredyth Lucas; *Producer:* Warren Lewis; *Writer:* Joel Murcott
   Cast: James Edwards, Maidie Norman, Ruby Goodwin, and McHenry Norman

Seven Angry Men (Allied Artists)   *Director:* Charles Marquis Warren; *Writer-Producer:* Vincent M. Fennelly
   Cast: Raymond Massey, Debra Paget, Jeffrey Hunter, Larry Pennell, Leo Gordon, James Best, James Edwards, Dennis Weaver, Tom Irish, James Anderson, and Smoki Whitfield

Alfred Hitchcock Presents (CBS Television)   *Episode:* "Breakdown"; *Airdate:* November 13, 1955; *Director:* Alfred Hitchcock; *Producers:* Alfred Hitchcock and Joan Harrison; *Writer:* Louis Pollock

Cast: Joseph Cotten, Raymond Bailey, Forrest Stanley, Mike Ragan, and James Edwards

The Phenix City Story (Allied Artists) *Director:* Phil Karlson; *Producers:* Samuel Bischoff and David Diamond; *Writers:* Daniel Mainwaring and Crane Wilbur
Cast: John McIntire, Richard Kiley, Kathryn Grant, Edward Andrews, James Edwards, Lenka Peterson, and Biff McGuire

TV Reader's Digest (CBS Television) *Episode:* "Mr. Pak Takes Over"; *Airdate:* June 13, 1955; *Director:* Leslie H. Martinson; *Writers:* Unknown, from a story by Daniel Haight III
Cast: Philip Ahn, James Edwards, Dan Barton, Walter Kelly, and Kenneth Tobey

Navy Log (CBS Television) *Episode:* "Hiya Pam"; *Airdate:* September 27, 1955; *Director:* Samuel Gallu et al.; *Producer:* Sam Gallu
Cast: James Archer, Douglas Easton, Douglas Dick, and James Edwards

General Electric Theatre (CBS Television) *Episode:* "D.P."; *Airdate:* January 9, 1955
Cast: James Edwards, Julius Jackson, Roy Glenn, Lisa Golm, and Bernie Hamilton

Medic (NBC Television) *Episode:* "What Is the Color for Courage?"; *Airdate:* Never aired; *Producers:* Frank LaTourette, Worthington Miner
Cast: Richard Boone and James Edwards

1956

Battle Hymn (Universal) *Director:* Douglas Sirk; *Producer:* Ross Hunter; *Writers:* Charles Grayson and Vincent B. Evans
Cast: Rock Hudson, Anna Kashfi, Dan Duryea, Don DeFore, Martha Hyer, James Edwards, Jock Mahoney, Alan Hale, Jr., Carl Benton Reid, Richard Loo, and Philip Ahn

The Killing (United Artists) *Writer-Director:* Stanley Kubrick; *Producers:* James B. Harris and Alexander Singer
Cast: Sterling Hayden, Coleen Gray, Vince Edwards, James Edwards, Jay C. Flippen, and Marie Windsor

Alfred Hitchcock Presents (CBS Television) *Episode:* "The Big Switch"; *Airdate:* January 8, 1956; *Director:* Don Weiss; *Writer:* Richard Carr, from a story by Cornell Woolrich; *Producers:* Alfred Hitchcock and Joan Harrison
Cast: George Matthews, George E. Stone, and James Edwards

1957

African Manhunt (Republic Pictures) *Director:* Seymour Friedman; *Writer:* Arthur Hoerl; *Producer:* Jerry Thomas
Cast: Myron Healey, Karin Booth, John Kellogg, Ross Elliott and Ray Bennett

Men at War (Security Pictures) *Director:* Anthony Mann; *Writer:* Philip Yordan; *Producer:* Sidney Harmon
Cast: Vic Morrow, Scott Marlowe, Robert Keith, James Edwards, Aldo Ray, Robert Ryan, Phillip Pine, and Anthony Ray

This Is Your Life (NBC Television) *Episode:* "Frank Lovejoy"; *Airdate:* October 16, 1957

Meet McGraw (NBC Television) *Episode:* "The New Orleans Story"; *Airdate:* July 27, 1957
Cast: Frank Lovejoy and James Edwards

1958

Tarzan's Fight for Life (MGM) *Director:* Bruce Humberstone; *Producer:* Sol Lesser; *Writer:* Thomas Hal Philips
Cast: Gordon Scott, Eve Brent, Rickie Sorenson, Woody Strode, James Edwards, Jill Jarmyn, Harry Lauter, and Carl Benton Reid

Fraulein (20th Century–Fox) *Director:* Henry Koster; *Producer:* Walter Reisch; *Writer:* Leo Townsend

Cast: Dana Wynter, Mel Ferrer, Luis Van Rooten, Theodore Bikel, Jack Kruschen, and James Edwards

Thunder Over Sangoland (Lippert Pictures) *Director:* Sam Newfield; *Producer:* Rudolph C. Flothow

Cast: Jon Hall, Myron Healey, Ray Montgomery, Marjorie Lord, House Peters, Jr., Nick Stewart, Frank Richards, and Louis Franklin

Assembled from episodes of the television program *Ramar of the Jungle*. The extent of Edwards' appearance is unknown.

Westinghouse Desilu Playhouse (CBS Television) *Episode:* "Silent Thunder"; *Airdate:* November 24, 1958; *Director:* Ted Post; *Writer:* John McGreevey, from a story and original screenplay by James Edwards

Cast: John Barrymore, Jr., Earl Holliman, and Wallace Ford

1959

Anna Lucasta (United Artists) *Director:* Arnold Laven; *Producer:* Sidney Harmom; *Writer:* Philip Yordan

Cast: Rex Ingram, Eartha Kitt, Georgia Burke, Isabelle Cooley, James Edwards, Sammy Davis, Jr., Claire Leyba, Rosetta Le Noire, Frederick O'Neal, and Henry Scott

Pork Chop Hill (United Artists) *Director:* Lewis Milestone; *Producer:* Sy Bartlett; *Writer:* James Webb

Cast: Gregory Peck, Woody Strode, Harry Guardino, George Shibata, Rip Torn, Barry Atwater, George Peppard, Robert Blake, and James Edwards

Zane Grey Theatre (CBS Television) *Episode:* "Mission"; *Airdate:* January 28, 1959; *Director:* William Daniel Favalia; *Producer:* Dick Powell; *Writer:* Aaron Spelling

Cast: Abraham Sofear, Felix Nelson, Roy Glenn, Ernie Anderson, Hari Rhodes, Bobby Johnson, Sammy Davis, Jr., and James Edwards

Blood and Steel (20th Century–Fox) *Director:* Bernard Kowalski; *Producer:* Gene Corman; *Writer:* Joseph C. Gilette

Cast: Brett Halsey, James Edwards, Allen Jung, John Lupton, James Hong, Ziva Rodann, and Bill Saito

Night of the Quarter Moon (MGM) *Director:* Hugo Haas; *Producer:* Albert Zugsmith; *Writers:* Frank Davis and Franklin Coen

Cast: Julie London, John Drew Barrymore, James Edwards, Nat "King" Cole, Anna Kashfi, Dean Jones, Agnes Moorehead, Cathy Crosby, Jackie Coogan, Charles Chaplin, Jr., Billy Daniels, and Marguerite Belafonte

Accused (ABC Television) *Airdate:* April 22, 1959; *Cast:* Edgar Allan Jones, Jr., William Gwinn, Tim Farrell, Jim Hodson, Violet Gilmore, and James Edwards

(Dramatization of actual court cases with a real judge and actors playing the defendants and witnesses)

1960

Peter Gunn (NBC Television) *Episode:* "Sing a Song of Murder"; *Director:* Lamont Johnson; *Producer-Creator:* Blake Edwards; *Writers:* Lewis Reed and Tony Barrett

Cast: Craig Stevens, Lola Albright, Herschel Bernardi, Diahann Carroll, and James Edwards

Texas John Slaughter (NBC Television) *Director:* Harry Keller; *Producer:* James Pratt; *Writer:* Teleplay by Maurice Tombrugel, from a story by Cyril Hume; *Episode:* "Apache Friendship"; *Airdate:* February 19, 1960

Cast: Tom Tryon, Nora Marlow, James Edwards, Betty Lynn, Brian Corcoran, Darryl Hickman, Annette Gorman, Jay Silverheels, and Gene Evans

Texas John Slaughter (NBC Television) *Episode:* "Kentucky Gunslick"; *Airdate:* February 26, 1960; *Director:* Harry Keller; *Producer:* James Pratt

Cast: Tom Tryon, Harry Carey, Jr., Norma Moore, James Edwards, Betty Lynn, Brian Corcoran, and Darryl Hickman

Texas John Slaughter (NBC Television) *Episode:* "Geronimo's Revenge"; *Airdate:* April 4, 1960; *Director:* Harry Keller; *Producer:* James Pratt; *Writers:* David Harmon and Bill Anderson
Cast: Tom Tryon, Darryl Hickman, Betty Lynn, James Edwards, Brian Corcoran, Alan Lane, Charles Maxwell, Annette Gorman, and Jay Silverheals

1962

The Manchurian Candidate (United Artists) *Director:* John Frankenheimer; *Writer-Producer:* George Axelrod
Cast: Frank Sinatra, Laurence Harvey, Angela Lansbury, Janet Leigh, James Gregory, James Edwards, John McGiver, and Henry Silva

The Clear Horizon (CBS Television) Daytime soap opera aired from 1960 to 1962; *Producer:* Charles Pollacheck; *Writer:* Irving Vendig, from a concept developed by Manya Starr
Cast: Beau Bridges, Phyllis Avery, Richard Coogan, James Edwards, Hal England, Earl Hammond, Ted Knight, Rusty Lane, and Lee Meriwether

The Lloyd Bridges Show (CBS Television) *Episode:* "Testing Ground"; *Airdate:* October 23, 1962; *Producer:* Four Star Television
Cast: Paul Richards, James Edwards, and Lloyd Bridges

The Joey Bishop Show (NBC Television) *Episode:* "Double Exposure"; *Airdate:* February 7, 1962; *Director:* Mel Ferber; *Producers:* Milt Josefsberg and Charles Stewart; *Writer:* Ernest Chambers
Cast: Joey Bishop, Lee Van Cleef, Abby Dalton, and James Edwards

1963

East Side/West Side (CBS) *Episode:* "Where's Harry"; *Airdate:* December 9, 1963; *Producer:* Talent Associates Productions; *Writer:* Millard Lampell; *Director:* Herschel Daugherty
Cast: George C. Scott, Norma Crane, Simon Oakland, James Edwards, Royce Wallace, Joseph Bernard, Melva Goodwin, and Muni Seroff

The Fugitive (ABC Television) *Episode:* "Decision in the Ring"; *Airdate:* October 22, 1963; *Director:* Robert Ellis Miller; *Producers:* Quinn Martin and Allan Armer; *Writer:* Arthur Weiss
Cast: David Janssen, Barry Morse, James Dunn, Jacqueline Morse, Bill Raisch, James Edwards, Hari Rhodes, and Ruby Dee

The Eleventh Hour (NBC Television) *Episode:* "Who Chopped Down the Cherry Tree?"; *Airdate:* June 10, 1963; *Producer:* Norman Felton; *Writer:* Dick Nelson
Cast: Ralph Bellamy, Harvey Korman, Richard Anderson, Robert Ryan, Peggy Ann Garner, and James Edwards

Going My Way (ABC Television) *Episode:* "Run, Robin, Run"; *Airdate:* March 20, 1963; *Director:* Fielder Cook; *Writer:* Arnold Bernstein
Cast: Gene Kelly, Leo G. Carroll, Dick York, Nydia Westman, Ivan Dixon, Robert Dugan, Juanita Moore, and James Edwards

1964

The Nurses (CBS Television) *Episode:* "The Roamer"; *Airdate:* February 6, 1964
Cast: Shirl Conway, Zina Bethune, Edward Binns, Stephen Brooks, James Edwards, Michael Tolan, and Joseph Campanella

The Dupont Show of the Week (NBC Television) *Episode:* "Ambassador at Large"; *Airdate:* June 14, 1964; *Director:*

Franklin Schaffner; *Producer:* Philip Barry, Jr.; *Writer:* Loring Mandel

Cast: Peter Falk, Oscar Homolka, Arthur Kennedy, Andrew Duggan, James Edwards, and Larry Hagman

Death Valley Days (Syndicated) *Episode:* "The Other White Man"; Aired on NBC Television on October 8, 1964; *Director:* Murray Golden; *Writer:* Melvin Levy

Cast: Lisa Gaye, Valentin De Vargas, Rodolfo Acosta, Don Haggerty, Roy Engel, James Edwards, Michael Hinn, Gregg Barton, and Perry Cook

1965

The Sandpiper (MGM) *Director:* Vincente Minnelli; *Producer:* Martin Ransohoff; *Writer:* Dalton Trumbo

Cast: Richard Burton, Elizabeth Taylor, Eva Marie Saint, Tom Drake, Torin Thatcher, Charles Bronson, and James Edwards

Dr. Kildare (NBC Television) *Episode:* "Wives and Losers"; *Airdate:* October 26, 1965; *Director:* Marc Daniels; *Producer:* Douglas Benton; *Writer:* Jerome Ross

Cast: Richard Chamberlain, Raymond Massey, Philip Bourneuf, Cloris Leachman, James Edwards, Donna Loren, Lee Kurty, Hazel Court, Viola Harris, Leslie Nielsen, Hayden Rorke, and Robert Reed

Dr. Kildare (NBC Television) *Episode:* "The Life Machine"; *Airdate:* November 2, 1965; *Director:* Marc Daniels; *Producer:* Douglas Benton; *Writer:* Jerome Ross

Cast: Richard Chamberlain, Raymond Massey, Philip Bourneuf, Cloris Leachman, James Edwards, Donna Loren, Lee Kurty, Hazel Court, Viola Harris, Leslie Nielsen, Hayden Rorke, and Robert Reed

1966

Amos Burke, Secret Agent (ABC Television) *Episode:* "Terror in a Tiny Town" Parts 1 & 2; *Airdate:* January 5 & 12, 1966; *Director:* Howard Henkels; *Producer:* Aaron Spelling for Four Star Television; *Writer:* Murray Golden

Cast: Gene Barry, Michael Fox, Carl Benton Reid, Harry Basch, Don Haggerty, Skip Homeier, and James Edwards

1968

Cowboy in Africa (ABC Television) *Episode:* "A Man of Value"; *Airdate:* February 26, 1968; *Director:* Earl Bellamy; *Producer:* Arthur M. Nadal; *Writers:* Jay Simms and John O'Dea

Cast: Chuck Connors, Tom Nardini, Ronald Howard, Gerald Edwards and James Edwards

The Outsider (NBC Television) *Episode:* "I Can't Hear You Scream"; *Airdate:* November 27, 1968; *Director:* Michael Ritchie; *Producer:* Gene Levitt; *Writers:* Roy Huggins, Adrian Joyce, and Frank Fenton

Cast: Darren McGavin, Ena Hartman, Myron Healey, Marc Cavell, Juanita Moore, Bobo Lewis, and James Edwards

The Outsider (NBC Television) *Episode:* "Tell It Like It Was...And You're Dead"; *Airdate:* December 4, 1968; *Director:* Michael Ritchie; *Producer:* Gene Levitt; *Writer:* Bernard C. Schoenfeld

Cast: Darren McGavin, Ted Knight, Marilyn Maxwell, Jackie Coogan, and James Edwards

Coogan's Bluff (Universal) *Producer-Director:* Don Siegel; *Writers:* Herman Miller, Dean Riesner, Howard Rodman, from a story by Herman Miller

Cast: Clint Eastwood, Lee J. Cobb, Susan Clark, Tisha Sterling, Don Stroud, Betty Field, Tom Tully, Meg Miles, and James Edwards

The Young Runaways (MGM) *Director:* Arthur Dreifuss; *Producer:* Sam Katzman; *Writer:* Orville H. Hampton

Cast: Kevin Coughlin, Lloyd Bochner, James Edwards, Richard Dreyfuss, Norman Fell, Isabel Sanford, Dick Sargent, and Patty McCormack

The Virginian (NBC Television) *Episode:* "The Mustangers"; *Airdate:* December 4, 1968; *Director:* Charles S. Dubin; *Writer:* Norman Jolley; *Producer:* David Levison

Cast: James Drury, John Agar, John McIntyre, William Paul Burns, Chuck Daniel, James Edwards, David Hartman, and Don Knight

The Outcasts (ABC Television) *Episode:* "My Name Is Jemal"; *Airdate:* November 18, 1968; *Director:* Harvey Hart; *Writers:* Ben Brady and Gerry Day

Cast: Don Murray, Otis Young, Jamey Michelle, and James Edwards

1969

Experiment in Television (NBC Television) *Episode:* "Color Me German"; *Airdate:* February 16, 1969; *Director:* Victor Vicus; *Writer:* Manya Starr

Cast: James Edwards, Rosemarie Fendel, and Ron Williams

Mannix (CBS Television) *Episode:* "The Sound of Darkness"; *Airdate:* December 6, 1969; *Director:* Corey Allen; *Writer:* Barry Trivers

Cast: Mike Conners, Gail Fisher, Robert Reed, Joby Baker, James Edwards, Gilbert Green, Glenn C. Wilder, Peter Brocco, Eddie Barth, and Arthur Eisner

1970

Patton (20th Century–Fox) *Director:* Franklin Schaffner; *Producers:* Frank McCarthy and Frank Caffey; *Writers:* Francis Ford Coppola and Edmund H. North

Cast: George C. Scott, Karl Malden, Michael Bates, Edward Binns, Lawrence Dobkin, John Doucette, James Edwards, Frank Latimore, and Richard Münch

1972

Doomsday Voyage aka ***Questions*** (Futurama International) (Released posthumously) *Writer-Director:* John Vidette; *Producers:* Al Adamson and John Vidette

Cast: Joseph Cotten, Charles Durning, John Gabriel, James Edwards, and Anne Randall

Chapter Notes

Chapter 1

1. Eugene Schrott, "Uncrowned Champion," *Negro Digest*, December 1949, 23–26.
2. Email received from Northwestern, 17 June 2005.
3. "Chicagoans Make Good Start in Hollywood; Two Cast in Pictures," *Chicago Defender*, 15 January 1949, 32. The article devoted six paragraphs to Edwards' exploits and one sentence to Robert Davis, another Skyloft Players member who, that year, appeared in the 1949 Columbia Pictures production of *Knock on Any Door*.
4. *Ibid.*
5. Schrott, 25.
6. Ossie Davis and Ruby Dee, *With Ossie and Ruby: In This Life Together* (New York: William Morrow, 1998), 145.
7. "Chicagoans Make Good"; "James Edwards' Varied Background Fitted Him for *Brave*." *Chicago Defender*, 28 May 1949, 34.
8. "Chicagoans Make Good"; "James Edwards' Varied Background"; Thomas D. Pawley, "Three Views of the Returning Black Veteran," *Black American Literature Forum*, Vol. 16, No. 4 (Black Theatre Issue, Winter 1982): 164.
9. Miles M. Jefferson, "The Negro on Broadway, 1945–1946," *Phylon*, Vol. 7, No. 2 (1946): 186.
10. James Gow and Arnaud d'Usseau, preface to *Deep Are the Roots* (published playscript). New York: Scribner's, 1946.
11. Gow and d'Usseau, *Deep Are the Roots*, 64.
12. Gow and d'Usseau, preface to *Deep Are the Roots*, xxxii.
13. Gordon Heath, *Deep Are the Roots: Memoir of a Black Expatriate* (Amherst: University of Massachusetts Press, 1992), 180.
14. "*Deep Are Roots* Advance Sale Sets Ten-Year Record." *North Hollywood (CA) Valley Times*, 16 January 1948.
15. "NAACP Endorses *Deep Are Roots*." *Los Angeles Sentinel*, 5 February 1948.
16. Henry Blankfort, "Review: *Deep Are the Roots*," *Los Angeles Tribune*, 31 January 1948.
17. "Drama Critics Agree on *Deep Are the Roots*." *Valley Jewish News*, 30 January 1948.
18. Blankfort, "Review"; "Other LA Theatre News," *Los Angeles Fortnight*, 13 February 1948.
19. Andrew Hatcher, "*Roots* Cast Sue S.F. Hotels in Discrimination Ban," *San Francisco Reporter*, 2 April 1948, 1.
20. James Haskins, *Cecil Poole: A Life in the Law* (Pasadena, CA: Ninth Judicial Circuit Historical Society, 2000), 49–50.

Chapter 2

1. Gene Bock, "Jimmy Edwards Visits Relatives," *Anderson Daily Bulletin*, 30 January 1969, 4; Eugene Schrott, "Uncrowned Champion," *Negro Digest*, December 1949, 24.
2. Schrott, "Uncrowned Champion"; Bock, "Jimmy Edwards Visits"; "Actor James Edwards Is Gifted College Product," Baltimore (MD) *Afro-American*, 4 August 1951; "James Edwards, Actor, Visits Friends Here," *The Anderson (IN) Herald*, 10 September 1964, 10.

3. "3 File Suits For Divorces," *Hammond Times*, 2 February 1940, 2.
4. Bock, "Jimmy Edwards Visits."
5. "Crowd Cheers Legion Bouts," *Hammond Times*, 20 April 1938, 21; Robert Storey, "Fans Look to Nineteen Hard Hitting Bouts," *Hammond Times*, 24 April 1938, Sports page 1.
6. Schrott, "Uncrowned Champion."
7. Bock, "Jimmy Edwards Visits."
8. All dialogue cited in this chapter was transcribed directly from the film soundtrack.
9. "Movie Debut: Ex-GI James Edwards Passes First Film Test with Robert Ryan's Advice," *Ebony*, April 1949, 25.
10. *Ibid.*
11. "*Deep Are the Roots* Star in New Drama," *Chicago Defender*, 1 January 1949, 22.
12. Bosley Crowther, "'A' Movies on 'B' Budgets: A New Hollywood 'genius,' Stanley Kramer, combines films of high artistic content with low financing." *New York Times*, 12 November 1950, 183; Ezra Goodman, "'Champion' Producer," *New York Times*, 10 April 1949, X4.
13. Schrott, "Uncrowned Champion," 26.
14. Stanley Kramer noted that his uncle ran an actor's agency "that never grew very large but always earned him a decent living." Stanley Kramer with Thomas M. Coffey, *A Mad, Mad, Mad, Mad World: A Life in Hollywood* (New York: Harcourt Brace, 1997), 32.
15. Schrott, "Uncrowned Champion."

Chapter 3

1. "Arthur Laurents: Emotional Reality," in *Backstory 2: Interviews with Screenwriters of the 1940s and 1950s*, ed. Pat McGilligan (Berkeley: University of California Press, 1991), 134.
2. Arthur Laurents, *Original Story By: A Memoir of Broadway and Hollywood* (New York: Alfred A. Knopf, 2000), 50.
3. "Arthur Laurents: Emotional Reality," in *Backstory 2*.
4. Ezra Goodman, "*Champion* Producer," *New York Times*, 10 April 1949, X4; Stanley Kramer with Thomas M. Coffey, *A Mad, Mad, Mad, Mad World: A Life in Hollywood* (New York: Harcourt Brace, 1997), 33–34; Thomas F. Brady, "Play By Laurents Will Be Made Film," *New York Times*, 24 February 1949, 29. (Note: Kramer claims in some interviews that the price he paid for the rights to *Home on the Brave* was $35,000.)
5. "*Home of the Brave*: First Film about Anti-Negro Bias Made in Secret by Hollywood ex-GIs," *Ebony*, June 1949, 60.
6. Laurents, *Original Story By*, 51.
7. "*Home of the Brave*: First Film," 59.
8. All dialogue used in this chapter was transcribed directly from the film soundtrack.
9. Donald Spoto, *Stanley Kramer: Filmmaker* (New York: Putnam's, 1978), 53.
10. Eugene Schrott, "Uncrowned Champion," *Negro Digest*, December 1949, 26.
11. Hedda Hopper, "Robson Film All Complete in 3 Months," *Washington Post*, 12 June 1949; Spoto, 44.
12. Spoto, 44; "Home of the Brave," Baltimore (MD) *Afro-American*, 14 May 1949, 12.
13. Kramer, *Mad World*, 36.
14. *Ibid.*
15. Goodman, "*Champion* Producer."
16. "SP's *Brave* Probably the Record Long-Runner on Proj. Room Circuit," *Variety*, 27 April 1949, 3; Eddie Burbridge, "James Edwards Role in New Pic Powerful," *Los Angeles Sentinel*, 5 May 1949, 5; "Inside Stuff—Pictures," *Variety*, 11 May 1949, 3; Kramer, *Mad World*, 41.
17. Kramer, *Mad World*, 41; "Platter Chatter and Flicker Parade—By Flo," *Color*, August 1949, 43.
18. Kramer, *Mad World*, 35; Manny Farber, "Films," *The Nation*, 21 May 1949; "12 Birds Play the Spy in a Pacific War Movie," *New York Herald Tribune*, May 1, 1949, 18; Farber, "Films."
19. "The Current Cinema: The Color Line," *New Yorker*, 21 May 1949, 68.
20. "The New Pictures: *Home of the Brave*," *Time*, 9 May 1949, 64.
21. San Rafael (CA) Independent Journal, 22 February 1950, M-15.
22. Farber, "Films."
23. Gene Handsaker, "Hollywood," Clearfield (PA) *Progress*, 23 May 1949, 4.
24. Time, *Ibid.*
25. *Motion Picture Herald*, 30 April 1949, 4590.
26. "*Home of the Brave* Turns out to Be

Most-Talked About Film," *Annapolis (MD) Capital*, 10 October 1949, 8.
27. Wood Soanes, "*Home of the Brave*—Vital Moving Film," *San Mateo (CA) Times*, 25 July 49, 17.
28. "Home of the Brave," *Variety*, 4 May 1949.
29. Philip T. Hartung, "Blueberry Pie," *The Commonweal*, 20 May 1949, 149.
30. Bosley Crowther, "*Home of the Brave* at Victoria, and *The Stratton Story* at Music Hall, Well Rated," *New York Times*, 12 May 1949, 29; "A Negro G.I.'s Story," *New York Times*, 1 May 1949, SM56.

Chapter 4

1. Laura Haddock, "Negro Star Speaks Up on Race Problems," *Christian Science Monitor*, 11 June 1949, 2.
2. "Movies and the Negro," Letters to the Editor, *Washington Post*, 25 November 1949, 30.
3. "*Home of the Brave*," Baltimore (MD) *Afro-American*, 14 May 1949, 12–13.
4. *Ibid.*
5. Langston Hughes, "The Negro and American Entertainment," in *The Collected Works of Langston Hughes, Vol. 9: Essays on Art, Race, Politics, and World Affairs*, ed. Christopher De Santis (Columbia, MO: University of Missouri Press, 2002), 430.
6. Eddie Burbridge, "James Edwards Role in New Pic Powerful," *Los Angeles Sentinel*, 5 May 1949, 5.
7. James Edwards, "Hollywood. So What!" *Our World*, December 1953, 59.
8. Bosley Crowther, "*Home of the Brave*," *New York Times*, 13 May 1949, 29.
9. Charles B. Lazarus, "*Home of the Brave*," *Motion Picture Herald*, 30 April 1949, 4590.
10. Bill Chase, "All Ears," *New York Age*, 4 June 1949, 26.
11. Nadine Sobotnik, "Outstanding Movie: *Home of the Brave*," Cedar Rapids (IA) *Gazette*, 5 November 1949.
12. Rebel Jackson, "*Home of the Brave*, Controversial Movie about Racial Prejudice, Tops Screen Fare," *Abilene (TX) Reporter*, 24 July 1949, 12.
13. Sterling Sorensen, "*Home of the Brave* 'Work of Art' Should Be Seen," *Madison (WI) Capital Times*, 4 August 1949.
14. Crowther, "*Home of the Brave*."

15. Haddock, "Negro Star Speaks Up."
16. Stanley Kramer with Thomas M. Coffey, *A Mad, Mad, Mad, Mad World: A Life in Hollywood* (New York: Harcourt Brace & Co., 1997), 43; "Texas Plunge," *Time*, 18 July 1949.
17. Emily G. Reiman, "*Home of the Brave*," Letters to the Editor, *Washington Post*, 11 August 1949; "*Home of the Brave* Booked at Jim Crow DC House." *Chicago Defender*, 13 August 1949, 27.
18. "The Press: Land of the Free." *Time*, 27 June 1949.
19. "Clipper Binford Okays *Brave* in Memphis," *Chicago Defender*, 13 August 1949, 27.
20. Haddock, "Negro Star Speaks Up"; "*Home of the Brave* Premiere Draws Overflow Audience." *Chicago Defender*, 28 May 1949, 1.

Chapter 5

1. Ulysses Lee, *Special Studies: The Employment of Negro Troops, The United States Army in World War II* (Washington, DC: Center of Military History, United States Army, Office of the Chief of Military History, U.S. Army, 1966).
2. Almond's words were quoted in 1972 to Morris. J. McGregor, Jr., and printed in *Integration of the Armed Forces, 1949–1965* (Washington, D.C.: Center for Military History, 1989), 440–441.
3. "James Edwards' Varied Background Fitted Him for *Brave*," *Chicago Defender*, 28 May 1949, 34.
4. Laura Haddock, "Negro Star of *Home of the Brave* Speaks Up on Racial Problem," *Christian Science Monitor*, 11 June 1949, 21; Eugene Schrott, "Uncrowned Champion," *Negro Digest*, December, 1949, 25.
5. "*Home of the Brave*," *Motion Picture Herald*, 30 April 1949, 4590; "James Edwards' Varied Background," *Chicago Defender*; "*Home of the Brave*," *Variety*, 4 May 1949.
6. Nadine Subotnik, "Outstanding Movie: *Home of the Brave*." Cedar Rapids (IA) *Gazette*, 5 November 1949.
7. "Home of the Brave," *Monthly Film Bulletin*, 16:181/192 (1949): 193.
8. Bill Chase, "*Home of the Braves* [sic] A "Must Film; Hits Bias," *New York Age*, 21

May 1949; Wood Soanes, "*Home of the Brave*—Vital, Moving Film," *San Mateo (CA) Times*, 25 July 1949, 17; Gene Handsaker, "Hollywood," Clearfield (PA) *Press*, 23 May 1949, 4.
   9. Schrott, "Uncrowned Champion," 25.
   10. "Edwards, Film Star, Honored in Harlem," *New York Times*, June 4, 1949, 8; James L. Hicks, "All Wanted to Hitch on Star's Chariot: Edwards Gets Ovation; Harlem Mayor Gets Feelings Hurt; 'Twas a Great Day," Baltimore (MD) *Afro-American*, 5 June 1949, 6.
   11. "Edward [sic], Film Star, Honored in Harlem," *New York Times*, 4 June 1949, 8.
   12. "James Edwards' Varied Background," *Chicago Defender*.
   13. James Edwards, "You'll Like Bermuda," *Our World*, May 1950.

Chapter 6

   1. "*Brave* Star Did Film During His Spare Time," Baltimore (MD) *Afro-American*, 13 August 1949, 8.
   2. "National Box Office Survey," *Variety*, 25 May 1949, 2.
   3. Ibid.; "National Box Office Survey," *Variety*, 1 June 1949, 5; Display Ad, *Variety*, 1 June 1949, 10; "National Box Office Survey," *Variety*, 8 June 1949, 3; "Picture Grosses," *Variety*, 8 June 1949, 10; "National Box Office Survey," *Variety*, 15 June 1949, 3.
   4. Gertrude Gipson, "Candid Comments," *California Eagle*, 5 January 1950, 22; James Edwards, "Hollywood. So What!" *Our World*, December 1953, 55; Eugene Schrott, "Uncrowned Champion," *Negro Digest*, December 1949, 25.
   5. "James Edwards, Star, Very Busy," *Pittsburgh Courier*, 7 May 1949, 19; James Edwards, "You'll Like Bermuda," *Our World*, May 1950, 27–28.
   6. Gertrude Gipson, "Candid Comments," *California Eagle*, 1 September 1949, 14.
   7. "James Edwards to Star in *Anna Lucasta* at Regal," *Chicago Defender*, 24 September 1949; "James Edwards Cited by USNG," Baltimore (MD) *Afro-American*, 1 October 1949, 8.
   8. James L. H. Peck, "Hollywood's Bronze Valentino," *Our World*, February 1950, 26.
   9. "Entertainers to Be Honored," *New York Times*, 20 April 1950, 36.
   10. Gertrude Gipson, "Candid Comments" (column), *California Eagle*, 28 January 1950, 10; Delores Calvin, "Meet 'Mr. Ups and Down'; He's Jim Edwards of Films," *Chicago Defender*, 19 August 1950, 32; Display advertisement for *Nat Turner*, *New York Times*, 11 March 1951, 98; Display ad, *New York Times*, 11 March 1951, 98.
   11. Walter Winchell, "Broadway and Elsewhere," *Logansport (PA) Pharos Tribune*, 30 June 1949, 16; "Hollywood," *Los Angeles Sentinel*, 25 August 1949, 3; "Hollywood Wanted 'New Face' for *No Way Out*," *California Eagle*, 26 January 1950.
   12. James Edwards, "Hollywood. So What!" 55.
   13. Harry Levette, "*Lights Out*; *Show Boat* Ready to Roll," *Chicago Defender*, 30 September 1959, 7.
   14. Dorothy Kilgallen, "Voice of Broadway," Olean (NY) *Times-Herald*, 16 February 1950, 13.

Chapter 7

   1. "*Steel Helmet*: James Edwards Has Excellent Role in Korean War Movie," *Ebony*, March 1951, 79.
   2. Bosley Crowther, "*Steel Helmet*, Dealing with an American Infantry Patrol in Korea, at Loew's State," *New York Times*, 25 January 1951, 21.
   3. All dialogue in this chapter was transcribed directly from the film soundtrack.
   4. "*Steel Helmet*: James Edwards," *Ebony*.
   5. Richard L. Coe, "Film Brings Home the War in Korea," *Washington Post*, 8 March 1951, B8.
   6. Renwick Cary, "*Steel Helmet* Average War Film," *San Antonio (TX) Light*, 3 February 1951; Fred D. Moon, "*Steel Helmet* Called Great Motion Picture of the Korean War," *Statesville (NC) Record*, 2 February 1951.
   7. "*The Steel Helmet* Is Termed Real, Unpainted War Portrayal," *Charleston (SC) Gazette*, 2 February 1951.
   8. Crowther, "*Steel Helmet*."
   9. "*Steel Helmet*: James Edwards," *Ebony*.

10. "Iran Bars U.S. Film on Korea," *New York Times*, 3 October 1951, 12; Harry Schwartz, "Soviet Agents Explore Hollywood," *New York Times*, 13 May 1951, X5; Samuel Fuller, "War That's Fit to Shoot," *American Film*, November 1976, 62.
11. "Louella Parsons," *Lowell (MA) Sun*, 22 July 1950, 6.
12. Manny Farber, "Films," *The Nation*, August, 1951, 590–591.
13. Bosley Crowther, "Poignant Film of Blinded War Veteran's Problems, *Bright Victory* at the Victoria," *New York Times*, 1 August 1951, 19; "The New Pictures," *Time*, 13 August 1951.
14. Robin Dorr, "Picture at Playhouse Has Stirring Theme," *Washington Post*, 29 August 1951, B7; Richard L. Coe, "Movies Have a Beef, Too," *Washington Post*, 19 August 1951, L1; "The Screen: Eyeless in Penna," *The Commonweal*, 17 August 1951, 54.
15. "Lights Out: Story of Blind GIs Blasts Racial Bias in a Moving Way," *Ebony*, December 1950, 87.
16. Advertisement, *Abiline (TX) Reporter News*, 23 November 52, 24.
17. Thomas M. Pryor, "Happy, Happy Author: Baynard Kendrick Expresses Delight Over Film Version of His *Lights Out*," *New York Times*, 28 January 1951, X5.
18. Mark Robson, "Plea for a New Flock of Film Fledglings: Director Presents Views on the Dearth of Young Talent Needed These Days," *New York Times*, 22 July 1951, 67.
19. Dolores Calvin, "Meet 'Mr. Ups and Down'; He's Jim Edwards of Films," *Chicago Defender*, 19 August 1950, 32.

Chapter 8

1. "Dramatic Reading Goal of Edwards," *Syracuse (NY) Post Standard*, 2 February 1951, 14.
2. Thomas M. Pryor, "Hollywood Report," *New York Times*, 2 May 1954, X5.
3. Ibid.
4. Thomas M. Pryor, "Columbia to Film *Last Angry Man*," *New York Times*, 20 October 1956, 17; Bob Thomas, "Hollywood Has First Negro Movie Writer; Former Actor," *Danville (VA) Bee*, 8 April 1957, 12.
5. Bob Thomas, "Hammond Man Quits Acting..." *Hammond (IN) Times*, 8 April 1957, 3; "Jimmy Edwards Quits Acting, To Write Films," *Jet*, 2 May 1957, 54.
6. James Edwards, "Hollywood. So What!" *Our World*, December 1953, 59.
7. Ibid.
8. Bob Thomas, "Hammond Man Quits."
9. "Negro Actors at Hearing Assail Bias in Casting," *New York Times*, 30 October 1962, 37; "Networks Deny Employment Bias," *Variety*, 31 October 1962, 62.
10. Thomas M. Pryor, "Hollywood Report," *New York Times*, 2 May 1954, X5.
11. "The Boy from Korea," First draft screenplay and step outline by James Altieri and James Edwards, October 1956, Papers of Albert J. Cohen, Special Collections Library, University of Iowa Libraries.
12. "New Independent Enters Film Field: Robert Gordon Productions Plans 4 Movies for 1957 — Abortion First Subject," *New York Times*, 28 August 1956, 31.
13. "Silent Thunder," Script, John Greevey Papers, The Lilly Library, Indiana University.
14. A. S. (Doc) Young, "The Token Negro," *Los Angeles Sentinel*, 23 March 1962, 2C.
15. Bruce Cook, "The War Between the Writers and Directors. Part I: The Writers," *American Film*, May 1979, 26–32.
16. A. S. (Doc) Young, "Requiem for a Talented Black Actor," *Chicago Defender*, 13 January 1970, 10.
17. Ibid.
18. All dialogue cited in this chapter was transcribed from the program soundtrack.
19. "*Halls of Ivory* [sic] Termed Slap Against Intolerance," *Baltimore (MD) Afro-American*, 30 September 1950, 7.

Chapter 9

1. James Edwards, "Hollywood. So What!" *Our World*, December 1953, 58
2. Ibid.
3. Walker's words from a speech delivered November 1952; excerpts reprinted on the website of the Screen Actors Guild, www.sag.org.
4. Poitier speaks at length about his struggles at the time, particularly his failed restaurant, "Ribs in the Buff," in Aram Goudsouzian, *Sidney Poitier: Man, Actor, Icon* (Chapel Hill: University of North Carolina Press, 2004), 90–91.

5. Fred Hift, "Negro Actor's Impressions of South Africa," *New York Times*, 22 April 1951, 97.
6. "Arts Committee Head Hurls Defi at Werker," Baltimore (MD) *Afro-American*, 6 August 1949, 8.
7. Pearl Bailey, *The Raw Pearl* (New York: Harcourt, Brace, 1968), 103–104.
8. "The Age of Hollywood: A Working Script," *New Republic*, 31 January 1949, 11; "Movie Makers Meet Postwar Problems," *Business Week*, 1 October 1949, 26.
9. Bosley Crowther, "Hollywood Survey: Visiting Critic Finds Studios Humming Under New Streamlined Operations," *New York Times*, 4 June 1950, X3.
10. Woody Strode with Sam Young, *Goal Dust* (Lanham, MD: Madison Books, 1999), 189.
11. Bosley Crowther, "'Z' Movies on 'B' Budgets," *New York Times*, 12 November 1950, 183.

Chapter 10

1. Diahann Carroll with Ross Firestone, *Diahann: An Autobiography* (Little, Brown, 1999), 52–53.
2. James Edwards, "You'll Like Bermuda," *Our World*, May 1951, 26.
3. James Edwards, "Hollywood. So What!" *Our World*, December 1953, 59.
4. "Woman Says Film Star Beat Her, Sues," *Chicago Defender*, 10 September 1949, 1.
5. "$57,000 Suit Filed Against Star of *Home of the Brave*," *Los Angeles Sentinel*, 1 September 1949, 1.
6. Ibid.
7. Cover page, *Ebony*, March 1951; also see "On the Cover," 13.
8. "Actress Denies Fisticuffs with James Edwards," *Los Angeles Sentinel*, 1 September 1949, 1.
9. Ibid.
10. Gertrude Gipson, "Candid Comments," *California Eagle*, 1 September 1949, 14.
11. Wil Haygood, *In Black and White: The Life of Sammy Davis, Jr.* (New York: Alfred A. Knopf, 2003), 197; Ossie Davis and Ruby Dee, *With Ossie and Ruby: In This Life Together* (New York: William Morrow, 1998), 159.
12. Edwards, "Hollywood. So What!" 59.
13. Woody Strode with Sam Young, *Goal Dust* (Lanham, MD: Madison Books, 1999), 191; Edwards, "You'll Like Bermuda," 27.
14. Carroll, *Diahann*.
15. Carroll, *Diahann*, 53.
16. Edwards, "Hollywood. So What!" 55, 59.
17. Lillian Smith, "Around 'n' About," *New York Amsterdam News*, 11 June 1949, 12.
18. Strode, *Gold Dust*, 188, 193; Carroll, *Diahann*, 45–56.
19. Lee Marks, "Take One," *The Woodlawn (CA) Booster*, 13 January 1970.

Chapter 11

1. Display advertisement, *California Eagle*, 11 August 1950, 6.
2. The individuals who came to be known as the Hollywood Ten were Herbert Biberman, Lester Cole, Albert Maltz, Adrian Scott, Samuel Ornitz, Dalton Trumbo, Edward Dmytryk, Ring Lardner Jr., John Howard Lawson and Alvah Bessie.
3. "Radio Held Biased on Negro Problem: Canada Lee Charges Owners Distort Issues, Refuse to Hire Member of Race," *New York Times*, 10 July 1949, 10; Mona Z. Smith writes of Lee's travails in *Becoming Something: The Story of Canada Lee* (New York: Faber and Faber, 2004).
4. "Communist Infiltration of Intellectual Groups, June 15, 1951, to April 15, 1952," Hollywood Arts, Sciences and Professions Council; "Communist Infiltration of Intellectual Groups, February 15, 1953 — July 15, 1953," Committee for the Negro in the Arts.
5. Ossie Davis and Ruby Dee, *With Ossie and Ruby: In This Life Together* (New York: William Morrow, 1998), 149.
6. Karl Evanz, "Black Hollywood and the FBI," *Black Film Review*, #64 (Winter 1987/88): 17.
7. "Negro Actor Tells FBI Snooper Where to Go," *The Daily Worker*, 5 February 1950, 2A.
8. Aram Goudsouzian, *Sidney Poitier: Man, Actor, Icon* (Chapel Hill: University of North Carolina Press, 2004), 92.
9. Carey McWilliams, "Hollywood Gray List," *The Nation*, 19 November 1949.
10. FBI Memorandum (LA 100-15732), Los Angeles Office, November 14, 1958.

11. Leo Verswijver, "Jeff Corey," in "Movies Were Always Magical": Interviews with 19 Actors, Directors, and Producers from the Hollywood of the 1930s Through the 1950s (Jefferson, NC: McFarland, 2003), 18.

12. One formerly confidential FBI memorandum dated November 13, 1958, alleges that *The Defiant Ones* was written by blacklisted writers, but notes that there was no reliable evidence of Kramer having any affiliation with the Communist Party; Another formerly confidential FBI reports describes Foreman as having "never been completely cooperative." See Communist Infiltration of Motion Pictures and Plays, LA 100-15732, 10–11.

13. FBI Memorandum, LA 100-15732, 19; See "George Glass" and "Lloyd Bridges."

14. Samuel Fuller, "War That's Fit to Shoot," *American Film*, November 1976, 62.

15. Alice A. Dunnigan, "*Deep Are the Roots* Authors under HUAC Microscope: McCarthy Questions Author of the Story," *Chicago Defender*, 18 July 1953, 19; see the website of the Screen Actors Guild, http://www.sag.org.

16. Evan Finch, "Will Geer: Frankfort's Supporting Actor," Indiana Historical Society, http://www.indianahistory.org/pop_hist/people/geer.html.

17. "Nathaniel Adams Cole," Declassified confidential memorandum, Federal Bureau of Investigation, Los Angeles, California, May 8, 1961.

18. Otto Preminger, *Preminger: An Autobiography* (Garden City, NY: Doubleday, 1977), 118.

19. Harry Belafonte, "Speaking Freely" (transcript), firstamendmentcenter.org, recorded August 26, 2000.

20. "'I'm No Benedict Arnold,' Cries Hilda Simms on Ban," *Pittsburgh Courier*, 10 September 1960, 7.

Chapter 12

1. "*Amos 'n' Andy* Protest Rocks, Radio, TV Industry," Baltimore (MD) *Afro-American*, 21 July 1951, 1.

2. "Front and Center with Sonny," *New York Age*, 4 August 1951, 12.

3. *Ibid*.

4. Jack Gould, "Billy Rose Gives First Show on TV," *New York Times*, 4 October 1950, 46.

5. Television Column, *Variety*, 30 September 1953; Bud Harris, "Why I Left *Beulah*," *Chicago Defender*, 25 December 1950, 31.

6. George Daniels, "Swinging the News," *Chicago Defender*, 11 July 1952, 18.

7. *Ibid*.

Chapter 13

1. "Films Go Biographical," *New York Times*, 3 May 1953, SM26.

2. A. H. Weiler, "The Local Scene: Producers Eye *The Time of the Cuckoo*—Of *The Joe Louis Story*—Addenda," *New York Times*, 18 January 1953, X5.

3. See *American Experience: The Fight*, "Jack 'Chappie' Blackburn," http://pbs.org.

4. See photograph in *Chicago Defender*, 18 April 1953, 19.

5. "'Bankroll' Sags as Camera Slow Down," *Chicago Defender*, 25 April 1953, 18; "*Joe Louis Story* Pix Back in Production," *Chicago Defender*, 2 May 1953, 19; "Producer Tells of Many Problems He Faces When Making *Joe Louis Story*," *Pittsburgh Courier*, 28 November 1953, 18.

6. "Deny *Joe Louis Story* Pix Stymied By Distributors Ban: Blames Retakes, Editing For Delay in Release," *Chicago Defender*, 4 July 1953, 19.

7. A. H. Weiler, "*The Joe Louis Story*," *New York Times*, 4 November 1953, 29.

8. Gladys M. Johnson, "*Joe Louis Story* in Smashing Detroit Premiere," *Pittsburgh Courier*, 24 October 1953, 18.

9. Alan Ward, "On Second Thought," *Oakland Tribune*, 12 November 1953, 57; "*Louis Story* Struggles Against Ropes," *Stars and Stripes* (Pacific), 1 January 1954, 16.

10. Weiler, "Joe Louis Story"

11. Ward, "On Second Thought."

12. "Everybody Goes When the Wagon Comes," Chicago Defender, 28 November 1953, 9.

Chapter 14

1. Gertrude Gipson, "Candid Comments," *California Eagle*, 25 January 1951, 11; Gertrude Gipson, "Candid Comments," *California Eagle*, 5 April 1951, 11; "James

Edwards to MC New TV Series on KCOP," *Los Angeles Sentinel*, 6 October 1955, 11; Hazel L. Lamarre, "Applause," *Los Angeles Sentinel*, 6 October 1955, 10.

2. Martin Grams, Jr., *The History of the Cavalcade of America*, unnumbered book; Barnouw, *The Sponsor*, 34.

3. Barnouw, 34.

4. "James Edwards Stars as Dr. Ralph Bunche on TV Oct. 4," *Los Angeles Sentinel*, 29 September 1955, 1, 10; Gertrude Gipson, "Candid Comments" *California Eagle*, 6 October 1955, 5; Lamarre, "Applause."

5. Lamarre, "Applause."

6. "James Edwards Stars"; Gipson, 6 October 1955.

7. "Logs," *TV-Radio Life*, 9–15 October 1954.

8. Hazel L. Lamarre, "Applause!" *Los Angeles Sentinel*, 13 January 1955, 10; "Local Boy to Star with James Edwards on G.E. Show," *Los Angeles Sentinel*, 6 January 1955, 10; "TV Players," Captioned photograph of James Edwards and Julius Bryant Jackson, appearing in the teleplay, "D.P.," *Pittsburgh Courier*, 15 January 1955.

9. "TV Players."

10. "No Cheapies for Desilu Features," *Variety*, 16 March 1955, 4.

11. Aaron Spelling with Jefferson Graham, *Aaron Spelling: A Prime-Time Life* (New York: St. Martin's Press, 2005), 216.

Chapter 15

1. Al White, "From Tom-Toms to Television," *Our World*, February 1951, 30.

2. "Television: Negro Performers Win Better Roles in TV than in Any Other Entertainment Medium," *Ebony*, June 1950, 22.

3. "Agency Rep Sees Rosy Year Ahead," Baltimore (MD) *Afro-American*, 9 December 1950, 8.

4. Erik Barnouw, *The Sponsor: Notes on a Modern Potentate* (New York: Oxford University Press, 1982), 50.

5. "Soundtrack with 'Chazz' Crawford," *California Eagle*, 5 March 1955, 9; See "Medic," at the website of the Museum of Broadcast Communications, http://www.museum.tv.com.

6. Charles Crawford, "Soundtrack," *California Eagle*, 3 October 1955; Joseph Turow, *Playing Doctor: Television, Storytelling, and Medical Power* (New York: Oxford University Press, 1989), 43–44.

7. Nat King Cole, "Why I Quit My TV Show," *Ebony*, March 1958, 30.

8. "Talmadge Hits TV," *Variety*, 9 January 1952, 20; Pete Peterson, "The Mariners," *The Magazine of African-American History & Culture* (Spring 2005), 17–24.

9. "Performers Group and NAACP Slate TV 'Blackout' to Protest Race Bias," *Pittsburgh Courier*, 29 January 1955, 17.

10. Jeff Kisseloff, *The Box: An Oral History of Television, 1920–1961* (New York: Viking Press, 1995), 279.

11. *Ibid*.

12. "Television in Review: *Ramar of the Jungle* Starring Jon Hall, Is Hasty Adventure Filmed on the Coast," *New York Times*, 31 August 1953, 15.

13. Nancy Bernhard, *U.S. Television News and Cold War Propaganda, 1947–1960* (Cambridge: Cambridge University Press, 1994), 132–134.

14. Bernhard, 150–151; "Samuel Gallu," *The Gale Literary Database: Contemporary Authors*, The Gale Group, 14 May 2002, www.galenet.com (accessed December 2006).

15. "Navy Log" photograph and review, *TV Guide*, 29 October 1955, 21.

16. "James Edwards in *Accused* Next Week," *New York Amsterdam News*, 22 April 1959, 15.

17. All dialogue cited in this chapter was transcribed directly from the program soundtrack.

18. Laurence Laurent, "Radio and Television: WOOK-TV Faces Outsized Challenge," *Washington Post*, 15 June 1962, D13.

19. "Plan Is to Weave Race into Every Phase of U.S. Life," *Pittsburgh Courier*, July 28, 1951; "Regular Negro Employees Practically Non-Existent in Hollywood Studios," *Variety*, 14 January 1959.

Chapter 16

1. Dolores Calvin, "Meet 'Mr. Ups and Down'; He's Jim Edwards of Films," *Chicago Defender*, 19 August 1950, 32.

2. "*Home of the Brave* Locked out in Bermuda," *California Eagle*, 23 November 1950, 7; Jimmy Edwards, "You'll Like Bermuda," *Our World*, May 1950, 27–28.

3. Edwards, "You'll Like Bermuda."

4. Edwards, "You'll Like Bermuda." The premiere of *Home of the Brave* in segregated Bermuda was a momentous occasion and is still referred to as one of many catalysts for changes in race relations on the island. See "Bermuda's History from 2000 to the Present," at http://www.bermuda-online.org. (accessed December 2006).

5. James Edwards, "Hollywood. So What!" *Our World*, December 1953, 55.

6. Arthur Nolletti, Jr., *The Films of Fred Zinnemann: Critical Perspectives*, (New York: State University of New York Press, 1999), 103–104.

7. Nolletti, 117.

8. Carson McCullers. *The Member of the Wedding* (published playscript) (New York: New Dimensions, 1946), 43.

9. This dialogue was transcribed directly from the film soundtrack.

10. Karel Reiss, "*The Member of the Wedding*," *Sight and Sound* 22:4 (April-June 1953): 197; Bosley Crowther, "Stanley Kramer's Production of *The Member of the Wedding* Has Premiere at Sutton," *New York Times*, 31 December 1952, 10; Philip T. Hartung "*Member of the Wedding*," *The Commonweal*, 30 January 42.

11. George E. Brown, "No Cover Charge," *Pittsburgh Courier*, 15 January 1955, 14; Eric Harrison, "A Hard Lesson from Hollywood's Past," *Los Angeles Times*, 9 July 2000; See also ebonytheatre.org.

12. "The Sad, Semi-Secret Death of a Star," *Sepia*, February 1970, 74.

13. Hazel L. Lamarre, "Applause," *Los Angeles Sentinel*, 6 January 1953, 10; "Actor James Edwards ... Turns Director," *Hue*, October 1956, 10; "*No Exit* on Coast." *Pittsburgh Courier*, 10 October 1953, 19; "James Edwards Directs *Detective Story* at Geller," *Los Angeles Sentinel*, 11 August 1955, 10.

14. "Play Review: *A Streetcar Named Desire* (Ebony Showcase Theatre)," *Hollywood Reporter*, 3 December 1956, 3.

15. "James Edwards to Do *Voice of the Turtle*," *New York Amsterdam News*, 19 January 1952, 12.

16. "James Edwards Directs."

17. "Actor James Edwards ... Turns Director."

18. "Screen Test: Dorothy Dandridge Wins *Carmen Jones* Title Role with Sizzling Performance," *Ebony*, September 1954, 37.

19. Diahann Carroll with Ross Firestone, *Diahann* (New York: Little, Brown, 1999), 53.

20. "Misguided Saga: *Seven Angry Men* Opens at Palace," *New York Times*, 2 April 1955, 15.

21. A. H. Weiler, "*The Killing*," *New York Times*, 21 May 1956, 20; "*The Killing*," *Time*, 4 June 1956, 106.

22. "Barbecued Shish-Kebob," *Ebony*, August 1956, 99.

Chapter 17

1. "Jimmy Edwards: Best Soldier in Hollywood," *Hue*, June 1958, 38.

2. Mary S. Spargo, "Truman Orders End of Bias in U.S. Jobs and Armed Service," *Washington Post*, 27 July 1958, 1; Harry Truman, *Memoirs by Harry S Truman: Years of Trial and Hope, 1946–1952*. Vol. 2 (New York: Signet Books, 1965), 183.

3. Alan L. Gropman, *The Air Force Integrates: 1945–1964* (Washington, D.C.: Office of Air Force History, 1976), 32.

4. Stanley Kramer with Thomas M. Coffey. *A Mad, Mad, Mad, Mad World: A Life in Hollywood* (New York: Harcourt Brace, 1997), 110.

5. A.M. Sperber and Eric Lax, *Bogart* (New York, William Morrow, 1997), 481; James Edwards, "Hollywood. So What!" *Our World*, December 1953, 55.

6. All dialogue cited in this chapter was transcribed directly from the film soundtrack.

7. Richard L Coe, "One on the Aisle," *Washington Post*, 1 January 1954, 10; Bosley Crowther, "The Screen: *Caine Mutiny* Arrives," *New York Times*, 25 June 1954, 17; "Mutiny in the *Caine*: Stanley Kramer Re-Creates the Herman Wouk Naval Saga for the Screen," *New York Times*, 4 July 1954, X1.

8. National Museum of the U.S. Air Force, the Official National Museum of the United States Air Force, http://www.nationalmuseum.af.mil/

9. Bosley Crowther, "*Battle Hymn*," *New York Times*, 16 February 1957, 14.

10. Dean Hess, *Battle Hymn* (New York: McGraw-Hill, 1956), 38, 124.

11. Douglas Sirk and Jon Halliday, *Sirk on Sirk: Conversations with Jon Halliday* (London: Faber and Faber, 1997), 125–126.

12. Bosley Crowther, "Screen: Celluloid Infantry: *Men in War* Proves Sherman Was Right," *New York Times*, 20 March 1957, 32.
13. "Wynter Role as Fraulein Has Warmth," *Syracuse Post-Standard*, 17 May 1958, 2; "Fraulein," *Variety*, 2 May 1958; A.H Weiler, "Fraulein," *New York Times*, 9 June 1958, 27.
14. Theresa Loeb Cone, "*Pork Chop Hill* Tells How It Was," *Oakland (CA) Tribune*, 28 May 1959; "*Pork Chop Hill* Due This Week at Plaza," *Paris* (TX) *News*, 24 January 1960, 11; Jimmie Meyers, "Meyers' Mill," *California Eagle*, 28 May 1959, 10.
15. Woody Strode and Sam Young, *Goal Dust* (Lanham, MD: Madison Books, 1999), 193.
16. *Ibid.*
17. Joseph R. Millichap, *Lewis Milestone* (Boston: Twayne Publishers, 1981), 178–181.
18. "Pork Chop Hill," *Berkshire (MA) Eagle*, 28 May 1959, 5; Meyers, "Meyers' Mill"; Cone, "*Pork Chop Hill* Tells How It Was."
19. "Blood and Steel," *Oakland (CA) Tribune*, 28 January 1960, 38.

Chapter 18

1. Barbara Berch, "Hail to a New and Farewell to an Old Tarzan," *New York Times*, 2 January 1949, X5.
2. Berch, "Hail to a New."
3. "Regular Negro Employees Practically Non-Existent in Hollywood Studios," *Variety*, 14 January 1959.
4. A. H. Weiler, "Makeshift Safari," *New York Times*, 20 April 1957, 21.
5. "Tarzan's Fight for Life," *Variety*, 27 June 1957; Richard W. Nason, "Tarzan's Fight for Life," *New York Times*, 16 August 1958, 10.
6. Woody Strode with Sam Young, *Goal Dust* (Lanham, MD: Madison Books, 1999), 188–189, 193–194.
7. "A Star at Ten: Cub Scout Gets Featured Role in Tarzan Film," *Ebony*, July 1958, 59.
8. For more information about the history of the American Negro Theatre, see Renee Antoinette Simmons, *Frederick Douglass O'Neal: Pioneer of the Actors' Equity Association*.
9. "*Anna Lucasta* Pix Fight Rages in N.Y.," Baltimore (MD) *Afro-American*, 9 December 1959, 8.
10. All dialogue cited in this chapter was transcribed directly from the film soundtrack.
11. "*Anna Lucasta*, U.S.A., 1958," *Monthly Film Bulletin*, 26:300/311 (1959): 17.
12. "The New Pictures," *Time*, 26 January 1959.
13. T.H.C., "Seen at the Algona," *Algona (IA) Advance*, 26 May 1959, 3.
14. Albert Johnson, "*Anna Lucasta*," *Sight and Sound*, Spring 1959, 91.
15. Bosley Crowther, "*Anna Lucasta*," *New York Times*, 15 January 1959, 27; "*Anna Lucasta*: Eartha Kitt, Sammy Davis, Star in Film," *Ebony*, December 1958, 72; Richard Coe, "Oh, Where's Porgy's Bess?" *Washington Post*, 4 February 1959, A23.
16. Robert Beck, "Whose Chip?" Letters to the Editor, *New York Times*, 25 January 1959, X7.
17. Eartha Kitt, *I'm Still Here* (London: Sidwick & Jackson, 1989), 196.
18. Johnson, "*Anna Lucasta*."
19. "*Anna Lucasta*: Eartha Kitt," *Ebony*, 74.
20. Bernard F. Dick, *City of Dreams: The Making and Remaking of Universal Pictures* (Lexington: University Press of Kentucky, 1997), 151.
21. "Night of the Quarter Moon," *Monthly Film Bulletin*, 26:300/311 (1959): 73; See "Most Promising Performer," photograph caption, *California Eagle*, 4 June 1959, 9.
22. "Most Promising Performer," *California Eagle*.
23. Philip T. Hartung, "The Screen: How Melo Was My Drama," *The Commonweal*, 27 February 1959, 570.
24. Theresa Loeb Cone, "Stage and Screen: Racial Film on Fox Oakland Bill," *Oakland (CA) Tribune*, 16 March 1959, 43.
25. Jimmie Meyers, "Meyers' Mill," *California Eagle*, 19 March 1959, 9; "*Night of the Quarter Moon*," *Variety*, February 5, 1959.

Chapter 19

1. Emmett Perry, "The Story Behind Phenix City: The Struggle for Law in a

Modern Sodom," *American Bar Association Journal* 42 (1956): 1146.

2. All dialogue cited in this chapter was transcribed directly from the film soundtrack.

3. Carolyn Ewers, *Sidney Poitier: The Long Journey*, (New York: Signet Books, 1969), 76–77.

4. Fred Wordress, "Mobsters Intimidate B'ham Booksellers of *Phenix City* Expose," *Variety*, 29 June 1955, 61; Charles Crawford, "Soundtrack," *Los Angeles Sentinel*, 10 April 1955, 10; "Edwards had Armed Guard on *Phenix City* Location," *Pittsburgh Courier*, 19 May 1955, 22.

5. Hazel L. Lamerre, "Applause! In the Theatre," *Los Angeles Sentinel*, 10 September 1955, 10; "Cinema: The New Pictures," *Time*, 19 September 1955, 6.

6. "*Phenix City Story* Grim, Tense," Syracuse (NY) *Herald-Journal*, 16 October 1955, 34; Nadine Subotnik, "*Phenix City* Is Filled with Violent Fact," Cedar Rapids (IA) *Gazette*, 27 October 1955, 20.

7. Bosley Crowther, "Best Films of 1955," *New York Times*, 25 December 1955, X3.

8. Richard L. Coe, "Shadows Fell on Alabama," *Washington Post & Times Herald*, 21 October 1955, 32.

9. Coe, "Shadows Fell on Alabama"; "*Phenix City Story* Grim, Tense," Syracuse (NY) *Herald-Journal*; Subotnik, "*Phenix City* Is Filled"; Wood Soanes, "Violence of *Phenix City Story* Filmed as Semi-Documentary," *Oakland Tribune*, 24 October 1955, 22.

10. See display ad appearing in the Kokomo (IN) *Tribune*, 28 February 1956, 11.

11. Bosley Crowther, "Small But Potent: The *Phenix City Story* an Exciting Film," *New York Times*, 11 September 1955, X1.

Chapter 20

1. Bennie J. McRae, Jr., "Black Cowboys," http://www.coax.net/people/lwf/bkcwboy2.htm.

2. Richard Gheman, "Black and White Television?" *TV Guide*, 27 June 1964, 32.

3. "Regular Negro Employees Practically Non-Existent in Hollywood Studios," *Variety*, 14 January 1959.

4. See "Dick Powell," Museum of Broadcast Communications, http://www.museum.tv.com.

5. All dialogue used in this chapter was transcribed from the soundtrack.

6. Gary Fishgall, *Gonna Do Great Things: The Life of Sammy Davis, Jr.* (New York: Scribner, 2003), 133–134.

7. "Aaron Spelling: Dialogue on Film. The Man Who Brought You *Dynasty, Hotel*, and *Family*, Talks about the Agony and Ecstasy of Producing for Network Television," *American Film*, May 1984, 55.

8. Aaron Spelling with Jefferson Graham, *Aaron Spelling: A Prime-Time Life* (New York: St. Martin's Press, 2005), 59.

9. Charles Crawford, "Soundtrack," *California Eagle*, 10 December 1959.

10. Douglas Brode, *Multiculturalism and the Mouse: Race and Sex in Disney Entertainment* (Austin: University of Texas Press, 2005), 128; Eric Barnouw, *Tube of Plenty: The Evolution of American Television* (New York: Oxford University Press, 1982), 193; Gary A. Yoggy, *Riding the Video Range: The Rise and Fall of the Western on Television* (Jefferson, NC: McFarland, 1995), 71.

11. "Front and Center with Sonny," *New York Age*, 4 August 1951, 12.

12. Brode, 76–77.

13. Yoggy, 78.

Chapter 21

1. Hazel L. Lamarre, "Applause: In the Theatre," *Los Angeles Sentinel*, 11 June 1961, 12.

2. Ethan Mordden. *Medium Cool: The Movies of the 1960s* (New York: Knopf, 1990), 88.

3. Mordden, 87.

4. Robert C. Wylder, "Puzzle Pinnacle: Jean Genet's *Blacks* Gripping — Way Out," *Long Beach (CA) Independent Press Telegram*, 18 March 1962, A-10.

5. Bosley Crowther, "*The Manchurian Candidate*: Laurence Harvey and Frank Sinatra Star, Brainwashing Is the Theme of New Film," *New York Times*, 25 October 1962, 48.

6. All dialogue cited in this chapter was transcribed directly from the film soundtrack.

7. McGilligan, Pat, "George Axelrod: Irony!" *Backstory 3: Interviews with Screen-*

writers of the 1960s (Berkeley: University of California Press, 1997), http://ark.cdlib.org/arkL/13030/ft138nb0zm/.

8. Crowther, *ibid*; "Down South in North Korea," *Time*, 2 November 1962.

9. Vincent Canby, "*The Manchurian Candidate*," *Variety*, 18 October 1962.

10. Vincente Minnelli with Hector Arce, *I Remember It Well* (Garden City, NY: Doubleday, 1974), 356.

11. *Ibid.*

12. Richard L. Coe, "*The Sandpiper*," *Variety*, 17 June 1965; Minnelli, 356; Crowther, *New York Times*; Display ad, *The Woodlawn Booster*, 5 April 1966, 3.

13. Samuel A. Boyea, "Most Grateful to Be Away: 'Talk Film' Probes Exile of U.S. Negroes Abroad," *Long Beach (CA) Independent*, 12 June 1966, A-14.

Chapter 22

1. Lawrence Laurent, "TV Recognizing Negro Citizens at Last," *Washington Post*, 29 October 1963, D6.

2. David Anderson, "Negro Actors at Hearing Assail Bias in Casting," *New York Times*, 30 October 1962, 37.

3. Laurent, "TV Recognizing Negro Citizens"; "Crossing the Bar," *Time*, 8 November 1963.

4. Radiogram from director of FBI to SAC, New Orleans, dated November 18, 1963.

5. Paul Buhle and Dave Wagner, *Hide in Plain Sight: The Hollywood Blacklistees in Film and Television, 1950–2002* (New York: Palgrave/Macmillan, 2003), 47.

6. "David Susskind: U.S. Producer and Talk Show Host," The Museum of Broadcast Communications, http://www.museum.tv.org.

7. Lawrence Laurent, "*East Side* Proving Estimate of Quality," *Washington Post/Times Herald*, 18 December 1963, B9.

8. All dialogue cited in this chapter was transcribed from the program soundtrack.

9. "Southern Stations Don't Carry," *TV Guide*, 16 November 1963, A-5; "George C. Scott," *TV Guide*, 30 November 1963, 16–19; "Review," *TV Guide*, 14 December 1963, 4; Val Adams, "Lewis's TV Show May Be Curtailed," *New York Times*, 13 November 1963, 65; Vincent Brook, "Checks and Imbalances: Political Economy and the Rise and Fall of *East Side/West Side*," *Journal of Film and Video*, 50:3 (Fall 1988): 24.

10. "Television," *Bridgeport (CT) Post*, 6 February 1964, 16.

Chapter 23

1. Gene Bock, "Jimmy Edwards Visits Relatives," *Anderson Daily Bulletin*, 30 January 1969, 4.

2. *Ibid.*

3. "Brightening the Tube," *Newsweek*, March 1969, 94.

4. "Stimuli of Experiment," *Time*, 18 April 1969, 96.

5. *Ibid.*

6. "Test Tube," Display ad for NBC Television, *New York Times*, 28 February 1969; "Television This Week," *New York Times*, 16 February 1969, D21; Jack Gould, "TV: P.B.L. Scouts Cable," *New York Times*, 17 February 1969, 71; "Critics Corner," Long Beach (CA) *Independent Press-Telegram*, 23 February 1969, 21.

7. Aaron Spelling with Jefferson Graham, *Aaron Spelling: A Prime-Time Life* (New York: St. Martin's Press, 2005), 48.

8. *Ibid.*

9. "Television," *Kokomo (IN) Tribune*, 16 June 1969, 13.

10. All dialogue cited in the chapter was transcribed from the video or film soundtrack.

11. A. S. "Doc" Young, "Requiem for a Talented Black Actor," *Chicago Defender*, 13 January 1970, 10.

Chapter 24

1. All dialogue cited in this chapter was transcribed from the film soundtrack.

2. George J. Mitchell, "War Films: The Photography of Patton," *After the Battle* No.7 (1975), 42; Erwin Kim, *Franklin Schaffner* (Lanham, MD: Scarecrow Press, 1985), 62.

3. "James Edwards," *Variety*, 14 January 1970, 70; "Milestones," *Time*, 19 January 1970, 49; Obituary, *Newsweek*, 19 January 1970, 95; "James Edwards, Film Actor, Dead: Gained Fame in Film, *Home of the Brave*— Also Did TV," *New York Times*, 8 January 1970, 41.

4. "The Sad, Semi-Secret Death of a

Star," *Sepia*, March 1970, 72–77; A.S. "Doc" Young, "Requiem for a Talented Black Actor," *Chicago Defender*, 13 January 1970, 10.

5. Young, "Requiem."

6. "Edwards," *Hammond (IN) Times*, 7 January 1970, B-6.

7. "Edwards Rites Tomorrow," *New York Times*, 9 January 1970, 33; "Memorial Service Planned Tomorrow for James Edwards," Van Nuys (CA) *The News*, 8 January 1970, 6-A.

8. Young, "Requiem."

9. "Gertrude Gipson's Candid Comments," *Los Angeles Sentinel*, 8 January 1970, E4.

10. Young, "Requiem."

11. *Ibid.*

12. *Ibid.*

13. Patricia Sullivan, "Paul Winfield," *Washington Post*, 11 March 2004, B6.

14. "Gertrude Gipson's Candid Comments," *ibid.*

15. "Dialogue on Film: Sidney Poitier, Since He's Come to Dinner, He's Helped Change Hollywood's Manners," *American Film*, September/October 1991, 18.

16. Young, "Requiem."

Bibliography

Books

Anderson, Christopher. *Hollywood: The Studio System in the Fifties.* Austin: University of Texas Press, 1994.
Bailey, Pearl. *The Raw Pearl.* New York: Harcourt, Brace, 1968.
Baker, Vernon J., with Ken Olsen. *Lasting Valor.* Columbus, MS: Genesis Press, 1997.
Barnouw, Eric. *The Sponsor: Notes on a Modern Potentate.* New York: Oxford University Press, 1978
_____. *Tube of Plenty: The Evolution of American Television.* New York: Oxford University Press, 1982.
Basinger, Jeanine. *The World War II Combat Film: Anatomy of a Genre.* New York: Columbia University Press, 1986.
Bergan, Ronald. *The United Artists Story.* New York: Crown, 1996.
Bernhard, Nancy. *U.S. Television News and Cold War Propaganda, 1947–1960.* New York: Cambridge University Press, 1994.
Binkin, Martin, et al. *Blacks and the Military.* Washington, D.C.: The Brookings Institute, 1982.
Biskind, Peter. *Seeing Is Believing.* New York: Pantheon, 1983.
Blum, John M. *V Was for Victory: Politics and Culture During World War II.* New York: Harcourt Brace Jovanovich, 1976.
Bogart, Leo, ed. *Social Research and the Desegregation of the U.S. Army.* Chicago: Markham, 1969.
Bohn, Thomas W., and Richard Sromgren. *Light and Shadows: A History of Motion Pictures.* Palo Alto, CA: Mayfield, 1978.
Brode, Douglas. *Multiculturalism and the Mouse: Race and Sex in Disney Entertainment.* Austin: University of Texas Press, 2005.
Brooks, Tim, and Earle Marsh. *The Complete Directory to Prime Time Network TV Show, 1946–Present.* New York: Ballantine, 1985.
Brownstein, Ronald. *The Power and the Glitter: The Hollywood-Washington Connection.* New York: Pantheon, 1990.
Buhle, Paul, and Dave Wagner. *Hide in Plain Sight: The Hollywood Blacklistees in Film and Television, 1950–2002.* New York: Palgrave/Macmillan, 2003.
Campbell, Edward D.C., Jr. *The Celluloid South: Hollywood and the Southern Myth.* Knoxville: University of Tennessee, 1981.
Carroll, Diahann, with Ross Firestone. *Diahann: An Autobiography.* Boston: Little, Brown, 1999.
Castleman, Harry, and Walter J. Podrazik. *Watching TV: Six Decades of American Television.* Syracuse, NY: Syracuse University Press, 2003.
Chung, Hye Seung. *Hollywood Asian: Philip Ahn and the Politics of Cross-Ethnic Performance.* Philadelphia: Temple University Press, 2006.

Conant, James B. *Slums and Suburbs: A Commentary on Schools in Metropolitan Areas.* New York: McGraw-Hill, 1961.
Custen, George F. *Twentieth Century's Fox: Darryl F. Zanuck and the Culture of Hollywood.* New York: Basic Books, 1997.
Davis, Ossie, and Ruby Dee. *With Ossie and Ruby: In This Life Together.* New York: William Morrow, 1998.
Davis, Sammy, Jr., Jane Boyar, and Burt Boyar. *Yes I Can: The Story of Sammy Davis, Jr.* New York: Pocket Books, 1966.
De Santis, Christopher, ed. *The Collected Works of Langston Hughes, Vol. 9: Essays on Art, Race, Politics, and World Affairs.* Columbia: University of Missouri Press, 2002.
Dick, Bernard F. *City of Dreams: The Making and Remaking of Universal Pictures.* Lexington: University Press of Kentucky, 1997.
Dunning, John. *On the Air: The Encyclopedia of Old Time Radio.* New York: Oxford University Press, 1998.
Ellis, Jack C. *A History of Film.* Englewood Cliffs, NJ: Prentice-Hall, 1979.
Ely, Melvin Patrick. *The Adventures of Amos 'n' Andy: A Social History of an American Phenomenon.* New York: Free Press, 1991.
Ewers, Carolyn. *Sidney Poitier: The Long Journey.* New York: Signet, 1969.
The Fight for Freedom in a Transition Year. NAACP Annual Report, Fifty Fourth Year, 1962. National Association for the Advancement of Colored People, New York; *Address to the 50th Annual NAACP Convention,* July 17, 1959, Library of Congress, Manuscript Division, Papers of the NAACP.
Fishgall, Gary. *Gonna Do Great Things: The Life of Sammy Davis, Jr.* New York: Scribner, 2003.
Gianakos, Larry James. *Television Drama Series Programming: A Comprehensive Chronicle 1947–1959.* Lanham, MD: Scarecrow Press, 1978.
_____. *Television Drama Series Programming: A Comprehensive Chronicle 1959–1975.* Lanham, MD: Scarecrow Press, 1980.
Gilbert, James. *Another Chance: Postwar America 1945–1985.* Chicago: Dorsey Press, 1986.
Gomery, Douglas. *The Hollywood Studio System.* London: Macmillan, 1986.
Goudsouzian, Aram. *Sidney Poitier: Man, Actor, Icon.* Chapel Hill: University of North Carolina Press, 2004.
Gould, Lewis L., ed. *Watching Television Come of Age: The New York Times Reviews by Jack Gould.* Austin: University of Texas Press, 2001.
Gow, James, and Arnaud d'Usseau. *Deep Are the Roots* (published playscript). New York: Scribner's, 1946.
Grams, Martin, Jr. *The History of the Cavalcade of America,* Kearny, NE: Morris, 1998.
Green, Paul. *A History of Television's* The Virginian, *1962–1971.* Jefferson, NC: McFarland, 2006.
Gropman, Alan L. *The Air Force Integrates, 1945–64.* Washington, D.C.: Office of Air Force History, 1978.
Halberstam, David. *The Fifties.* New York: Villard Books. 1993.
Harrington, Michael. *The Other America.* New York: Penguin, 1963.
Haskins, James. *Cecil Poole: A Life in the Law.* Pasadena, CA: Ninth Judicial Circuit Historical Society, 2000.
Haygood, Wil. *In Black and White: The Life of Sammy Davis, Jr.* New York: Alfred A. Knopf, 2003.
Head, Sydney, and Sterling Kittross. *Broadcasting in America: A Survey of Electronic Media.* 6th ed. Boston: Houghton Mifflin, 1990.
Heath, Gordon. *Deep Are the Roots: Memoir of a Black Expatriate.* Amherst: University of Massachusetts Press, 1992.
Heldenfels, R. D. *Television's Greatest Year: 1954.* New York: Continuum, 1994.
Hess, Dean. *Battle Hymn.* New York: McGraw-Hill, 1956.
Hope, Richard O. *Racial Strife in the U.S. Military: Toward the Elimination of Discrimination.* New York: Praeger, 1979.

Issacs, Ethel J. R. *The Negro in the American Theatre*. College Park, MD: McGrath, 1968.
Izod, John. *Hollywood and the Box Office, 1895–1986*. New York: Columbia University Press, 1988.
Jones, James Earl, and Penelope Niven. *James Earl Jones: Voices and Silences*. New York: Scribner's, 1993.
Kagan, Norman. *The War Film*. New York: Pyramid, 1974.
Kalisch, Philip A., Beatrice J. Kalisch and Margaret Scobey. *Images of Nurses on Television*. New York: Springer, 1983.
Kane, Kathryn. *Visions of War: Hollywood Combat Films of World War II*. Ann Arbor: UMI Research Press, 1982.
Kim, Erwin. *Franklin Schaffner*. Lanham, MD: Scarecrow Press, 1985.
Kisseloff, Jeff. *The Box: An Oral History of Television, 1920–1961*. New York: Viking Press, 1995.
Kitt, Eartha. *I'm Still Here*. London: Sidwick & Jackson, 1989.
Kittross, John M., and Christopher Sterling. *Stay Tuned: A Concise History of American Broadcasting*. Belmont, CA: Wadsworth, 1990.
Koppes, Clayton R., and Gregory Black. *Hollywood Goes to War: How Politics, Profits and Propaganda Shaped World War II Movies*. New York: Free Press, 1987.
Kramer, Stanley, with Thomas M. Coffey. *A Mad, Mad, Mad, Mad World: A Life in Hollywood*. New York: Harcourt Brace, 1997.
Laurents, Arthur. *Original Story By: A Memoir of Broadway and Hollywood*. New York: Alfred A. Knopf, 2000.
_____. *Selected Plays of Arthur Laurents*. New York: Back Stage Books, 2004.
Levering, Ralph B. *The Cold War: 1945–1972*. Arlington Heights, IL: Harlan Davidson, 1982.
Lichter, S. Robert, Linda Richter, and Stanley Rothman. *Watching America*. New York: Prentice Hall Press, 1991.
Lightfoot, Claude M. *Ghetto Rebellion to Black Liberation*. New York: International Publishers, 1968.
MacDonald, J. Fred. *Blacks and White TV: African Americans in Television Since 1948*. Chicago: Nelson-Hall, 1992.
Mast, Gerald. *A Short History of the Movies*. Indianapolis: Bobbs-Merrill, 1976.
McCarty, John M., and Brian Kellher. Alfred Hitchcock Presents: *An Illustrated Guide to the Ten-Year Television Career of the Master of Suspense*. New York: St. Martin's Press, 1985.
McCullers, Carson. *The Member of the Wedding* (published playscript). New York: New Dimensions Paperback, 1946.
McGilligan, Patrick. *Alfred Hitchcock: A Life in Darkness and Light*. New York: Regan Books/HarperCollins, 2003.
McGilligan, Pat, ed. *Backstory 2: Interviews with Screenwriters of the 1940s and 1950s*. Berkeley: University of California Press, 1991.
Millichap, Joseph R. *Lewis Milestone*. Boston: Twayne, 1981.
Minnelli, Vincente, with Hector Arce. *I Remember It Well*. Garden City, NY: Doubleday, 1974.
Mordden, Ethan. *Medium Cool: The Movies in the 1960s*. New York: Knopf, 1990.
Naremore, James. *The Films of Vincente Minnelli*. Cambridge: Cambridge University Press, 1993.
Navasky, Victor S. *Naming Names*. New York: Viking Press, 1980.
Nolletti, Arthur, Jr. *The Films of Fred Zinnemann: Critical Perspectives*. New York: State University of New York Press, 1999.
Patterson, Lindsay, ed. *Anthology of the American Negro in the Theatre: A Critical Approach*. New York: Publishers Co., 1967.
Phillips, Cabell. *The Truman Presidency: The History of a Triumphant Succession*. Baltimore: Penguin, 1969.
Poitier, Sidney. *The Measure of a Man: A Spiritual Autobiography*. San Francisco: HarperSan Francisco, 2005.
Preminger, Otto. *Preminger: An Autobiography*. Garden City, NY: Doubleday, 1977.

Ravitch, Diane, ed. *The American Reader: Words That Moved a Nation.* New York: HarperCollins, 1990.
Ray, Robert B. *A Certain Tendency of the Hollywood Cinema, 1930–1980.* Princeton, NJ: Princeton University Press, 1985.
Sampson, Henry T. *Swingin' on the Ether Waves: A Chronological History of African Americans in Radio and Television Broadcasting, 1925–1955, Volumes 1 & 2.* Lanham, MD: Scarecrow Press, 2005.
Schwartz, Nancy L., and S. Schwartz. *The Hollywood Writer's Wars.* New York: McGraw-Hill, 1983.
Shulman, Arthur, and Roger Young. *How Sweet It Was: Television, A Pictorial Commentary on Its Golden Age.* New York: Bonanza Books, 1966.
Simmons, Renee Antoinette. *Frederick Douglass O'Neal: Pioneer of the Actors' Equity Association.* New York: Garland, 1996.
Sirk, Douglas, and Jon Halliday. *Sirk on Sirk: Conversations with Jon Halliday.* London: Faber and Faber, 1997.
Sitkoff, Harvard. *The Struggle for Black Equality, 1954–1980.* New York: Hill & Wang, 1981.
Smith, Mona Z. *Becoming Something: The Story of Canada Lee.* New York: Faber and Faber, 2004.
Sorlin, Pierre. *The Film in History: Restaging the Past.* Totowa, NJ: Barnes & Noble, 1980.
Spelling, Aaron, with Jefferson Graham. *Aaron Spelling: A Prime-Time Life.* New York: St. Martin's Press, 2005.
Sperber, A.M., and Eric Lax. *Bogart.* New York: William Morrow, 1997.
Spoto, Donald. *Stanley Kramer, Film Maker.* New York: Putnam's, 1978.
Stevens, George, Jr., ed. *Conversations with the Great Moviemakers of Hollywood's Golden Age at the American Film Institute,* New York: Knopf, 2006.
Strode, Woody, with Sam Young. *Goal Dust.* Lanham, MD: Madison, 1999.
Strucken, Frank. *Live Television: The Golden Age of 1946–1958 in New York.* Jefferson, NC: McFarland, 1990.
Taylor, Ella. *Prime Time Families: Television Culture in Postwar America.* London: University of California Press, 1989.
Terrace, Vincent. *Fifty Years of Television: A Guide to Series and Pilots, 1937–1988.* New York: Cornwall, 1991.
Truman, Harry S. *Memoirs by Harry S Truman: Vol. 2, Years of Trial and Hope, 1946–1952.* New York: Signet, 1965.
Turow, Joseph. *Playing Doctor: Television, Storytelling, and Medical Power.* New York: Oxford University Press, 1989.
Verswijver, Leo. *"Movies Were Always Magical": Interviews with 19 Actors, Directors, and Producers from the Hollywood of the 1930s through the 1950s.* Jefferson, NC: McFarland, 2003.
West, Richard. *Fifty Years of Television: A Guide to Series and Pilots.* Jefferson, NC: McFarland, 1987.
Winkler, Alan M. *The Politics of Propaganda: The Office of War Information, 1942–1945.* New Haven, CT: Yale University Press, 1978.
Wolper, David, with David Fisher. *Producer: A Memoir.* New York: Scribner, 2003.
Year of the Great Decision. NAACP Annual Report, Fifty-fourth Year, 1952. National Association for the Advancement of Colored People, New York.
Yearwood, Gladstone, ed. *Black Cinema Aesthetics: Issues in Independent Black Filmmaking.* Athens: Ohio University, Center for Afro-American Studies, 1982.
Yoggy, Gary A. *Riding the Video Range: The Rise and Fall of the Western on Television.* Jefferson, NC: McFarland, 1995.
Yordan, Philip. *Anna Lucasta.* New York: Random House, 1945.

Archival Collections

John McGreevey Papers. The Lilly Library Manuscripts Collection, Indiana University.
Albert J. Cohen Papers, Special Collections Department, University of Iowa Libraries.

Websites

The Harry S Truman Library, trumanlibrary.org.
Museum of Broadcast Communications, museum.tv.com
TCM Turner Classic Movies, tcm.com

Index

Accused 98
Adams, Julie 47
The Adventures of Ellery Queen 8, 55
African Manhunt 129
Ahn, Philip 87, 117, 120
Aletter, Frank 90
Alexrod, George 154
Alfred Hitchcock Presents 88–89, 161
Almond, Major Gen. Edward M. 31
Almost Faithful 14
Altieri, James 53
American Negro Theatre 130
Amos Burke, Secret Agent 178–179
Amos 'n' Andy 59, 75–77, 97
Anderson, Eddie "Rochester" 84
Anderson, Ernie 148
Anderson, Richard 171
Anderson High School 10
Andrews, Edward 142
Anna Lucasta 38, 68, 73, 79, 130, 131, 132, 134, 147, 173
anti–Semitism 16–17
Ardrey, Robert 4

Backus, Jim 51
Bailey, Pearl 61, 94
Bailey, Raymond 88
Barnouw, Erik 85, 93
Barrow, Joe Louis 11, 78
Barry, Gene 178
Barrymore, John Drew 54, 135
Battle Hymn 54, 116–120, 127, 135
Baxter, Alan 13
Beavers, Louise 76
Belafonte, Harry 37, 59, 61, 68, 73, 84, 107
Bellamy, Ralph 171
Bennett, Ray 129
Berch, Barbara 128

Bermuda 35, 65, 101, 102
Berry, John 7, 8
Best, James 108
Beulah (television show) 76, 77
bigotry 4, 26, 27, 59, 61, 62, 104, 148, 153
Binford, Lloyd T. 30
biopics 78
Blackburn, Jack "Chappie" 79
Blair, Betsy 7, 72
Blake, Robert 126
Blandel, Marc 178
Blankenship, John 106
Blankfort, Henry 7
Blayton, J.B., Sr. 56
Blood and Steel 127, 190
Body and Soul (Lux Theatre radio program) 9
Body and Soul (1947 film) 68
Bogart, Humphrey 20, 72, 113–116, 128, 131, 175
Booth, Karen 129
The Boy from Korea 54
Brando, Marlon 39, 106, 158
Breen, Joseph 44
Bridges, Lloyd 20, 71, 90, 146, 152, 175
Bright Victory 45–51, 58, 72, 74, 173
Brinkley, John 127
Brode, David 149
Brodie, Steve 20, 43, 113
Bronson, Charles 158, 159, 181
Brown vs. the Board of Education 94
Bryant, Nana 47
Buckner, Robert 51
Bunche, Ralph 84–85, 172
Bundy, Brooke 161
Burbridge, Eddie 22, 28
Burton, Dan 87
Burton, Richard 157
Byrd, Holland 54

The Caine Mutiny 52, 72, 113, 115–116
Calumet District Amateur Boxing Tournament 11
Calumet Steel Mill 12
Cannady, Camille 106
Carey, Tim 110
Carmen Jones 67, 73, 107, 175
Carroll, Diahann 63, 66, 67, 73, 99, 108, 164, 165
Carroll, Leo 172
Champion 15, 17, 33, 50, 194
The Charioteers (musical group) 38
Childress, Alvin 75
Chrysler, Walter 81
civil rights 34, 68, 69, 73, 76, 84, 94, 100, 153, 163, 164, 169, 172, 191
Clark, Susan 160
The Clear Horizon 100, 176, 180
Clemons, Joseph P. 126
Cobb, Lee J. 160, 181
Coe, Richard 50, 115, 132, 143, 161
Cohn, Albert J. 54
Cohn, Harry 114, 152
Cole, Nat "King" 61, 73, 94, 135, 175
Colman, Benita Hume 56
Colman, Ronald 56
Color Me German 176, 177
Committee for the Negro in the Arts 69
Committee on Equality and Opportunity in the Armed Forces 26
Communist influence in the motion pictures 68
Communist Party 69, 72
COMPIC (Communist Influence in Motion Pictures), FBI Report on 71, 72
Condon, Richard 154
Confession 56
Conners, Chuck 180
Conners, Mike 183
Coogan, Jackie 135, 180
Coogan's Bluff 160, 161
Coordinating Council for Negro Performers 95
Corey, Earl 181
Corey, Jeff 20, 71
Correll, Charles 75
Cosby, Bill 184
Cotten, Joseph 88, 161
Coughlin, Kevin 161
Crawford, Charles 106, 142
Crowther, Bosley 25, 28, 41, 49, 105, 115, 119, 121, 132, 143, 156, 159
Culp, Robert 98, 164
Cumber, Lillian 37
Cunningham, Rosalind "Roz" 64–65
Curtis, Tony 61

The Daily Worker 45, 72
Dana, Mark 89
Dandridge, Dorothy 37, 102, 107, 151, 175
Daniel, Chuck 182
Davis, Ossie 4, 37, 39, 53, 59, 65, 69, 79, 84, 164, 165, 194
Davis, Sammy, Jr. 65, 73, 94, 131, 132, 147, 158
A Day of Absence 164
Death Takes a Holiday 4
Death Valley Days 150
de Corsia, Ted 110
Dee, Ruby 37, 59, 69, 165, 169, 173, 194
Deep Are the Roots 5–9, 12, 14, 61, 72, 175, 189, 194
The Defiant Ones 71
Department of Defense 44, 73, 97
Desilu Studios 87
The Detective Story 106
DeWilde, Brandon 104
Dick, Douglas 20, 98, 152
Disney, Walt 92, 148, 152
Dixon, Ivan 172
Dmytryk, Edward 12, 72, 114
Dr. Kildare 173
Donegan, Dorothy 37
Doomsday Voyage 161, 162, 185
Douglas, Kirk 15, 17
Dow, Peggy 47
Downing, Joseph 89
Drake, Tom 158
dramatic anthology programs on early television 83–84
Dreyfuss, Richard 161
Drury, James 182
Druten, John Van 106
Duggan, Andrew 173
Dunn, James 169
DuPont Cavalcade of America 84
Duryea, Dan 12, 117
d'Usseau, Arnaud 5, 72, 189, 194

East Side, West Side 165, 166
Eastwood, Clint 160
Ebony Showcase (television show) 192
Ebony Showcase Theatre 83, 106, 188, 189
Edwards, Eugenia (Eugia) 154, 171, 185
Edwards, Everdinne 153, 171, 185, 188
Edwards, James Valley 10, 175, 188
Edwards, Vince 110
Egan, Richard 50, 51
Eisenhower, Dwight 94
The Eleventh Hour 164, 171
Elliott, Ross 129
Evans, Gene 42

Index

Evans, Vincent B. 117
Executive Order 9980 26
Executive Order 9981 112
The Exiles 159
Experiment in Television 176, 177

Falk, Peter 172
Farber, Manny 24, 49
FBI 69, 70, 71, 72, 73
Fell, Norman 126, 161
Fendel, Rosemarie 177
Ferrer, Jose 72, 114
Ferrer, Mel 61, 123
Festival de Cannes 50
The Fireside Theatre 86
Fisher, Gail 183, 184, 189
Flippen, Jay C. 110
Flothow, Rudolph 96
Fong, Harry 43
Ford, Tennessee Ernie 94
Ford, Wallace 13, 14, 54, 88
Foreman, Carl 16, 71
Four Star Productions 90, 146, 175
Fox, William 152
Francis, Robert 114
Frankel, Gene 154
Frankenheimer, John 154
Fraulein 122, 124
Friedman, Seymour 129
The Fugitive 168
Fuller, Samuel 41, 44–45, 72, 135

Gallu, Sam 97
Garfield, John 9
Garner, Peggy Ann 171
Geer, Will 47, 72
The General Electric Theatre 84, 87, 177
Genet, Jean 154
Gipson, Gertrude 38, 188
Glass, George 16, 22, 71, 72
Glenn, Roy 87, 148
Godfrey, Arthur 94
Godman, Howard A. 161
Going My Way 172
Golden, Murray 178
Golden Globe Awards 50
Goodwin, Ruby 85
Gordon, Robert 54, 78, 88
Gosden, Freeman 75
Gow, James 5, 175, 189, 194
Grayson, Charles 117
Grayson, Jessie 7
Gregory, James 154, 155
greylisting 70, 71
Gribble, Harry Wagstaff 14
Guardino, Harry 126

Haas, Hugo 134
Hagman, Larry 172
Haight, Capt. Frederick II 87
Hairston, Jester 56
Hale, Alan 117
Hall, Jon 95
The Halls of Ivy 56, 58
Halsey, Brett 127
Hamilton, Bernie 51, 84, 85, 87, 97
Harlem Detective 74, 93
Harris, Bud 76
Harris, Julie 103, 104
Hartman, David 181, 182
Harvey, Lawrence 154
Hayden, Sterling 12, 110
Healy, Myron 129, 180
Heath, Gordon 7, 194
Helton, Percy 13
Hernandez, Juano 39
Hervey, Irene 12
Hess, Dean 117
HICCASP (Hollywood Independent Citizens Committee of Arts, Sciences & Professions) 69
Hickman, Darryl 13
Hitchcock, Alfred 20, 88, 99, 161, 190
Hobart, Rose 7
Hoerl, Arthur 129
Holliman, Earl 54, 88
Hollywood Ten 68, 72, 114, 157
Home of the Brave 15, 16–25, 26–29, 30, 33, 36, 37, 38, 40, 43, 45, 48, 50, 51, 58, 60, 61, 66, 71, 72, 74, 90, 101, 102, 104, 110, 112, 113, 120, 127, 128, 151, 152, 175, 176, 185, 189, 190, 191
Homolka, Oscar 173
Horne, Lena 39, 64, 68, 73
Hotel Cecil 8
House Committee on Education and Labor 53, 164
House Un-American Activities Committee (HUAC) 69–74, 114, 121
Hudson, John 51
Hudson, Rock 51, 117, 122, 128
Hughes, Howard 12
Hughes, Langston 4, 27
Hunter, Jeffrey 108
Hunter, Ross 117

Indiana University 11
Ingram, Rex 97, 131
The Ink Spots 79
International Film and Radio Guild 73
Irish, Tom 108

Jackson, Julius 87
Jackson, Mahalia 92
James Edwards School of Dramatics 38
Janssen, David 169
Jason, Katherine 161
Jeb 4, 5
Jeffries, Herb 92
Jim Crow 6, 32, 61, 112, 113
The Joe Louis Story 54, 61, 78, 82, 173
The Joey Bishop Show 171
Johnson, Annie Mae 10, 188
Johnson, Bobby 148
Johnson, Dots 79, 84
Johnson, Van 36, 114
Jolley, Norman 183
Jones, Dean 135
Jones, Edgar Allen 98
Jones, James Earl 166
Julia 164

Karlson, Phil 139
Kashfi, Anna 117, 119, 135
KCOP 83
Keith, Robert 121
Kellogg, John 129
Kelly, Gene 7, 172
Kendrick, Baynard 50
Kennedy, Arthur 45, 50, 173
Kennedy, John F. 98, 157, 168
Kiley, Richard 142
The Killing 109, 110
King, Walter 171
Kingsley, Sidney 106
Kitt, Eartha 128, 131, 132, 134
Knoxville College 11
Korean Conflict 41, 44, 45, 120, 122, 125, 154
Korman, Harvey 171
Koster, Henry 122
Kowalski, Bernard 127
Kramer, Stanley 14–17, 20–28, 29, 38, 71, 39, 50, 61, 62, 66, 71, 103, 114–115, 153, 189, 190
Krasner, Milton 157
KTTV 83
Ku Klux Klan 165
Kubrick, Stanley 109

Labor and Industry Committee 95
Lansbury, Angela 154, 155
Laurents, Arthur 16
Leachman, Cloris 3, 174
Lee, Canada 5, 9, 68, 84, 130
Lee, Johnny 75, 86
Leigh, Janet 154, 155
LeNoire, Rosetta 84, 130
Lesser, Sol 129

Lippert, Robert 41
London, Julie 135
Long, Avon 84
Loo, Richard 43, 117
Lord, Leon 106
Lost Boundaries 60
Lovejoy, Frank 20, 98, 152, 175
Lucille Ball–Desi Arnaz partnership 87
Lux Theatre 9, 29, 55
Lynde, Paul 3
Lynn, Jay Loft 56

Maddow, Ben 72
Mahoney, Jock 117
Mainwaring, Dan 140
The Manchurian Candidate 154, 156, 190
Manhandled 12, 36
Mann, Anthony 121
Mannix 183
March, Joseph Moncure 12
Marshall, Brig. Gen. S.L.A. 124
Marshall, William 74, 93
Martin, Buzz 171
Marvin, Lee 114, 181
Mason, Morgan 158
Massey, Raymond 108
Mathews, George 89
Mayer, Louis B. 152
McCarthy, Sen. Joseph P. 70, 72
McCormack, Patty 161
McCullers, Carson 103
McDaniel, Hattie 76
McGavin, Darren 179
McGreevey, John 54, 88
McIntire, John 142
McIver, Ray 56
McMurray, Fred 113
Medic 93, 94
Meet McGraw 98
The Member of the Wedding 103, 104, 105
The Men 39, 49, 103
Men in War 72, 120–122
Metromedia Producers Corporation 188
Milestone, Lewis 44, 72, 124, 127
Miller, Herman 161
Minelli, Vincente 157
Minow, Newton 166
Montgomery, Dan 37
Montgomery, Lillie 37
Montgomery, Ray 95
Moore, Juanita 97, 106, 154, 172, 180
Moore, Tim 75
Moorehead, Agnes 136
Moreland, Mantan 84
Morrow, Vic 121
Mosley, Leola 63, 82, 153, 188

Murcott, Joel 85
Muse, Clarence 147

Nat Turner 39
National Association for the Advancement of Colored People (NAACP) 7, 8, 35, 38, 39, 64, 76, 95
National Negro Labor Council 69
Navy Log 97, 98
Negro Actors Guild 69
Negro problem (in America) 26, 34
Nelson, Felix 148
Nichols, Nichelle 164
Night of the Quarter Moon 54, 73, 134, 137, 175, 180
No Way Out 37, 39, 60
Norford, George 145
Norman, Maidie 12, 56, 85, 106
Norman, McHenry 85
Northwestern University 3, 4, 16
The Nurses 173

Oakland, Simon 167
O'Morrison, Kenny 14
On Whitman Avenue 4, 68
O'Neal, Frederick 38, 84, 130, 131
Operation Kiddy Car 117
The Outcasts 181
The Outsider 179

Patterson, Albert 139, 142
Patton 173, 175, 185, 186, 187, 190
Peck, Gregory 125, 126
Pennell, Larry 108
Peppard, George 126
Perl, Arnold 168
Persoff, Nehemiah 121
Peter Gunn 99
Peters, Paul 39
The Phenix City Story 139, 142, 143, 144
Poitier, Sidney 37, 39, 53, 59, 60, 61, 70, 84, 113, 131, 141, 151, 164, 189, 192
Poole, Cecil 8
Pork Chop Hill 65–67, 72, 124–127
Post, Ted 88
Powell, Adam Clayton 53, 164
Powell, Dick 90, 146, 147, 175, 178
Pratt, James 52
Preminger, Otto 67, 73, 107, 151, 154
Production Code Administration (PCA) 44

race prejudice 23, 28, 49, 61
race radio stations 56
racial discrimination 8, 23, 27, 28, 34, 49, 60, 69, 70, 72, 73, 153, 160, 163, 167, 190

Ramar of the Jungle 95, 97, 105
Randolph, Amanda 75, 76, 92, 93
Randolph, Lillian 75
Ransohoff, Martin 158
Ray, Aldo 121
Rayburn, Donna 64
Red Ball Express 70
Red Channels 70, 73
Red Scare 68, 70, 74, 97
Rhodes, Hari 148, 169
Richards, Paul 90
Riesner, Dean 161
Riley, Anne Edwards *see* Johnson, Annie Mae
Robert Gordon Productions 54
Robeson, Paul 68, 69, 70, 74
Robinson, Jackie 23
Robinson, Sugar Ray 39, 81, 83
Robson, Mark 16, 45, 50
Rodann, Ziva 127
Russell County Betterment Association 139
Ryan, Robert 12, 121, 171

Saint, Eva Marie 158
Sampson, Bill 56
The Sandpiper 157, 158, 159
Sands, Diana 165, 166
Sargent, Dick 161
Sartre, Jean-Paul 67, 106
Schaffner, Franklin 66, 173
Schenck, Joseph 152
Scott, George C. 83, 166, 168, 181, 185
Scott, Hazel 74, 92, 93
Scott, Henry 7, 131
Screen Actors Guild 60, 72, 100, 128, 146
Screen Extras Guild 100, 129
Screen Plays, Inc. 16
screenwriting 52, 54, 71, 88, 117
Seligsman, Selig 98
Selznick, David O. 152
The Set-Up 12, 36, 54, 121, 171
Seven Angry Men 108, 109
Shibata, George 125
Shulberg, B.P. 152
Silent Thunder 53, 54, 71, 88, 135
Siliphant, Stirling 78
Silverheels, Jay 148
Simms, Hilda 38, 73, 79, 84, 130, 131, 164, 173
Sinatra, Frank 39, 154, 157
Sirk, Douglas 116
Skyloft Players 4, 12, 67, 194
Smith, John 108
Smith, Lillian 67
Sofear, Abraham 148

Spaulding, Helen 4
Spelling, Aaron 66, 91, 147, 178, 179
Spencer, Ray 7
spoken-word recordings 52
Spotlight Wednesday 83
Stanley, Forrest 88
Starr, Manya 100, 176, 177
The Steel Helmet 41, 43, 44, 45, 64, 71, 72, 190
Stevens, Craig 98
Stevens, Inger 61
Stewart, Nick 75, 86, 97, 105, 130, 192
Stewart, Paul 79
Stillman, John 17
Stone, George E. 89
A Streetcar Named Desire 106, 189
Strickland, Edwin 143
Strode, Woodrow "Woody" 62, 65–67, 125–126, 130
Susskind, David 166
Swing Street 83
Sylvester, Robert 78

Talmadge, Herman 94
Tarzan 128
Tarzan's Fight for Life 65, 129–130
Taylor, Elizabeth 155, 157
Thorpe, Buddy 79
Thunder Over Sangoland 97
Toast of the Town 83
Tobey, Kenneth 87
Tobias, George 13
Tomikin, Dmitri 23
The Torch Grows Dim 14
Torn, Rip 126
Totter, Audrey 13
Trans-Lux Theatre Chain, Washington, DC 29
Truman, Harry 26, 27, 112
Trumbo, Dalton 157
TV Reader's Digest 86
Tyron, Tom 148
Tyson, Cecily 166

Ullman, Daniel B. 108
United States Air Force 117
United States Army 31, 41, 71, 112, 185
United States Commission on Civil Rights 94
United States Information Agency 85
United States Navy 97, 114

Vandercook, John 86
Vicus, Victor 176, 177
Vidette, John 161
The Virginian 181
The Voice of the Turtle 106

Wade, Ernestine 75
Walker, William 60, 128, 146
Wallace, Coley 79
Walling, H.F. 87
Walt Disney Studios 148
War Production Board 12
Ward, Douglas Turner 164
Warfield, William 84
Warner, Albert 152
Warner, Harry 152
Warren, Charles Marquis 108
Warwick, Robert 7
Washington, Dinah 83, 93
Waters, Ethel 38, 76, 84, 103, 104
Weaver, Dennis 108
Webb, James 124
Webber, Robert 158
WERD (Radio) 56
Werker, Alfred 60
Westerns, on television 92, 95, 148
Westinghouse-Desilu Playhouse 54, 87, 88
White, Jane 35, 39, 64
White, Walter 35, 39, 64
Whitfield, Jordan "Smoki" 109
Wilbur, Crane 140
Wilder, Thornton 3
Williams, Clarence, III 164
Williams, Guy 108
Williams, Ron 177
Williams, Spencer, Jr. 75
Williams, Tennessee 106, 189
Wilson, Everdinne *see* Edwards, Everdinne
Windsor, Marie 110
Wisbar, Frank 86
Wise, Robert 12
Woods, Maxine 4
World War II 17, 23, 27, 41, 42, 48, 49, 62, 97, 98, 105, 131, 153, 186
Worstman, Gene 143
Wouk, Herman 113
Writers Guild 55
Wynn, May 114
Wynter, Dana 122

Yoggy, Gary 149
Yordan, Philip 38, 79, 121, 130, 134
Young, Otis 181
The Young Runaways 161

Zane Grey Theatre 73, 146, 147, 148, 175
Zanuck, Darryl F. 39
Zinnemann, Fred 103
Zugsmith, Albert 134

www.ingramcontent.com/pod-product-compliance
Ingram Content Group UK Ltd.
Pitfield, Milton Keynes, MK11 3LW, UK
UKHW041946140426
5217IPUK00014B/681